W9-BEU-088

parents aren't supposed to like it

VOLUME 2

parents aren't supposed to Like It

Rock & Other Pop Musicians of the 1990s

David P. Bianco, Editor

South Side Middle School
LIBRARY

AN IMPRINT OF GALE

Detroit · New York · Toronto · London

Parents aren't supposed to like it

Rock & Other Pop Musicians of the 1990s

David P. Bianco, Editor

Staff

Sonia Benson, U·X·L Senior Editor
Carol DeKane Nagel, U·X·L Managing Editor
Thomas L. Romig, U·X·L Publisher

Mary Beth Trimper, Production Director
Evi Seoud, Assistant Production Manager
Shanna Heilveil, Production Associate

Cynthia Baldwin, Product Design Manager
Barbara Yarrow, Graphic Services Director
Michelle DiMercurio, Art Director
Jessica L. Ulrich, Permissions Assistant
Marco Di Vita, Graphix Group, Typesetter

Library of Congress Cataloging-in-Publication Data
Bianco, David P., 1947-
    Parents aren't supposed to like it: rock and other pop musicians of the 1990s/David P. Bianco
      p. cm.
    Includes bibliographical references, discographies, and index.
    Summary: Profiles over 100 contemporary musicians and bands in the categories of alternative rock, rap, folk music, and others..
    ISBN 0-7876-1731-8 (alk. paper).—ISBN 0-7876-1732-6 (alk. paper).—ISBN 0-7876-1733-4 (alk. paper).—0-7876-1734-2
    1.Musicians—Biography—Dictionaries, Juvenile. 2. Musical groups—Dictionaries, Juvenile. 3. Popular music—Dictionaries, Juvenile. [1. Musicians.] I. Title.
    ML3929.B5 1997
781.66'0922--dc21
[B]
    97-34040
    CIP
    AC MN

This publication is a creative work copyrighted by U·X·L and fully protected by all applicable copyright laws, as well as by misappropriation, trade secret, unfair competition, and other applicable laws. The authors and editors of this work have added value to the underlying factual material herein through one or more of the following: unique and original selection, coordination, expression, arrangement, and classification of the information. All rights to this publication will be vigorously defended.

Copyright © 1998
U·X·L, An Imprint of Gale
All rights reserved, including the right of reproduction in whole or in part in any form.

∞™ This book is printed on acid-free paper that meets the minimum requirements of American National Standard for Information Sciences—Permanence Paper for Printed Library Materials, ANSI Z39.48-1984.

10 9 8 7 6 5 4 3 2

Printed in the United States of America

contents

volume 1

Green Day

VOLUME 3

Reader's Guide

There's something for just about every young music fan in *Parents Aren't Supposed to Like It: Rock & Other Pop Musicians of the 1990s.* This comprehensive resource contains more than 135 biographical/critical entries on the hottest bands and musicians of the 1990s, from a wide range of musical tastes and genres, including grunge, rap, traditional rock and roll, folk, heavy metal, British pop, ska, art rock, techno, rhythm and blues, and much more.

Perfect for browsing or for research, the three volumes are arranged by general musical categories with an overview of each category preceding the alphabetically arranged profiles of musicians in that genre. Volume 1 is devoted entirely to alternative rock; volume 2 contains Brit pop, dance music, and hip-hop and rap; and volume 3 features folk and folk rock, heavy metal, rhythm and blues and urban soul, rock and roll, and singers/songwriters.

Portraits and other black-and-white photos of the musicians accompany most entries. Fun facts and fascinating anecdotes ap-

k. d. lang

pear in sidebars throughout the volumes, and pertinent quotes by and about the musicians begin each entry and can be found highlighted within the text. The entries conclude with sections listing awards, selected discographies, further reading sources, and contact information, with web sites for nearly all the musicians. Along with a thorough subject index for the three-volume set, there are three tables of contents to aid the reader, listing entries in the order in which they appear, in alphabetical order by musician, and in a breakdown by specific genres.

Scope

All of the bands and artists selected for inclusion are relevant to current popular music of the late 1990s. Most sold a lot of records in the 1990s, are on the cutting edge of a musical trend, or have been highly influential to music of the 1990s. The bands featured in *Parents* provide a representative cross-section of different styles of pop music, reflecting the wide variety of tastes exhibited by the record-buying public. The musicians included differ greatly not only in musical style, but in attitude, image, political messages, belief systems, and lifestyles.

Placing musicians in general genre sections provides a unique opportunity to compare the stories and experiences of artists with those of their peers. With overviews introducing these sections, a reader can quickly come up with an overall picture of the particular musical scene in which their favorite bands participate. Many modern musicians, of course, play in several genres, or have combined genres for new sounds. The editors of *Parents* have made an effort to place musicians in the category they are generally associated with, knowing that in many cases the musicians could easily fit well into another category. The tables of contents are provided in order to facilitate quick reference.

The profiles in *Parents* present the stories of the lives and careers of the featured artists, revealing childhood and family life and the inspirations and obstacles involved in the rise to stardom. Descriptions of the artists' recorded music and live performances are provided along with views of the critical and commercial response to their work. Beyond this, the entries contextualize the musical scene and the pop music business in the various genres as they relate to the musicians' experiences. Music festivals, major and independent record labels, innovative producers, musical technology, social and political controversy, and many other behind-the-scene aspects of pop music are brought out in the context of the musicians' life stories.

About the Contributors

David P. Bianco, editor of *Parents Aren't Supposed to Like It,* is a freelance writer, editor, and publishing consultant. His longstanding interest in popular music has resulted in the publication of two previous music reference books, *Who's New Wave in Music: An Illustrated Encyclopedia, 1976-1982, The First Wave* and *Heat Wave: The Motown Fact Book.* Other contributors are listed on the following page:

Kathy Bilitzke: freelance writer.

Charity Anne Dorgan: writer and editor with thirteen reference books to her credit, and a classically trained amateur singer and harpist.

Brian Escamilla: former editor of *Contemporary Musicians,* a biographical reference series, and a freelance writer.

Jo-Ann Greene: contributor to a wide variety of music publications in both the United States and the United Kingdom, including *Hits, Goldmine, CMJ Monthly, Alternative Press,* and *NME: New Musical Express.* She is also the author of *The Cure* and co-author of *U2: A Visual Documentary.*

Jill Hamilton: contributor to *Rolling Stone, Entertainment Weekly,* and *Playgirl.* Winner of 1996 award from the National Society of Newspaper Columnists.

Ralph Heibutzki: contributor to *Goldmine, DISCoveries, Bass Player* and *Guitar Player,* among other publications. Author of liner notes for Rhino's *Sugar Hill* CD boxed set and for the *Dub Chill Out* compilation by Music Collectors International.

Tim James: cofounder and active member of the non-profit Detroit Musicians Alliance (DMA). Promoter of music festivals and concerts; manager of several Detroit-area bands. Contributor to *Jam Rag* magazine and *Musiczine,* the newsletter of DMA.

Allison Jones: freelance writer and contributor to various music publications, including *Contemporary Musicians* and *Canadian Newsmakers.*

Peter Schorn: multiple-award winning and nominated record producer, songwriter, guitarist, and performer with the band Red September. A founder and past president of the Detroit Musicians Alliance (DMA), he has worked to educate musicians and promote quality music in southeast Michigan. He is a columnist and reviewer for *Musiczine,* the newsletter of the DMA.

Sue Summers: cofounder and vice president of the Detroit Musicians Alliance (DMA); freelance writer for *Musiczine,* the fanzine of the DMA; manager of the independent label Static Records; music promoter and band manager.

Dave Thompson: author of more than sixty rock books, including biographies of Kurt Cobain, Depeche Mode, Red Hot Chili Peppers, Perry Farrell, and U2; regular contributor to *Alternative Press* and *Goldmine* magazines.

Patricia Whipple: co-owner of recording studio; manager, booking agent, and critic in music industry; freelance music writer.

Suggestions

We welcome any comments or suggestions on *Parents Aren't Supposed to Like It: Rock and Other Pop Musicians of the 1990s.* Please write: Editors, *Parents Aren't Supposed to Like It,* U•X•L, Gale Research, 835 Penobscot Bldg., Detroit, Michigan 48226-4094; call toll-free: 800-877-4235; or fax to 313-961-6348.

ALPHABETICAL LISTING OF MUSICIANS

(Boldface numeral indicates volume number, which is followed by page number.)

Tupac Shakur

musicians by genre

(Boldface numeral indicates volume number, which is followed by page number.)

Sheryl Crow

Picture Credits

The photographs appearing in *Parents Aren't Supposed to Like It: Rock & Other Pop Musicians of the 1990s* were received from the following sources:

Cover: Grant Lee Phillips of Grant Lee Buffalo: © **Ken Settle. Reproduced by permission.**

AP/Wide World Photos. Reproduced by permission: pp. 1, 5, 24, 57, 60, 78, 93, 138, 164, 174, 219, 220, 230, 241, 249, 310, 330, 344, 368, 378, 387, 418, 420, 439, 451, 473, 542, 574, 585, 588, 594, 597, 611, 621, 626, 627, 630, 643, 644; © **Larry Hulst/Michael Ochs Archives/Venice, CA. Reproduced by permission:** pp. 4, 27, 75, 584; **Archive Photos. Reproduced by permission:** pp. 6, 178, 180, 257, 314, 468, 504; ©**Ken Settle. Reproduced by permission:** pp. 7, 12, 16, 37, 43, 45, 50, 61, 69, 89, 96, 110, 130, 134, 145, 148, 160, 163, 169, 172, 190, 199, 231, 237, 248, 266, 267, 277, 284, 350, 382, 412, 454, 461, 465, 479, 482, 485, 545, 548, 552, 565, 572, 576, 579, 606, 613, 618, 636, 639, 653; **Photograph by Danny Clinch. Columbia, Sony Music. Reproduced by permission:**

The Fugees

p. 11; © Denise Sofranko/Michael Ochs Archives/Venice, CA. Reproduced by permission: pp. 20, 511; Photograph by Rafael Fuchs. Matador Records. Reproduced by permssion: p. 30; Photograph by Christine Alicino. Corbis. Reproduced by permission: p. 33; Photograph by Tim Mosenfelder. Corbis. Reproduced by permission: pp. 34, 182, 253, 254; Photograph by Timothy White. Arista Records. Reproduced by permission: p. 42; Photograph by Frank Ockenfels. Outline Press Syndicate. Reproduced by permission: p. 46; Photograph by Jeff Christensen. Archive Photos/Reuters. Reproduced by permission: pp. 49, 53, 322; Photograph by Tina Paul. Archive Photos. Reproduced by permission: p. 65; Photograph by Jon Hammer. Archive Photos. Reproduced by permission: p. 70, 196, 222, 270; Photograph by Pauline St. Denis. Courtesy of Rykodisc: p. 81; Photograph by Tibor Bozi. Corbis. Reproduced by permission: p. 84, 291, 443; Michael Ochs Archives/Venice, CA. Reproduced by permission: p. 87, 355, 366, 382, 383, 622; Photograph by Scott Harrison. Archive Photos. Reproduced by permission: pp. 101, 153, 187, 559; Photograph by Sin/Tony Mott. Corbis. Reproduced by permission: pp. 105, 123, 497; Photograph by Scope/John Wallace. Corbis. Reproduced by permission: p. 106; Photograph by James Smolka. Reproduced by permission: p. 111; © Anna Luken/Michael Ochs Archives/Venice, CA. Reproduced by permission: pp. 115, 155, 617; Photograph by Gary Hershorn. Reuters/Archive Photos. Reproduced by permission: p. 117; Photograph by Mike Hashimoti. Corbis. Reproduced by permission: p. 124; Photograph by Lance Mercer. Columbia Records. Reproduced by permission: p. 127; © Joe Hughes/Michael Ochs Archives/Venice, CA. Reproduced by permission: pp. 150, 312; Photograph by Richard Drew. AP/Wide World. Reproduced by permission: p. 192; Photograph by Henry Diltz. Corbis. Reproduced by permission: p. 203; Photograph by Paul Banks. Corbis. Reproduced by permission: pp. 223, 224; Archive Photos/Popperfoto. Reproduced by permission: pp. 227, 516, 541, 634; Archive Photos/Big Pictures. Reproduced by permission: p. 228; Photograph by Mike Segar. Archive Photos/Reuters. Reproduced by permission: pp. 238, 265; © Waring Abbott/Michael Ochs/Archives/Venice, CA. Reproduced by permission: pp. 275, 287, 403, 405, 458, 528; Photograph by Tom Gates. Archive Photos. Reproduced by permission: p. 283; Corbis-Bettmann. Reproduced by permission: 303, 317, 343, 362, 376, 392, 403, 410, 446, 50, 5241, 655; © Al Pereira/Michael Ochs Archives/Venice, CA. Reproduced by permission: pp. 306, 360, 399, 520; © Raymond Boyd/Michael Ochs Archives, Venice, CA. Reproduced by permission: pp. 321, 340, 372, 424, 525; Photograph by Bob Grant. Fotos international/Archive Photos. Reproduced by permission: p. 326; Ruthless Records. Reproduced by permission: p. 338; Photograph by Miranda Shen. Fotos international/Archive Photos. Reproduced by permission: **p. 415**; Photograph by Sin/Roy Tee. Corbis. Reproduced by permission: **p. 441**; Photograph by Michael Miller. Eastwest Records. Reproduced by permission: **p. 490**; ©David Corio/ Michael Ochs Archive, Venice, CA. Reproduced by permission: **p. 493**; Photograph by Fred Prouser. Archive Photos. Reproduced by permission **p. 506**; Photograph by Adam Nadel. AP/Wide World Photos. Reproduced by permission: **p. 535**; © 1996 Rick Olivier. All Rights Reserved. Reproduced by permission: **p. 591**; Photograph by Ken Franckling. Corbis. Reproduced by permission: **p. 603**; Photograph by Ian Waldie. Archive Photos/Reuters. Reproduced by permission: **p. 647**; Photograph by Stephen Apicella-Hitchcock. Atlantic Records. Reproduced by permission: **p. 650**.

parents aren't supposed to like it

Brit POP

Roots of British alternative/pop

If one artist helped push the rock envelope throughout the 1970s, it was **David Bowie** (see entry). With his theatrical, emotive singing, wide-ranging taste in musical styles and experimental approach, Bowie kept fans and critics guessing with a string of important releases for the length of the decade. From the "glam" pop-rock of his *Ziggy Stardust, Space Oddity, Hunky Dory* and *Aladdin Sane* albums, through his arty *Thin White Duke* phase (*Station to Station*), through the warm, canny soul of *Young Americans* and the chilly, innovative records he made with producer/artist Brian Eno in Berlin (*Low, Heroes* and *Lodger*), Bowie remained a vital presence. Though 1983's *Let's Dance* (featuring blues-guitar wizard Stevie Ray Vaughn) was his biggest album, Bowie seemed to lose focus in the 1980s, trying out a variety of new forms that weren't as successful as his earlier efforts.

The late 1970s brought not only British punk groups like the Sex Pistols and The Clash (see introduction to Alternative/Pop in volume 1), but a host of inventive singer/songwriters who brought

David Bowie

The Cure in 1989

punk energy, new-wave smarts and old-fashioned pop songwriting skills to the table. Chief among these was **Elvis Costello** (see entry), who burst onto the scene with his 1977 debut, *My Aim Is True,* and proceeded to stun fans and critics with album after album of sharp, passionate material. Costello's ability to pen memorable pop songs in the vein of the Beatles was so strong that he found himself working with a Beatle, Paul Mc-Cartney, in the 1990s, as well as with another important songwriter and personal idol, Burt Bacharach. Though one of the most admired artists to come about during this period, Costello never achieved big sales. The same was true of gifted singer/songwriters like Graham Parker

and Costello's frequent collaborator, Nick Lowe. Kindred spirits Squeeze managed to score a couple of hits, notably "Tempted" and "Black Coffee in Bed," with their energetic, clever pop.

Other influential alternative rockers of the 1970s and 1980s

Though fronted by an American living in London—singer/songwriter/guitarist Chrissie Hynde—the otherwise English band The Pretenders were one of the most successful alternative rock bands to emerge from the U.K. in the late 1970s, and the group went from the underground to the charts in short order. Two deaths in the band slowed things down, but the band remained a vital force in alternative music through the first half of the 1980s.

Joy Division—arguably rock's gloomiest band ever—fused punk and industrial sounds and won over critics and legions of underground fans before singer Ian Curtis' suicide caused them to reform as dance-pop favorites New Order. Even such radical acts as post-punk/funk quartet Gang of Four achieved some measure of success in the 1980s, though it paled next to the fame won by the funk-rock and rap acts they influenced. The "new wave"/alternative boom of the 1980s also helped such forward-looking British pop bands as Echo and the Bunnymen, the Psychedelic Furs and others who drew on acid rock, classic pop, and avant-garde music.

Another hugely influential band that benefitted from the development of alternative radio and MTV was **The Cure** (see entry). Fronted by wild-haired, lipsticked singer/songwriter Robert Smith, the group's dark, often despairing pop caught on with teenagers; they not only knew the group's songs by heart, but imitated Smith's style of dress and makeup. The "goth" school owes a great deal to Smith's anguished presentation.

But surely **Morrissey** (see entry), lead singer of the gifted pop band The Smiths, also deserves some of the same credit. Though less extreme in costume— he favored 1950s style—Morrissey's tearful warbling and smart lyrics had a strong influence on the alternative rock that followed, as did the crafty, melodic playing of Smiths guitarist Johnny Marr.

Melody as an alternative

Drawing on the influence of earlier punk and alternative musicians, England's so-called "Brit Pop" movement of the 1990s gave the world a number of gifted, melodic rock bands. The first to become superstars were **Oasis**, fronted by two brothers—guitarist/songwriter Noel and singer Liam—who made headlines for fighting and insulting everyone else. What made Oasis huge in America, however, had more to do with their ability to write songs with big, singable choruses, like "Wonderwall" and "Don't Go Away." Oasis offended some rock purists by comparing themselves to the Beatles, but even McCartney and Beatle producer George Martin expressed admiration for their well-made rock.

The Brit Pop school also produced such adventurous groups as **Blur** (see entry), who had a bitter public rivalry with Oasis that helped both groups get more publicity, experimental tune smiths Radiohead, new-wave revivalists **Elastica** (see entry), and many others. These bands offered a catchier, more tuneful alternative to the angst-ridden, metallic blast of the grunge music that was overwhelming U.S. radio waves. Of course, all of these groups owed a massive debt to The Beatles, who helped invent "power pop" in the 1960s by putting sweet melodies (and beautiful vocal harmonies) together with guitar-rock energy. But other bands, like The Kinks, The Who, and The Zombies from England and The Beach Boys and The Byrds from the U.S., were very influential in the development of this style.

Suede

sure on MTV and heavy radio rotation turned their first two albums into multi-platinum smashes despite generally bad reviews and charges that their popularity had more to do with Rossdale's looks than with the group's music.

Among the less obviously commercial British alternative music that emerged in the 1990s, two of the more important names are **PJ Harvey** (see entry) and Nick Cave. Polly Jean Harvey and her rotating crew of musicians served up heavy, uncompromising rock, citing influences like 1970s "rock priestess" Patti Smith and 1960s avant-garde artist Captain Beefheart. Harvey also showed a flair for modernizing classic blues. Cave, meanwhile, provided always dark and sometimes gloomy songs with varied forms of instrumentation.

Part of the Brit Pop school aped the high fashion and androgyny (like lipstick and eye makeup on males) of such "glam rock" acts of the 1970s as David Bowie, T. Rex, and Roxy Music. Groups like **Suede** (see entry), known as The London Suede in America, drew not only on the look of these earlier acts, but on their dramatic, emotional blend of guitar rock and pop melody. Though they hailed from England, the band Bush—fronted by heart throb singer/guitarist Gavin Rossdale—sounded very American indeed, with a grunge/alternative guitar-based roar and anguished lyrics, and became superstars thanks to their rabid young fans. Expo-

Brett Anderson, of Suede, simply laughs when people ask him about the mid-decade explosion of Brit Pop. "I don't think anyone who knew the ins and outs of Brit Pop would actually take notice of those bands who jumped on the coat tails of the original factions, and make third rate xeroxes of everything."

In 1996, Blur proclaimed Brit Pop was dead, perhaps because they themselves were bored with the term. But Anderson said, "Everyone says 'we're not Brit Pop, or whatever,' but bands making the sort of music they are, they just are. And to American ears, we're totally that category. We're not **Nirvana** [see entry], we're not **Bjork** [see entry], so we totally fit into that category."

THE
BEAUTIFUL SOUTH

British alternative pop/rock band

Formed 1989 in Hull, England

A band as well-known for their gin-soaked cynicism as their catchy and lush pop melodies, the Beautiful South have had enormous impact in their native England, while success in America has been limited. Music critics on both shores and beyond, however, have praised the South. In particular, they've praised lyricist and singer Paul Heaton for his cockeyed views on love, the music business, and whatever else comes up. Heaton and songwriting partner Dave Rotheray seem to easily invent hummable tunes with irresistible pop hooks. Named for the not-so-beautiful run-down neighborhoods of South London, their band's name, like their songs, is an exercise in irony.

The Beautiful South was formed from the remnants of the breakup of the Housemartins, another cynical band from northern England with a more political bent. Singer/songwriter Heaton, along with Housemartin drummer Dave Hemingway, started the Beautiful South in 1989 in their hometown of Hull, a gray, working-class city in the north of England. With guitarist/songwriter Rotheray, bassist Sean Welch, drummer David Stead, and vocalist Brianna Corrigan,

"It's all a question of putting people on the right train, telling them to watch out, there's things in people and society to be angry about."–

Paul Heaton, singer and songwriter

The Beautiful South is known in England for its biting irony, particularly about the music business

the South presented a more expansive musical playing field than what was offered by the Housemartins. Their sound featured the vocal characterizations of three quite different lead vocalists. Commenting on the band's pop vocals and overall sound, Parke Puterbaugh observed in *Stereo Review,* "Their voices, one a croon of limited range [Heaton], the other more of a sing-speak [Hemingway]—are joined by Corrigan's girlish mouse-squeak and backed by a crack three-piece band of guitar, bass, and drums."

Songs for whoever

The Beautiful South released their first single, "Song for Whoever," in May 1989, five months before their debut album, *Welcome to the Beautiful South.* "Make a list of qualities that define great pop music," *People Weekly's* Michael Small suggested in his review, "and you've got a pretty fair description of the Beautiful South." The album did exceptionally well in England but received a cooler response in America.

Their second album, *Choke,* released in 1990, cemented their reputation as biting ironists. *Stereo Review's* Puterbaugh described the album as a "mix of lyrical quirks and music-hall and cabaret-influenced pop.... [which] stops just shy of being cute and charming, however, and gives the songs here a devilishly droll

Parents Aren't Supposed to Like It

[humorous] edge." The album included one of the band's best-known singles, "A Little Time," a Hemingway-Corrigan duet.

In 1992 the band released *0898 Beautiful South*. On the album the band's three lead vocalists deliver subtle social commentary and humor over fragile pop melodies and harmonies. Vocalist Corrigan left the band soon after that album's release, supposedly due to the sexist lyrics of a song from *0898*. Corrigan claimed that wasn't the reason for leaving. "I left really because it was the right time for me to go," she told Gary Crossing of England's *The Big Issue*. "My reservations about some of the lyrics became like a trigger to spur me on." Following the departure of Corrigan the band took some time off and returned with *Miaow,* a 1994 album featuring new vocalist Jacqueline Abbott, whom the band discovered singing at a party. While only available as an import in America, the album didn't fare well in England despite critical praise.

Heaton and company wouldn't have to worry about record sales much longer. In November 1994, *Carry On Up the Charts: The Best of the Beautiful South* was released and became the third-fastest selling British album of all time. At the same time Heaton was questioning how much further he could go with the band. "I was feeling a bit unconvinced about me own future in music," he told Sylvia Patterson of *Melody Maker.* "Because I just feel a bit old for it.... I was just thinking how I'm not sure, as a singer-songwriter in a band, how long you can go in the pop industry."

Toward the end of 1996 the band released *Blue Is the Colour,* another album available only as an import in America. Jennifer Nine of *Melody Maker* described it as, "charming, subversively luscious business as usual." So it seems Heaton will carry on with the Beautiful South. He admitted to Patterson in 1995 that he's, "starting to write really good lyrics now. I'm starting to get proud." Heaton also admitted that the Beautiful South, aside from exploring the undiscovered hooks and melodies of pop, is furthering the mission begun by British punk and new wave bands such as the Clash, the Jam, and the Sex Pistols. "It's all a question of putting people on the right train," he told Patterson, "telling them to watch out, there's things in people and society to be angry about."

Selected Awards

BRIT Award for Best Music Video, for "A Little Time," 1991.

Carry On Up the Charts: The Best of the Beautiful South, quintuple platinum.

Selected Discography

Welcome to the Beautiful South (Elektra), 1989.

Choke (Elektra), 1989.

0898 Beautiful South (Elektra), 1992.

Miaow (Go! Discs), 1994, United Kingdom.

Carry On Up the Charts: The Best of the Beautiful South (Mercury), 1995.

Blue Is the Colour (Go! Discs), 1996, United Kingdom.

Further Reading

The Big Issue (England), May 27, 1996, p. 29.

Chicago Sun-Times, June 26, 1992.

Melody Maker (England), September 29, 1990, p. 8; November 10, 1990, p. 47; April 2, 1994, p. 34; December 2, 1995, p. 20; November 9, 1996, p. 51.

New Musical Express (England), November 11, 1995.

New York Times, October 24, 1994, p. C14.

People, May 7, 1990, p. 31.

Q (England), March 1995, p. 42.

Spin, May 1990, p. 75; July 1992, p. 18.

Parents Aren't Supposed to Like It

BLUR

British pop/rock band

Formed in London, England, in 1988

Blur has made a career as music chameleons, changing its music from record to record. Blur first came to the public's attention as part of England's "baggy" scene with bands like The Happy Mondays and The Stone Roses. After that fad passed the band adopted a very British sound taken from classic English bands like the Kinks. Then on 1997's album titled *Blur,* the band suddenly started sounding like American lo-fi bands like **Pavement** (see entry) and **Guided by Voices** (see entry). The band's changing ways hasn't hurt it in England. There, Blur is one of the top bands of the 1990s, and the United States is belatedly catching on.

Blur has had a hard time making it as big in America as they have in England. On *Blur,* singer Damon Albarn seems to be trying to court America. "Look inside America / She's alright, she's alright," he sings on "Look Inside America."

Middle class kids

In England, a well-publicized feud exists between Blur and fellow English band **Oasis** (see entry). The rivalry has to do with

> "When you're dealing with people who don't understand you and don't like your music, it gets to be a bit frustrating."
>
> —Damon Albarn in *Rolling Stone* on Blur's former lack of success in the United States

Damon Albarn

Blur, signing their book, 1996

the differences in the bands' upbringings. Oasis's members came from a poor working-class background, while the members of Blur came from the middle-class. Albarn's parents were unconventional artists, and he grew up in Colchester, a town outside London. When he was fifteen he won a regional "Young Composer of the Year" award.

While they were all attending art school, Albarn, guitarist Graham Coxon, and drummer Dave Rowntree decided to form a band. They recruited bassist Alex James and called the new band Seymour. At one of their early gigs, a representative from a record label spotted them and agreed to sign them on the condition that

they change their name. Thus, Blur was born.

A hit in England, tough luck in the United States

Their single "She's So High," reached number two on the British charts; when the album *Leisure* came out, it debuted on number seven on the British charts. The single, "There's No Other Way," was discovered by a few American fans, but for the most part, Blur remained unknown in the United States.

The follow-up record, *Modern Life Is Rubbish*, took a long time. Both the English and U.S. label sent the band back to the studio because they wanted to hear a

Parents Aren't Supposed to Like It

single. Blur went back to work and scored with another hit record in England. In the United States the record tanked, mainly because Americans were in the middle of grunge's popularity.

Albarn hated grunge, thinking it to be whiny. "If you tell a whole nation it's dysfunctional [not functioning right], it becomes dysfunctional," he said to *Rolling Stone*. So instead of going grunge, Blur made the record *Parklife* that was even more upbeat and melodic. *Rolling Stone* described the record as "some hopped-up soap opera, a potent collection of dance-hall floor stompers and sweeping ballads that sparkle with knowing winks at English pop stylists from the Small Faces to Wire to Madness." The record spawned a British hit with the new wave dance single "Girls and Boys." The single was a minor hit in the United States.

The follow-up, 1995's glossy pop record *The Great Escape*, took the usual Blur path—a hit in England, a miss in the United States. "The conflicts between U.K. and American tastes seemed too decisive for Blur," commented Rolling Stone Online, saying the record "struck many Americans as too perfect."

Breaking the chain?

Blur completely switched gears on their 1997 record *Blur*, picking up some influences from American bands. Entertainment Weekly Online gave the record a B+ and applauded the style change, saying that Blur does "pull it off." MTV Online said the group is "shying away from crowd-pleasing pop in favor of self-indulgent experimentation."

Among the new sounds on *Blur*, the thrashy, upbeat "Song 2" made a hit with American audiences and critics, paving the way for the U.S. exposure that had previously eluded the band.

Selected Awards

BRIT Awards, Best Single and Best Video, for *Parklife*, 1995.

New Music Express Single of the Year ("Girls and Boys").

Selected Discography

Leisure (SBK), 1991.

Modern Life Is Rubbish (SBK), 1993.

Parklife (SBK), 1994.

The Great Escape (Virgin), 1995.

Blur (Virgin), 1997.

Further Reading

Daly, Steven, "Britain's Class Act: Blur Stand Up for Their Mod-rock Roots on 'Parklife,'" *Rolling Stone*, November 3, 1994.

Krugman, Michael, "The Reading Festival," *Rolling Stone*, October 19, 1995, p. 33.

Sinclair, Tom, "Blur," *Entertainment Weekly*, March 14, 1997, p. 78.

Sprague, David, "Blur Get Introspective on Their New Album," *Rolling Stone*, November 2, 1995.

Wallace, Bruce, "Rock of Aged: The Old-timers Dominate Britain's Pop-music Exports," *Maclean's*, March 13, 1995, p. 62.

Contact Information

Virgin Records
338 N. Foothill Road
Beverly Hills, CA 90210

Web Site

http://www.blur.co.uk/

DaViD BoWiE

Influential British singer/songwriter

Born David Jones on January 8, 1947,
in Brixton, England

"I could make a transformation as a rock n' roll star / I could play the wild mutation as a rock n' roll star." —from David Bowie's "Star"

The "Rock and Roll Chameleon," David Bowie, is one of the most changing and mysterious figures in rock music. The "man who sold the world" through his different personas and unique sound and vision, has maintained an astonishing career that has spanned three decades into the 1990s and beyond. Light years ahead of the times, Bowie has channeled his musical and stage images to match the ever-changing world of music. Vocalist, songwriter, actor, artist, and visionary are just a few of the titles that fit this multifaceted, multitalented performer.

Rebel, rebel

Born David Jones on January 8, 1947, in Brixton, England, his difficult childhood led him to take refuge in rock and roll. His parents exposed him to the music of American rhythm and blues artists Fats Domino and Little Richard, which inspired him to learn to play guitar and saxophone at a young age. His teenage years were spent exploring the art world. He studied commercial art at Bromley Technical High School, but left to

Bowie (left) performing with Nine Inch Nails, 1995

work at an advertising agency before graduating. He studied the art of mime with the Lindsay Kemp Mime Troupe and painted and acted in small stage roles. Finding religion in the teachings of Buddhism, Bowie even considered entering a Buddhist monastery at one point.

His first of many "changes" was his name. To avoid confusion with Davey Jones of the Monkees, David Jones became "David Bowie." He started performing in many 1960s rock bands, including George and the Dragons, The Lower Third, The Nazz, and the King Bees. It was by striking out on his own, though, that the performer struck gold.

Starman

"Space Oddity" introduced Bowie's 1969 debut album, *Man of Words/Man of Music* to become *the* song of David Bowie's career. Inspired by Stanley Kubrick's film, *2001: A Space Odyssey,* the song told the story of Major Tom, an astronaut lost in space. The single was his first hit on both sides of the Atlantic.

Changes continued with the release of his next two albums, *The Man Who Sold the World* and *Hunky Dory*. On a trip to New York, he met pop artist Andy Warhol who, along with the avant-garde music of New York-based Velvet Underground, would heavily influence his sound and image. Both album covers display the first of Bowie's many looks. Taking tips from the flamboyant Little Richard, Bowie's new androgynous (mixing of male and female elements), *femme fatale* appearance caused many to wonder about his sexuality. (After admitting his bisexual experimentation in an interview, despite being married with a child, Bowie would later say it was a major mistake to have made such a statement.) This ambiguous male/female look started a whole new movement called "Glitterrock" or "Glam Rock," and left a lasting impression on music fashion for years to come.

Rock superstardom fell upon David Bowie in 1972 with the release of his stellar album, *The Rise and Fall of Ziggy Stardust and the Spiders from Mars.* Bowie became the "Ziggy" persona, an androgynous, space-alien rock star. In real life, he adopted the wild lifestyle of the make-believe rock idol he created. **Lou Reed** (see entry), another influential glam rocker, would observe, "When Bowie gets drunk, he thinks he's Ziggy." When the character became his alter ego, Bowie disbanded Ziggy Stardust and the Spiders from Mars (which featured guitarist Mick Ronson). A final show capturing Bowie's performance in all its glory was documented on film.

Changes: from Ziggy Stardust to Aladdin Sane

The Aladdin Sane character, revealed on the 1973 album of the same name, didn't venture far from the glittery make-up and stage costumes of Ziggy. The album featured "Panic in Detroit" and "Jean Genie," a song he wrote in Detroit about the infamous **Iggy Pop** (see entry), who later became Bowie's partner in other musical adventures .

Bowie's dark apocalyptic album *Diamond Dogs* appeared in 1974. Songs like the (British novelist) George Orwell-inspired "1984" glimpsed the future of rock and roll according to David Bowie. The theatrical tour behind the album revolutionized rock stage shows forever. Reaching back into his theater background, Bowie hired a team of Broadway designers to construct an elaborate stage design that included Bowie levitating over the audience for the encores. These inventive stage productions were borrowed by other rock legends like Kiss, Alice Cooper, and Pink Floyd.

With slicked-back hair and crisp white suits, Bowie conceived his next visage, "The Thin White Duke." This persona lasted through the next two albums. While the world was tuning into disco, he turned to funk, soul, and rhythm and blues (R&B) for inspiration. *Young Americans* featured the hit song "Fame," two tracks with John Lennon, and Bowie playing the saxophone. *Station to Station* hit gold with its single "Golden Years" in 1976, but it was far from a golden time in his life.

After problems involving drugs stood in the way of his illustrious career, Bowie took a break and went to Berlin, Germany, to recover. Bowie's fondness for the city and its culture gave birth to a trilogy of albums that incorporated a new electronic, futuristic sound for Bowie. *Low, Heroes,* and *Lodger* were all produced by

Brian Eno, an innovator in ambient music, a form of electronic music meant especially for listening. This emotionally cold, turbulent period from the late 1970s is captured in the song "Heroes," a definitive Bowie classic.

Let's dance

The 1980s was a time of continued musical exploration for Bowie. *Scary Monsters* had him venturing further into the new art of music video. He returned to the Major Tom character, who met his demise in the video for the hit single "Ashes to Ashes." Unfortunately, this new medium stifled his musical creativity for the next three albums.

Let's Dance, released in 1983, reached commercial success thanks to its new wave sound. The new clean cut image wasn't what old Bowie fans wanted from their hero, though. He seemed to many to be on his way as a mainstream pop artist as the album reached number one. The albums *Tonight* and *Never Let Me Down* were forgettable and let his fans down. Bowie would later admit, "They were just awful," due to the fact he had fallen out of love with writing music at the time. He did produce the first long form video for the song "(Jazzin for) Blue Jean."

During the video revolution, Bowie paired up with other 1970s rock idols for duets. A collaboration between glam-rockers Queen and Bowie produced the remarkable song, "Under Pressure," which appeared on *Queen's Greatest Hits.* Mick Jagger of the Rolling Stones teamed up with him for a rendition of Martha

The actor and artist

Determined not to be confined to rock music, Bowie embarked on an acting career. Infatuated with the silver screen, he appeared in numerous films throughout the years. First was a cameo live performance in Christianne F in 1980, followed by a feature role as an alien in The Man Who Fell to Earth, a role that won him a best actor award from the U.S. Academy of Science Fiction Fantasy and Horror Films. Just a Gigolo, The Hunger, Merry Christmas, Mr. Lawrence, Labyrinth, Absolute Beginners, and The Linguini Incident all showcased his acting talents through the years. He appeared as his onetime creative muse, Andy Warhol, in the 1997 movie Basquiat. His performance as the lead character in a Broadway production of The Elephant Man in the fall of 1980 brought him critical acclaim. His artistic vision as a painter was showcased in many art exhibitions through the years as well.

and the Vandellas' 1960s Motown hit, "Dancing in the Streets," for the Live Aid concert in 1985. Both songs and videos followed the early success of his legendary duet with Bing Crosby, performing the Christmas song "The Little Drummer Boy," on Crosby's TV special back in 1977.

The 1990s brought *Tin Machine.* Tin Machine wasn't just the latest Bowie incarnation; it was a full band. Stepping back from the limelight, he stayed in the background and enjoyed being just one of the band. He let guitar virtuoso Reeves

Golden years

In 1996 David Bowie was inducted into the Rock and Roll Hall of Fame. He refused to show up at the event, saying that he wasn't dead yet. Madonna presented and accepted the award on his behalf. He also received the 2,083rd star on the Hollywood Walk of Fame for his musical and acting efforts.

In addition, Bowie put a price on his future career moves and became the first rock star to sell "Bowie Bonds." Fifty-five million dollars worth of the bonds were bought up by Prudential Insurance. This allowed him to get Wall Street to front him future revenues and have him pay it back as his back catalog of music continues to sell. Since his twenty-five-plus albums still sell over a million copies a year, this should be an easy task.

On January 8, 1997, David Bowie turned 50. The new alternative music world came out to celebrate his birthday at a benefit concert. All the young dudes like Sonic Youth, Billy Corgan of the **Smashing Pumpkins** (see entry), and David Grohl of the **Foo Fighters** (see entry), joined Bowie onstage to pay tribute to the man and perform his songs. The encore had Bowie take the stage to perform his classic "Space Oddity," the song that started it all.

Gabrels and the Sales Brothers (Tony and Hunt) step to the front. Tin Machine released three albums altogether, but they only had moderate success.

The next solo Bowie album, *Black Tie, White Noise,* topped the U.S. charts with the single, "Jump They Say," and was accompanied by the release of an interactive CD-ROM, which allowed users to edit their own versions of the video. Bowie was entering the future he once wrote about.

Fame

Bowie returned to experimenting with music again and reteamed with Brian Eno for his concept album, *Outside.* *Outside* recalls Bowie's *Low* album, but with a twisted, metallic, industrial sound. The album tells the story about a fictional detective, Nathan Adler, and the ritual murder of Baby Grace Blue. The song and video to "The Heart's Filthy Lesson" recaptured his unique visionary style. The coinciding tour was a double bill with **Nine Inch Nails** (see entry), a collaborative effort to gain the new alternative, modern rock audience for Bowie. This also benefited Nine Inch Nails, who were already electronic music superstars. In fact, Trent Reznor, the man behind the band, readily admits that he owes his music career and success to Bowie. *Low* was the album that influenced Nine Inch Nails the most and paved the way for Reznor's music. In concert Bowie resurrected a few *Heroes* and *Low* era songs. Reznor and Bowie even sang each other's songs on the tour, hoping to catch each other's fans.

Cyberspace

Bowie's next world to conquer was cyberspace. He released his next single "Telling Lies" on the Internet. He was the first major artist to do so, setting yet another trend for others to follow. *Earthling*, the 1997 album, promises to continue the Bowie tradition of musical innovation. Exploring the sounds and electronic textures of dance music and electronica, he fuses hyperkinetic, aggressive rock with modern jungle-beat rhythms. His distinctive vocals soar above the metallic, jarring guitar work of Reeves Gabrels, his former Tin Machine collaborator. A return to "Alien" form and a newfound energy is evident on the album. Bowie is still changing with the times, but putting his own spin to the music.

The end of the 1990s finds David Bowie still reinventing himself, breaking new musical ground, and remaining in the spotlight. Taking his sound and vision into the next decade, David Bowie will always be the man who sold the world.

Selected Awards

U.S. Academy of Films, Best Actor Award, for "Man Who Fell to Earth," 1977.

BRIT Awards, Best British Male Artist, 1984.

MTV Video Music Awards, Best Performance, for "Dancing in the Streets," 1986.

Silver Clef Awards, Outstanding Achievement, 1987.

Grammy Awards, Best Album Package, for *Sound + Vision,* 1990.

Irvo Novello Awards, Outstanding Contribution to British Music, 1990.

Q Awards, Inspiration Award, 1995.

Inducted into the Rock and Roll Hall of Fame, 1996.

BRIT Awards, Outstanding Contribution to British Music, 1996.

Selected Discography

David Bowie: Man of Words/Man of Music (Mercury), 1969; reissued as *Space Oddity* (RCA), 1984.

The Man Who Sold the World (Mercury), 1971.

Hunky Dory (Mercury), 1971.

The Rise and Fall of Ziggy Stardust and the Spiders from Mars (RCA), 1972.

Alladin Sane (RCA), 1973.

Pin Ups (RCA), 1973.

Diamond Dogs (RCA), 1974.

David Live (RCA), 1974.

Young Americans (RCA), 1975.

Station to Station (RCA), 1976.

Changesonebowie (RCA), 1976.

Low (RCA), 1977.

Heroes (RCA), 1977.

Stage (RCA), 1978.

Lodger (RCA), 1979.

Scary Monsters (RCA), 1980.

(All of the preceding have been reissued by Rykodisc.)

Let's Dance (EMI America), 1983.

Tonight (EMI America), 1984.

Never Let Me Down (EMI America), 1987.

Sound + Vision (Rykodisc), 1989, 4-disc box set.

Changesbowie (Rykodisc), 1990.

Black Tie, White Noise (Savage), 1993.

Outside (Virgin), 1995.

Earthling (Virgin), 1997.

Further Reading

Gordinier, Jeff, "Stardust Memories," *Entertainment Weekly,* January 31, 1997.

Gore, Joe, "Changes 2.1: New Digital Stimulation from David Bowie and Reeves Gabrels," *Guitar Player,* June 1997, p. 44.

Levine, Robert, "Cyberspace Oddity: The David Bowie Interview," *The Web Magazine,* March 1997.

Sischy, Ingrid, "The Artist Who Fell to Earth," *Interview,* February 1997, p. 46.

Books:

Bowie, Angela, and Patrick Carr, *Backstage Passes,* Jove Publications, 1994.

Buckley, David, *Complete Guide to the Music of David Bowie,* Omnibus Press, 1996.

Miles, *David Bowie,* Omnibus Press, 1996.

Thompson, Dave, *David Bowie,* Publishers Group West, 1994.

Contact Information

Virgin Records
1790 Broadway
20th Floor
New York, NY 10019

Web Sites

http://www.virginrecords.com/

http://www.davidbowie.com/

BUSH

British alternative pop/rock band
Formed in 1992 in London, England

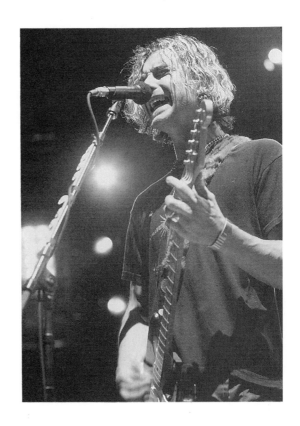

The story of Bush is one of modern rock's extraordinary tales. After two albums, the quartet is rated among the most successful British groups to visit America since the Beatles. But at home, they are virtual unknowns, a band who didn't even score their first hit single until 1997. The hard-rocking Bush exploded onto the American music scene in 1995. They had already been playing together for nearly three years at that point, but no one was able to anticipate the events to come.

Early history

Of the four members of Bush, bassist Dave Parsons was the best known, having tasted some success with the 1980s pop group Transvision Vamp, themselves best remembered for the hit singles "I Want Your Love" and "Baby I Don't Care." By 1989, however, the group's success had dried up. Singer/songwriter and guitarist Gavin Rossdale, meanwhile, had never entered the spotlight, despite his band, Midnight, having released a string of singles through the early 1990s. Lead guitarist Nigel Pulsford, too, was still searching for

> "If anyone compares us to Nirvana, I take that as a big compliment." –Gavin Rossdale (vocals, guitar)

Gavin Rossdale

Bush at the 1996 MTV Video Music Awards

that first lucky break following the breakup of his band, King's Blank. He never dreamed it would happen while he was checking out another band entirely, at a London club in 1992. That was where he first met Rossdale, and the first seeds of Bush were planted.

Joined by Parsons and drummer Robin Goodridge, a London session musician, Bush recorded an album's worth of demos, heavily influenced by the grunge sound that was just entering Britain from America. Rossdale told *Spin*, "if anyone compares us to Nirvana, I take that as a big compliment." **Nirvana** (see entry) drummer Dave Grohl was one of the people who complimented him; ac-

cording to *Spin*, Grohl reckons Rossdale sings just like Kurt Cobain. "I didn't teach myself to sing that way," Rossdale answered. "You can't manufacture that, you know."

Bush's first demos

Rossdale's vocals were a deep, throaty roar, bellowed over the growling of his bandmates, and the perfect match for song titles like "Bomb," "Glycerine," and "Testosterone." It was an interesting sound, but it was also an unfashionable one; Brit Pop bands like **Oasis** (see entry) and **Suede** (see entry) were just beginning to make an impact in the United

Parents Aren't Supposed to Like It

Kingdom, and few record labels even looked at Bush.

It was late 1993 before Bush landed a deal, signing to the American Trauma label (headed by George Michael's former manager, Rob Kahane), and heading into the studio to record their first album, *Sixteen Stone*. (A stone is an English measurement of weight, equal to 14 pounds.) Just as heavy as their demos, but with producers Clive Langer and Alan Winstanley layering the songs with the bright hooklines and irresistible choruses that became Bush's trademark, *Sixteen Stone* was an instant classic. Released in late 1994, *Sixteen Stone* was already heading for the American charts when Bush opened their first American club tour in the new year.

Sudden success in America

By the time the band was halfway through the visit, "Everything Zen"—Rossdale's reflections on what he sees as the hollowness of modern life—was topping the alternative charts, the first of a staggering five successive hits to be taken from the album. It was an excellent choice for a single, blending the band's sound with some amusing references to a few of their heroes. The line "Mickey Mouse is on sale again," for instance, was borrowed from an old **David Bowie** (see entry) song.

Over the next year, "Little Things," "Comedown," "Glycerine," "Machinehead" (featuring Rossdale's dog, Winston, on backing growls), and of course, "Everything Zen," would become some

of the most familiar sounds on American radio.

Bush intended to tour the United States for a matter of months. Instead they ended up on the road for the next year and a half, playing 230 shows and watching *Sixteen Stone* take up residence in the Top Ten.

Bush came off the road in May 1996, following two shows at Red Rocks, Colorado. They returned directly to the studio. Hooking up this time with underground producer Steve Albini, they headed over to London to record at the famed Abbey Road, where the Beatles recorded all their classics in the 1960s. There were, the band said, less distractions in London simply because nobody had heard of them!

Into the studio with Steve Albini

Aiming to draw their energies from the past eighteen months of live experience, Bush and Albini intended slamming the album down in record time, no more than two takes per song, and every song a firestorm of down-to-earth energy and intensity. The success of the experiment can be gauged from the speed with which *Razorblade Suitcase* hit the streets. It was released just six months after the band finished touring, in November 1996, and just weeks after Bush won the MTV Viewers' Choice video award. Shortly after, Rossdale was included within *People Weekly*'s "50 Most Beautiful People" issue. "Women have always lost it over Gavin," video director Shawn Mortensen shrugged by way of explanation.

Razorblade Suitcase was an immediate smash. It was just as aggressive as *Sixteen Stone,* but even more immediate. *Spin* called it one of the best albums Albini ever worked on—a role call that includes everyone from Nirvana to the Jesus Lizard, and Pod to **PJ Harvey** (see entry)—and the American public agreed. *Razorblade Suitcase* was an immediate chart topper, while the first single, "Swallowed," entered Billboard's Modern Rock Monitor chart at #6, the highest debut in history. "Cold Contagious" and "Personal Holloway," named after a London women's prison and featuring another guest appearance from Winston the dog, swiftly followed it up the chart.

Meanwhile, back in Britain

And still nobody at home knew who they were. While Bush was recording *Razorblade Suitcase,* it was sharing the studio with Mark Owen, formerly of British teenybop sensation Take That. Armies of Owen's fans waited outside hoping to catch a glimpse of their hero and cornering everyone who left the building to find out if they knew him. Rossdale was one of the people they stopped. And when they asked who he was, he'd simply reply, "I'm just the dishwasher, and nobody tells me anything." They usually believed him.

Selected Awards

MTV Viewers Choice Video, for "Machinehead," 1996.

Selected Discography

Sixteen Stone (Trauma/Interscope), 1994.

Razorblade Suitcase (Trauma/Interscope), 1996.

Further Reading

Daly, Steven, "Nirvanawannabes: Bush," *Rolling Stone,* April 18, 1996, p. 40.

Diehl, Matt, "Bush: Razorblade Suitcase," *Rolling Stone,* December 12, 1996, p. 84.

Hannaham, James, "Drop In on a Neighbour" *Spin,* December 1996.

Kelly, Christina, "Bush Whacked!," *Rolling Stone,* July 13, 1995, p. 29.

Web Sites

http://www.Bushnet.com/home/

he band's official site features news, photos, and audio and video material.

http://www.ici.net/cust_pages/petper/linkpage.htm

The Burning Bush features photos, tour histories, readers surveys, and plenty of links to other Bush sites.

http://www.cybercomm.net/-jon/winston.html

The only page devoted to Gavin's dog, Winston.

ELViS COSTELLO

British alternative pop/rock singer and songwriter

Born Declan Patrick McManus in London, England, on August 25, 1954, and raised in Liverpool, England

Elvis Costello is one of the most productive and constantly changing songwriters of his generation. An innovative composer whose music defies classification by genre, he's written and performed all types of music, from country-and-western songs to classical compositions. His first hit, 1977's "Watching the Detectives" from the album *My Aim is True,* combined snarly punk with a reggae beat. From there he went on to explore American rhythm and blues, country and western, and other styles. Called a "brilliant, multifaceted artist" by *Billboard,* Costello became known for drawing from various sources of music, such as the marriage of punk and reggae in his early work, and later the ability to write and perform songs in virtually any genre from Motown to country to classical. Although diverse in form, all of his compositions are challenging musically, and his melodies always are inventive. His lyrics are literate and complex. A Costello song can be either personal or political in nature, but—whatever the topic—the material shows Costello's passion through sharp wit and cynicism or through pointed descriptions and dialogue.

"You don't even need to talk in terms of strict divisions or crossover anything anymore—that's ancient history." –Elvis Costello

The great risk taker

Throughout his career, Costello has willingly experimented with different forms and styles of music, giving little regard to the effect these flights from mainstream pop music may have on his commercial success. "We applaud Elvis for the risks he takes," noted Warner Bros. executive Jeff Gould in *Billboard*. "His side projects may be less accessible to a general audience, but they keep him interesting to his core fans and show his continuing viability as a cutting-edge artist."

Musical upbringing

Costello—originally named Declan Patrick McManus (some sources say MacManus)—had a fairly traditional musical upbringing. His father Ross McManus, a singer with the Joe Loss Dance Orchestra, introduced him to music. As a child, Costello would save his pocket money to buy records, a habit that continued into adulthood. As an avid record collector, Costello developed a deep knowledge of popular songs by tracing musical pieces that he found interesting back to their origins. The singer regularly searched out old recordings to expand his knowledge. "When I became a musician," he told *Billboard*, "I started tracing back stuff. I'd know one song that had filtered back to England, and I'd want to hear more. When I came to America, I went to all these thrift stores and got another layer of music."

Costello began writing songs when he was about fifteen years old, the same age that he left school. He eventually started working as a computer programmer for Elizabeth Arden cosmetics in 1973. In 1975, married with one son, Costello formed his first band—Flip City—a country combo that disbanded one year later.

In 1976 Costello embarked upon a career as a solo artist with newly formed British independent label Stiff Records. He began billing himself as D.P. Costello—the new surname being his grandmother's maiden name—instead of using his given name. By 1977, Costello was able to quit his day job at the cosmetic factory, concentrating solely on his musical career. Costello changed his first name to Elvis and released his first single—"Less Than Zero," which described English fascism—that same year.

Profound and productive

Since then, Costello has released seventeen albums in approximately nineteen years, beginning with the groundbreaking punk rock album *My Aim Is True* in 1977. Called one of the greatest first albums in the history of pop music, *My Aim Is True* mixed new wave punk with other musical forms and, in fact, established new wave punk as a legitimate form of pop music. Three of the songs from the album went on to become rock classics: the hard-rocking and whimsical "(The Angels Wanna Wear My) Red Shoes," the incredibly romantic and evocative ballad "Alison" (which contains the line, "My aim is true"), and "Watching the Detectives." Four years after its release, *My Aim Is True* received certification as a gold record from the Record Industry Association of America for selling

500,000 copies. Ten years later, the album earned platinum certification in 1991 when sales topped one million copies.

Costello followed *My Aim Is True* with *This Year's Model* in 1978. Costello assembled his road band The Attractions—Steve Nieve on keyboards, Pete Thomas on drums, and Bruce Thomas on bass—for this album. With a harder edge, *This Year's Model* enjoyed even greater commercial success than its predecessor. Critically, reviewers praised the album as an example of "intelligent pop," and it produced two hit singles in "Pump It Up" and "(I Don't Want to Go to) Chelsea."

Costello closed the 1970s with *Armed Forces,* one of his best selling albums. More ambitious, melodic, and diverse than earlier albums, *Armed Forces* contained "Oliver's Army"—a single that sold more than 400,000 copies—and demonstrated Costello's skill with political pop. Two other notable singles emerged from *Armed Forces* as well: Costello's "Accidents Will Happen" and "(What's So Funny 'bout) Peace, Love, and Understanding," written by the album's producer Nick Lowe.

Bigger Musical Experiments

During the 1980s, Costello became more commercial and started experimenting with other sounds. *Get Happy!,* a twenty-song album, incorporated the 1960s rhythm and blues sounds of Motown, Stax, and Atlantic Records. Continuing the songwriter's exploration of American sounds, 1981's *Almost Blue* included country covers recorded under the direction of Billy Sherrill, famous for producing country stars Charlie Pride and George Jones. Costello appeared at the Grand Ole Opry in Nashville, Tennessee, to promote *Almost Blue* while touring the United States.

"There is some expressive life left in rock 'n' roll, even for us."

Costello continued releasing new and different records. *Imperial Bedroom,* from 1982, was heavily orchestrated and critically acclaimed. Next year's *Punch the Clock* featured upbeat pop songs and enjoyed commercial success. Costello's 1984 release, *Goodbye Cruel World,* fared poorly, however. The album suffered from trendy synthesized production that overshadowed the strength of Costello's songs. Costello's performance on the album seemed uninspired.

At this time, Costello's marriage ended. He toured without the Attractions for a while, but remained quiet for the rest of the year. In 1985, still keeping a low profile, Costello produced the Irish rock/traditional band The Pogues' second album. He married Caitlin O'Riordan, the group's bass player, that same year and returned to recording, still without the Attractions.

Now exploring more of a folk sound, Costello released *King of America* in 1986, an experimental mixture of Tex/Mex, country, Cajun, and Irish styles performed in mostly acoustic versions but also with some rockabilly musicians who used to back up the other Elvis

Public Relations

Early on in his career, Elvis Costello gained a reputation in the music industry for promoting himself and his work in novel ways. "We want to do things that people won't forget in an hour, things that'll leave 'em talking," Costello explained to Billboard when discussing his promotional strategies in 1996.

Costello first earned notoriety in 1977 with a public-relations ruse outside of the London Hilton Hotel. The songwriter heard that CBS sales executives were meeting at the hotel, and he wanted their attention, believing that if they heard his material they might offer him a recording contract. Costello performed some songs right on the street outside of the hotel. He was, however, promptly arrested and fined five pounds.

Undeterred, Costello continued to use impromptu performances to promote himself throughout the years. While appearing on Saturday Night Live later in 1977, for example, Costello began singing his first single release "Less Than Zero," but he stopped mid-song and told the audience: "I'm sorry, ladies and gentlemen, there's no reason to do this song." He then changed tunes and sang "Radio, Radio"—a song critical of the then-current state of rock 'n' roll radio—which Saturday Night Live personnel had specifically requested that he not sing. That performance was Costello's introduction to American television audiences.

Other notable Costello performances included appearances at three New York clubs—the Great Gildersleeves, the Lone Star Cafe, and the Bottom Line—in one night during his U.S. tour for the Armed Forces album. During the 1980s Costello jammed with Jerry Garcia (of the Grateful Dead) and James Burton at a San Francisco club to commemorate the anniversary of a record store. In the 1990s he sang "You Can't Take That Away from Me" with Tony Bennett during Bennett's "Unplugged" performance on MTV and sang "Bama Lama Bama Loo" with Chuck Berry and Little Richard on The Late Show. (Costello holds the distinction of appearing on The Late Show from four different cities on two continents.) He likewise participated in special broadcasts, including appearances on the World Cafe radio program and on Storytellers broadcast on VH-1.

Costello also utilized promotional gimmicks—such as a spinning request wheel—while touring. He developed his own print ad campaigns for his albums as well, including one for All This Useless Beauty in 1996.

Costello's energy in promoting his material earned him respect in the music industry. Jeff Gould, executive vice president and general manager of Warner Bros., called Costello "a dream artist." "He manages himself," Gould explained, "and comes to the table with loads of his own marketing ideas."

(Presley). Produced by Nick Lowe and Colin Fairley, *Blood & Chocolate* was a 1986 collection of hard-rocking songs that was Costello's last recording with the Attractions for eight years and his last for Columbia.

Work with me on this

During the 1980s Costello began collaborating with other notable contemporary songwriters, including Ruben Blades. He also collaborated with Paul McCartney on "Back on My Feet," which led to other songwriting with the ex-Beatle. McCartney's *Flowers in the Dirt* album featured songs co-written with Costello. Costello's 1989 album *Spike,* his first with Warner Bros., included other collaborations—including "Veronica," the first Costello song to reach the top twenty in the United States. The 1991 *Mighty Like a Rose* album also included the McCartney-Costello compositions "So Like Candy" and "Playboy to a Man."

In addition, the two composers worked together on a royal charity performance for Prince Charles and 300 invited guests. Costello and McCartney performed their composition "Mistress and Maid" together at the benefit. "It's the first time Elvis and I have played live," the ex-Beatle revealed in *Billboard.* "We've written together, we made demos together, we've done a bit of recording together and always enjoyed it." In fact, McCartney once likened writing with Costello to working with John Lennon.

Later in the 1990s Costello also collaborated with Burt Bacharach, creator of sophisticated pop ballads, to recreate the sound of the 1960s for a film project. "Burt consciously breaks rules with bar lines," Costello observed in *Time.* "He's breaking the meter, but it still feels natural. And he expresses feeling so much better than the trumped-up romantic ballads of today, where the emotions seem

to have come off a shopping cart at Woolworth's."

Then on to something really different

The 1990s marked a time of even greater experimentation with musical form for Costello. His big chance to stretch out came in 1993, when he ventured into classical music with *The Juliet Letters,* a sequence of dramatic ballads for voice and string quartet. Recorded with the noted Brodsky String Quartet, the song cycle revolves around letters about love, betrayal, and death. Accomplished and moving, *The Juliet Letters* were a commercial and artistic success. The album sold 300,000 copies worldwide.

Brutal Youth, released the next year, also sold well (180,000 copies) and enjoyed critical praise. At last reunited with The Attractions, Costello created an album not unlike those of his early days

---

Costello's lyrics kept their edge

From "Radio Radio" (This Year's Model, 1978): "And the radio is in the hands / of a lot of fools / who are trying to anesthetize / the way that you feel."

From "No Action" (This Year's Model, 1978): "Everytime I phone you, I just want to put you down."

From "All the Rage" (Brutal Youth, 1994): "The twitching impulse is to speak your mind / I'll lend you my microscope, and maybe you'll find it."

---

from the 1970s and 1980s. The highly original *Kojak Variety* followed in 1995. Recorded in 1990 and 1991, this collection of covers included The Kinks' "Days" and Bob Dylan's "I Threw It All Away," among other largely unknown songs from the 1930s through the 1970s. Nevertheless Costello covered the original versions skillfully with new arrangements, leaving his own mark on the songs and showing his love of blues and rock.

Costello helped produce his 1996 release, *All This Useless Beauty,* which again reunited him with The Attractions. The album proved that his songwriting ability was as strong as ever. *Billboard* wrote that Costello was "pushing the limits of pop songcraft" and called the album "as lyrically complex and musically challenging as Costello's best work to date." Writing in *People Weekly,* Craig Tomashoff called it "one of the most sophisticated discs of Costello's career" and noted that "each song has a twist to it."

As one of the more productive contemporary songwriters, Costello will no doubt continue to add to his impressive body of work. But his future material will most likely be new and different. "There is some expressive life left in rock 'n' roll, even for us," Costello explained in *Billboard.* "Having a 'sound' can be dangerous. But I think we've dismantled ours successfully.... We have more to offer."

Selected Awards

Grammy Awards, Best New Artist nomination, 1979.

MTV Video Music Awards, Best Male Video Award for "Veronica," 1989.

Rolling Stone Critics' Awards, Best Songwriter Award, 1989.

Ivor Novello Awards, Outstanding Contemporary Song Collection Award, 1995.

Selected Discography:

My Aim Is True (Columbia), 1977.

This Year's Model (Columbia), 1978.

Armed Forces (Columbia), 1979.

Get Happy! (Columbia), 1980.

Trust (Columbia), 1981.

Almost Blue (Columbia), 1981.

Imperial Bedroom (Columbia), 1982.

Punch the Clock (Columbia), 1983.

Goodbye Cruel World (Columbia), 1984.

King of America (Columbia), 1986.

Blood & Chocolate (Columbia), 1986.

Spike (Warner Brothers) 1989.

Mighty Like a Rose (Warner Brothers), 1991.

The Juliet Letters (Warner Brothers), 1993.

Brutal Youth (Warner Brothers), 1994.

Kojak Variety (Warner Brothers), 1995.

All This Useless Beauty (Warner Brothers), 1996.

Further Reading

Bambarger, Bradley, "New Elvis Costello Set Stars Attractions," *Billboard,* May 18, 1996, p. 11.

Corliss, Richard, "'60s Going on '90s," *Time,* October 7, 1996, p. 92.

Flanagan, Bill, "Concert Gives McCartney a Stage for Fab Firsts," *Billboard,* April 1, 1995, p. 8.

Newman, Melinda, "WB Takes the Lid off Costello's Covers Album," *Billboard,* April 15, 1995, p. 8.

Contact Information

Warner Bros.
3300 Warner Blvd.
Burbank, CA 91510

Web Site

www.wbr.com\elvis

THE CURE

British alternative pop/rock band
Formed in Sussex, England, in 1976

♪ "So many groups fool themselves into believing they're artists. We strive for beautiful things, and occasionally—infrequently, really—we get there. But over the years, I've come to realize that a lot of what we do is purely entertainment."—Robert Smith

Among the grandfathers of alternative rock bands, The Cure stand out for their tremendous influence on the current generation of alternative rockers. Led by Robert Smith, whose teased hair and black eyeliner dominates the group's look, The Cure formed in 1976 as a trio and released their first single, "Killing an Arab," in 1978. Simplistic, harsh, and mocking, The Cure's albums contained disturbing laments about despair, hopelessness, and death. Their albums "have always been suffused with what can only be termed the Dread—an all-encompassing sense of futility," said *Rolling Stone* contributor Michael Azerrad. In album after album, the British rock band presented their dark, introspective music to an ever-increasing number of fans.

The Cure's 1979 debut album, *Three Imaginary Boys,* was indeed gloomy, featuring the themes of isolation and despair. The band followed it with more bleak records, such as *Seventeen Seconds* in 1980, *Faith* in 1981, and *Pornography* in 1982. These were followed by a string of albums, including a few live concert albums and singles compilations, up to (appropriately) the sound-

Robert Smith

The Cure in 1989, from left to right: Boris Williams, Porl Thompson, Robert Smith, Roger O'Donnell, Simon Gallup

track for Sylvester Stallone's *Judge Dredd* in 1995 and *Wild Mood Swings* in 1996. Critics found the albums intense, but somehow therapeutic, calling songs like "The Funeral Party" and "The Drowning Man" darkly radiant.

The Guru of Gloom

The primary conveyor of this overpowering angst was the always original and often inspired singer-songwriter Robert Smith, one of The Cure's founding members. According to Azerrad, Smith was "a virtual messiah of melancholy, a guru of gloom." Since Smith ultimately was the only permanent member

of the band as well as its songwriter, his introspective and anguished mood permeated The Cure's music. As Smith told *Rolling Stone,* "Knowing that everything's futile but still fighting, still raging against the dying of the light—that's what motivates me all the time."

On tour

The mournful nature of The Cure's music earned them a large cult base throughout the world. The band toured frequently and enjoyed a big following during their travels, beginning with their first tour of the United Kingdom in 1979. The Cure have performed everywhere

Personnel changes

Throughout the years, The Cure has undergone numerous personnel changes. Only founder Robert Smith, guitarist and vocalist, remained a permanent member throughout the first twenty years of the band's history. This time line tracks the comings and goings of members from 1976 to 1996:

1976 Robert Smith (vocals/guitar), Lol Tolhurst (drums), Michael Dempsey (bass), and Porl Thompson (guitar) form The Cure.

1978 Thompson quits the band.

1979 Smith creates his own label and plays guitar for British new wave punk band Siouxsie and the Banshees on their United Kingdom tour but continues with The Cure. Dempsey leaves the band and is replaced by bassist Simon Gallup. Mathieu Hartley also joins The Cure as a keyboards player. Smith, Tolhurst, Gallup, and Frank Bell (a Sussex postal worker) form the Cult Heroes.

1980 Hartley leaves band.

1982 Gallup leaves after fighting with Smith while on tour in France. Gallup starts his own group, The Cry. Steve Goulding joins as a bass player. Smith returns to Siouxsie and the Banshees to play guitar.

1983 Smith forms yet another group, The Glove, with Steve Severin of Siouxsie and the Banshees. The Glove makes an album Blue Sunshine. Although no longer technically together, The Cure—now comprised of Smith, Tolhurst, drummer Andy Anderson, and bassist Derek Thompson—perform on BBC-TV, which starts up the group again. Phil Thornley joins later as a bassist.

1984 Smith resumes a "full-time" roll with The Cure. Anderson attacks members of the band and is fired. Vince Ely joins as drummer for the first segment of a U.S. tour, with Boris Williams completing the tour on drums. Thornley leaves.

1985 Gallup returns to The Cure.

1986 Porl Thompson returns, and Boris Williams joins Smith, Tolhurst, and Gallup as The Cure.

1987 Roger O'Donnell guests as the keyboards player for a U.S. tour.

1988 The Cure now is comprised of Smith (vocals/guitar), Gallup (bass), Porl Thompson(guitar), Williams (drums), and O'Donnell (keyboard).

1989 Drummer Tolhurst leaves after disagreements with Smith and forms The Presence. (Tolhurst later sues Smith and for back payments on royalties, but loses.

1990 Keyboardist O'Donnell resigns, and Perry Bamonte, a former roadie, joins The Cure on keyboards and guitar.

1994 Guitarist Thompson leaves again.

1996 New and former band members are enlisted for the Wild Mood Swings album. The Cure is now Smith (vocals/guitar), Gallup (bass), Bamonte (keyboards/guitar), O'Donnell (keyboards), and Jason Cooper (drums).

since then—Spain, France, the Far East, South America, Eastern Europe, and throughout the United States. In 1992, for example, more than 14,680 people attended one performance in Rhode Island during a thirty-nine-date U.S. tour. That same year, the band's tour of Australia and New Zealand grossed more than one million Australian dollars. The band also completed thirty-three performances on a European tour, plus an additional nine dates in the United Kingdom. These live performances gave The Cure greater visibility and attracted even more followers.

> **"Knowing that everything's futile but still fighting, still raging against the dying of the light–that's what motivates me all the time."**

Occasionally, however, the band's message of despair and its cult base combined in unfortunate ways during tours. In 1979, for instance, the National Front rioted at a Cure performance in London because of controversy caused by the band's first single, "Killing an Arab," which was based on Albert Camus's existential novel *The Stranger.* Later, in 1986, a fan committed suicide during a concert in Los Angeles. The depressed and disillusioned man jumped on stage with The Cure and stabbed himself repeatedly. In a macabre twist, the audience applauded the act, thinking it was just part of the show.

The singles

The Cure also attracted new listeners through the changing sounds and attitudes of its singles. Unlike its albums, the group's single releases historically have been more upbeat. Several singles—from the early "Boys Don't Cry" to later works like "Friday I'm in Love"— were uncharacteristically whimsical. Though not reflective of the group's albums, the optimistic nature of the singles was deliberate. First, the emotional weight of typical album fare could be too overwhelming for even alternative radio or a video presentation. As The Cure moved more into the mainstream during the 1980s, radio play and MTV support became more critical to their success. Singles also became important for their pure performance value. As Smith explained in *Billboard:* "The singles, especially, are The Cure being entertaining."

Carrying on

Despite their veteran status in alternative rock, The Cure endures and probably will for years to come. Though rumors of the group's end frequently circulate, their 1996 dark and deep *Wild Mood Swings* album—with its forty-date tour and three single releases—proved The Cure's longevity among fans. As Paul Sexton noted in *Billboard,* "The band that's older than the modern rock format itself returns to once again confound its naysayers." Rejuvenated, The Cure is assured of its future in the music industry. Marsha Edelstein, a senior marketing director for Elektra Records, explained to *Billboard* that "The Cure have remained enormously influential.... They remain popular at alternative and pop radio, and they still receive air play at MTV." After more than twenty years, they still rage against the dying of the light.

Selected Awards

BRIT Awards, Best Music Video, 1990.

BRIT Awards, Best British Group, 1991.

MTV Video Music Awards, European Best International Video for "Friday I'm in Love," 1992.

Selected Discography

Three Imaginary Boys (Fiction), 1979, United Kingdom.

Boys Don't Cry (Elektra), 1980 (contains some songs from *Three Imaginary Boys*).

... Happily Ever After (A&M), 1981 (Double album combining *Seventeen Seconds,* 1980, and *Faith,* 1981).

Pornography (Elektra), 1982.

The Head on the Door (Elektra), 1985.

Standing on a Beach: The Singles (Elektra), 1986.

Staring at the Sea (Fiction), 1986, United Kingdom.

Kiss Me, Kiss Me, Kiss Me (Elektra), 1987 (double album).

Disintegration (Elektra), 1989.

Wish (Elektra), 1992.

Wild Mood Swings (Elektra), 1996

Further Reading

Atwood, Brett, "Cure Web Site Brings the Band Home," *Billboard,* July 13, 1996, p. 87.

Brambarger, Bradley, "The Modern Age," *Billboard,* June 29, 1996, p. 89.

Pearson, Roger, "Former Cure Member Loses Royalty Fight," *Billboard,* October 8, 1994, p. 22.

Sexton, Paul, "Cure Captures 'Wild Mood Swings,'" *Billboard,* March 30, 1996, p. 18.

Contact Information

Elektra Records
75 Rockefeller Plaza
New York, NY 10019

Web Site

www.elektra.com/alternative_club/cure/cure.html

Parents Aren't Supposed to Like It

ELASTICA

British alternative pop/rock band
Formed 1992 in London, England

Reviving British punk and new wave sounds from the late 1970s and early 1980s, Elastica quickly became a sensation in England in 1993. Led by singer/guitarist/songwriter Justine Frischmann (born September 16, 1969), Elastica blasted out short, angular, punk/pop songs reminiscent of British new wave punk groups such as the Buzzcocks, Wire, and the Stranglers. Frischmann's lyrics were usually sarcastic or humorous, and the songs only lasted two or three minutes apiece. After two years together, Elastica signed a major label deal with Geffen Records in 1994 and released their first album in 1995 to good reviews. They toured the United States several times during 1995 and replaced a pregnant Irish singer/songwriter **Sinead O'Connor** (see entry) on the 1995 Lollapalooza tour.

Band formed in London in 1992

Born and raised in Twickenham, Middlesex, England, Frischmann began playing guitar in her mid-teens and soon wanted to be in a band. After attending the fairly exclusive St. Paul's School

"I find it much more therapeutic to go out and sing very sarcastic songs. I don't feel a massive need to share my angst with other people."

—Justine Frischmann,
vocals/guitar/songwriter

Justine Frischmann

Elastica dazzled England and then the United States with its short, funny, punk/pop songs

in London, she went on to study architecture at London University. While there she met Brett Anderson of the British glam-rock band **Suede** (see entry). She played with Suede for about eighteen months but left after being fed up with being "the to-

ken girl standing at the back strumming a guitar." Suede also refused to perform any of the songs she had written.

Wanting to form her own band, Frischmann asked drummer Justin Welch

Parents Aren't Supposed to Like It

to join her. Welch was with Suede for a short time in 1990 and played drums on the A-side of their first single, "Be My God." Then, at the urging of a friend who knew about the band, semi-retired twenty-seven-year-old Annie Holland borrowed a friend's guitar and auditioned for Frischmann and Welch. The quiet and enigmatic Holland passed the audition.

The group wanted to add another member, so they placed an ad for a guitarist in the British music weekly, *Melody Maker*. Donna Matthews, from Newport, England, had just moved to London and answered the ad. Constantly changing the length and color of her hair, Matthews may have been sporting an orange Mohawk when she became Elastica's guitar player.

After rehearsing for about a month, the band lined up some studio time and recorded three tracks in three days, including the version of "Line Up" that was later released as a single. In "Line Up" Frischmann attacked all that she saw as wrong with the music business, including groupies. The band's first live performance took place on May 7, 1993, under the pseudonym Onk. It was a fast-paced, fifteen-minute, seven-song set. After a few more gigs around London's Southeast side, the band debuted as Elastica at London's Camden Falcon.

First single released in 1993

Toward the end of 1993 Elastica went on tour for the first time and released their first single, "Stutter"/"Pussycat," in a limited edition of 1500 copies. Written by Frischmann, "Stutter" made fun of boys who got too drunk to be effective lovers. The single sold out quickly and received rave reviews. Two of Britain's most influential music magazines, *Melody Maker* and *New Musical Express,* named it "Single of the Week." Elastica was also named "Best New Band of 1993" by the readers of those two weeklies.

Signed major label deal with Geffen (DGC) in 1994

After headlining their first tour in February, Elastica came to the attention of Geffen Records. By May they had signed a deal with the American record company and began recording their first album. For much of 1994 the band was involved with recording and playing the occasional date, but Frischmann's romance with **Blur's** (see entry) Damon Albarn kept the band's name in the British press. The tabloids, ever eager to sell papers, dubbed them the "Sonny and Cher" (after the 1960s folk-rock duo) and even the "King and Queen" of Brit Pop. The press even pursued them when they went on a holiday to the West Indies.

First album and American debut in 1995

Elastica's self-titled debut album came out in March 1995. It contained sixteen songs averaging about three minutes a song. Praising the album, *Rolling Stone* described the band's sound as "restless guitar pop with irreverent verve and brash vigor." Most of the songs were written by Frischmann, with others by vocalist/guitarist Donna Matthews. The songs on the album "exist not as conveyors of deep personal expression but rather as tightly wrapped packages of pop hooks and punk attitudes," according to *Addicted to Noise* reviewer Bud Scoppa.

Elastica began touring the United States in May in support of the album and returned again in June. Then Elastica was chosen to replace Sinead O'Connor on the Lollapalooza tour for July and August. All this touring was too much for bassist Annie Holland, who left the group because of tour fatigue and repetitive motion syndrome (a condition that affected the muscles and joints she used to play her instrument).

Fans await next album

After extensive touring Elastica landed back in the United Kingdom in February of 1996. It proved to be a relatively uneventful year for the band. After temporarily replacing bassist Annie Holland, they finally settled on a new lineup with bassist Sheila Chipperfield and Dave Bush (formerly with The Fall) on keyboards. In December *New Musical Express* revealed that Frischmann had become disillusioned with life in the public eye, but had gotten over it with help from her friend and bandmate Donna Matthews.

Selected Awards

Melody Maker and *New Musical Express,* Single of the Week, for "Stutter," 1993.

New Musical Express and *Melody Maker,* Readers' Polls, Best New Band, 1993.

Selected Discography

Elastica (DGC/Geffen), 1995.

Further Reading

DeLuca, Dan, "Brit-rock Band Elastica Hits the States for Its Second American Tour," Knight-Ridder/Tribune News Service, June 1, 1995.

DeRogatis, Jim, "Best New Band: Elastica," *Rolling Stone,* January 25, 1996, p. 44.

"Elastica: Britain's New New-wave Band for the '90s," *Entertainment Weekly,* December 29, 1995, p. 49.

Graff, Gary, "British Rock Band's Leader Says Music Career 'Sort of Snuck Up' on Her," Knight-Ridder/Tribune News Service, March 10, 1995.

Manning, Kara, "Burning Rubber: Elastica Hit the U.S. at Full Throttle," *Rolling Stone,* May 4, 1995, p. 23.

Panahpour, Nilou, "Elastica," *Rolling Stone,* May 18, 1995, p. 88.

Scoppa, Bud, "A Brit Band Gets Its Ducks Lined Up," Addicted to Noise Online.

Contact Information

Geffen Records
9130 Sunset Blvd.
Los Angeles, CA 90069

Web Sites

http://www.geffen.com/elastica/

http://www.actwin.com/

PJ Harvey

British alternative pop/rock
composer and singer and band of the same name

Born Polly Jean Harvey on October 9, 1969,
in Yeovil, Dorset, England

According to *Newsweek*'s Jeff Giles, Polly Jean Harvey is "the high priestess of subversiveness." Indeed, she has gone out of her way to overthrow the foundations of rock and roll, and her inventiveness has changed the shape and sound of modern music.

"I want to keep experimenting and trying different things." –PJ Harvey

In the Beginning

PJ Harvey was born Polly Jean Harvey in a small English village to a stonemason and sculptress. Her mother was very involved in music, and notable musicians—Charlie Watts of the Rolling Stones, for example—frequently visited her home. Harvey experienced and experimented with different instruments at home. When she joined bands as a teenager, she played saxophone. Although she was writing songs, they were only played occasionally. One group she was in, Automatic Dlamini, toured Europe and recorded two albums.

Wanting more songwriting opportunities, Harvey formed the band PJ Harvey with drummer Robert O. Ellis and bass player Ian

Olliver in 1991. The band's beginnings were inauspicious—a live debut at a bowling alley. They released two singles, "Dress" and "Sheela Na Gig" that year on the independent British label Too Pure. Both songs dealt with being a woman and with expectations based on gender.

Effecting Change

In 1992 the PJ Harvey band signed with Island Records and released its first recording. *Dry,* the band's debut album, was a low-budget record that was made for about $3,600. More importantly, the album produced a sound previously unheard. *Dry* featured harsh, powerful music—like the blues in form and style, but punk in its aggressiveness. The songs had no leads. The riffs were uncomplicated, the rhythms swinging. Songwriter Polly Jean Harvey added more songs containing strange sexual imagery to complement her other songs about gender roles. "Compared to *Dry,*" wrote Brain Cullman in *Request,* "most '90s releases sound vulgar, careerist, or simply beside the point."

A year later, PJ Harvey's second album had an equally great impact. *Rid of Me* featured harder, angrier songs with even more elementary dynamics than those of *Dry.* Well received by both critics and alternative music fans, Harvey's songs are about obsessive love, desire, disappointment, and hate. Many of her songs reveal a strange, sexual imagery—a sort of overt feminism that Harvey repeatedly denied in interviews. "I don't understand why people have this desire to pinpoint everything," she told *Spin.*

"It's a desire to control, which isn't necessary. Why not let it speak to you in some way, and not try to interpret it into words all the time." Many of the songs showed a refreshing inventiveness and sense of humor.

Writing in 1993, Evelyn McDonnell of *Rolling Stone* observed that Harvey's compositions showed a remarkable depth and range. That year *Rolling Stone* named Harvey songwriter of the year.

More Changes

Though 1993 was a pivotal year for popular and critical acceptance of the PJ Harvey band, it also was the breaking point for the personalities within the group. Earlier, Olliver left the band and was replaced by Steven Vaughan. Now the friction between Harvey and her band members caused both Ellis and Vaughan to leave. "It makes me sad," Harvey later said of her bandmates' departures. "I wouldn't have gotten here without them. I needed them back then—badly. But now I don't need them anymore. We all just changed as people."

New band, new album

Harvey ventured out alone. She reorganized her band for *4-Track Demos,* an album of demo versions of the songs on *Rid of Me* that showcased her songwriting abilities in a new light. Then, in 1995, she organized a new five-piece band for her third Grammy-nominated album *To Bring You My Love.* She also played several instruments on the album, wrote the songs, and delivered the vocals. As with her previous albums, many of the songs dealt with obsessive love. The album's title tune begins with the words, "I've lain with the devil / Cursed God above / Forsaken heaven / To bring you my love." These and other blues-inspired lyrics are delivered with a voice that "ranges from throaty grunge to ululating [howling] whoops," according to music critic Gene Santoro of *The Nation*.

Through all these changes, Harvey established herself as a self-sufficient artist—both brilliant and creative. "I want to keep experimenting and trying different things," she once said. "Maybe they won't work, but that's what keeps my interest in music."

Selected Awards

Melody Maker, Single of the Week, for "Dress," 1991.

Rolling Stone, Artist of the Year, 1995.

Spin, Artist of the Year, 1995.

Village Voice, Artist of the Year, 1995.

Grammy Awards, nominations for Best Female Rock Performance and Best Alternative Music Performance, for *To Bring You My Love,* 1995.

Village Voice Jazz and Pop Critic's Poll, Best Album of the Year, for *To Bring You My Love,* 1995.

Selected Discography

Dry (Island), 1992.

Rid of Me (Island), 1993.

4-Track Demos (Island), 1993.

To Bring You My Love (Island), 1995.

By John Parish and Polly Jean Harvey:

Dance Hall at Louse Point (Island), 1996.

Further Reading

Giles, Jeff, "Move Over, Tarzan—PJ Harvey Is Back," *Newsweek,* May 3, 1993, p. 67.

McDonnell, Evelyn, "PJ Harvey: 4-Track Demos," *Rolling Stone,* November 25, 1993, p. 112.

Pareles Jon, "PJ Harvey: To Bring You My Love," *New York Times,* March 19, 1995, sec. 2, p. 29.

Santoro, Gene, "PJ Harvey: To Bring You My Love," *The Nation,* April 17, 1995, pp. 539-540.

Spin, November 1992; May 1993; August 1993; December 1993; February 1995.

Strauss, Neil, "PJ Harvey," *Rolling Stone,* December 28, 1995, p. 68.

Contact Information

Island Records
400 Lafayette St., Fifth Floor
New York, NY 10003

Polygram Label Group
Worldwide Plaza
825 Eighth Ave.
New York, NY 10019

Web Site

www.polygram.com\polygram\island\artists\ harvey_pj\pjbio.html

morrissey

British alternative pop/rock singer and songwriter

Born Stephen Patrick Morrissey in Manchester, England, on May 22, 1959

"I simply stand alone." –Morrissey

Widely recognized as "the prince of melancholy [sadness]," Morrissey sings and composes passionate, attention-holding, and often disturbing songs of alienation and loneliness. His songs are characterized by sensitive lyrics, dramatic vocals, and honeyed tunes. An alienated artist, Morrissey is motivated by his deep and abiding love of music more than any desire to be a star or to deliver a special message.

Unlikely beginnings

Though Morrissey did not begin his professional career as a singer, he nevertheless started out in a field related to the music business. During the 1970s, Morrissey worked as a freelance music journalist for the *Record Mirror*. He also wrote a book, *James Dean Isn't Dead*, and served as the president of the New York Dolls Fan Club in the United Kingdom. He began performing with a band, The Nosebleeds, in the early 1980s.

His next band was the much-acclaimed The Smiths, which he founded with Johnny Marr in 1982. It was with The Smiths that

The Smiths

In 1983 guitarist Johnny Marr asked Morrissey to start a band. The odd pairing—the cheerful Marr and the reclusive Morrissey—called themselves The Smiths to be nondescript in the glamorous world of music. As The Smiths, the two carefully constructed their music to teach people about themselves, allowing them to grow. Their songs explored the immorality of eating meat, the cruelty of school, and other topics of despair or oppression. The result was immediate and unexpected success as youths all over Great Britain connected with the songs.

Radio producer John Walters discovered The Smiths, then supported them with BBC recording sessions and a contract with Rough Trade Records. The Smiths offered listeners a new and exotic style of music. "The sound of The Smiths," wrote Frank Rose in The Nation, "is a difficult but strangely compelling amalgam [or mixture] of American blues and British folk set to a spinning beat."

The Smiths self-titled first album created a following for the group and reached number two on the record charts. The band's second album in 1985, Meat Is Murder, earned gold certification by selling 500,000 copies within one week of its release, debuting at the number one position on charts in Great Britain. Critics took notice and still consider The Smiths one of the more musically accomplished pop groups of the 1980s.

At the height of The Smiths' success in 1987, the group disbanded. Marr decided to leave to work with other artists, leaving Morrissey to fend for himself. Many assumed Morrissey would fail without his partner. "The general opinion," explained Morrissey in Spin, "was that once Johnny Marr unplugged that umbilical cord I would just kind of deflate like a paddling pool." That, of course, was not to be as Morrissey went on to prominence as a successful solo artist.

Morrissey was first recognized as a unique and compelling lyricist. As a performer, he became something of an anti-hero, not wanting to be looked to as a leader or pop star. The Smiths were a successful, legitimate, and influential post-punk band, but Morrissey and Marr's personal and professional relationship could not last. By 1987 The Smiths dissolved. One year later Morrissey was performing as a solo artist.

Since that time, he has generated five well-received albums. Yet Morrissey shuns the idea that he is a celebrity. "I would rather be cut off at the knees than be perceived as selling myself," he told Billboard in 1994. "I am not even vaguely interested in the idea of being a pop star or a rock star or wearing leather trousers and telling everyone I am the most wonderful person on earth. I'd like to think that in some way, I'm helping move pop music away from those notions."

Only the lonely

Morrissey often composes songs about guilt, depression, and self-hate that describe a particular made-up person and often involve other characters. In fact, he presents alienation as a way of life through conversational lyrics that are both witty and cruel. His compositions show typically British references and a vulnerability that has inspired his loyal following of rebellious teens and young adults. According to Jim Farber, a *Seventeen* writer, Morrissey "inspires uncommon feelings of intimacy by writing about loneliness in a way no pop star before him has," and that has endeared him to many.

"I am not even vaguely interested in the idea of being a pop star or a rock star or wearing leather trousers and telling everyone I am the most wonderful person on earth. I'd like to think that in some way, I'm helping move pop music away from those notions."

Morrissey seems strangely connected to his fans, who regard him as the spokesperson of the lost and lonely. They copy his ordinary dress and demeanor, even his hair style—a slicked pompadour (in which hair is combed into a high mound in front). His fans are fiercely devoted, too. At concerts, Morrissey's devotees bring him gladioluses—his favorite flower—and embrace him in group hugs. Fans welcome the attention the singer shows them after concerts as well. Morrissey is known for his kind treatment of fans as he shyly accepts their gifts with hugs.

Morrissey's songs regularly top the charts overseas. He is especially popular in Europe. In the United States, however, he has never sold more than 500,000 copies of an album. "As far as I can tell," Morrissey observed to David Browne in *Entertainment Weekly,* "any fool can have a hit record in America—except me." Yet the singer's American fans remain enthusiastic. For example, when Morrissey appeared at a midnight album signing in Grand Rapids, Michigan, in 1992, fans bought more than 500 copies of the album *Your Arsenal* in one-and-a-half hours. In 1994, 2,000 fans converged on a New York City record store for an album signing.

"I hated my childhood. I hated my teen years. I hated school. I hated everything about life."

The fascination of his American fans endured through his tours as well. Morrissey easily sold out major concert venues such as Madison Square Garden in New York City. In 1992, his two-show performance at the Hollywood Bowl in California grossed more than $800,000. Morrissey's stage demeanor demonstrated an enthusiasm and energy unusual for the lonely-hearted thousands he came to represent. While at the shows, his fans—though alienated from the world—could be cool at last. As Bill Flanagan recalled in *Musician:* during a Morrissey concert "the wimpy kids stood on their chairs and pumped their fists in the air and screamed and the wimpy singer ripped off his shirt.... Morrissey, who in his lyrics, on his albums and in his interviews shows self-immolating weariness with the insensitivity of the world, comes alive in concert as a stomping, rocking, posing, sweating, handsome, and scream-inducing star."

Critical acclaim

Critically, Morrissey has been called one of the finest British singer-songwriters of the 1970s, 1980s, and 1990s. In 1988, for example, "Suedehead"—a dramatic song about racist, homophobic gangs—earned Morrissey critical applause for his interesting lyrics and unconventional interpretation. He followed "Suedehead" with other witty and sometimes cruel songs about contemporary issues. "Bengali in Platforms," for instance, warns immigrants of the hardships ahead of them. "The National Front Disco" covers fascism and racism, while "You're the One for Me, Fatty" looks at obesity. Some songs are self-pitying: "Seaside, Yet Still Docked," "Heaven Knows I'm Miserable Now," or "I Am Hated for Loving." Some—such as "I Know It's Gonna Happen Someday" and "Hold on to Your Friends"—are aching and emotional. Many study alienation of epic proportions, notably "Billy Budd."

"As far as I can tell, any fool can have a hit record in America—except me."

Of Morrissey's albums, *Vauxhall and I* is considered the most powerful and maybe his best work. Steven Volk of *Rolling Stone* called the work oddly beautiful, with its disturbing images of alienation conveyed through strong melodies. Overall, the critic found the album to be accessible pop despite the weighty themes of its songs. *Your Arsenal,* an earlier album, also received praise. Again, *Rolling Stone* critic Mark Coleman recognized Morrissey's lyric writing and conversational grace as high points of the album.

Later albums, including *Southpaw Grammar* and *World of Morrissey,* continued the exploration of the songwriter's familiar themes. Al Weisel lauded Morrissey in *Rolling Stone* for creating an aural (relating to the sense of hearing) landscape in *Southpaw Grammar.* Similarly, Paul Evans—also of *Rolling Stone*—commended the *World of Morrissey* album for providing fourteen new songs about vulnerability for the fascination of fans.

His life and times

Like his fans, Morrissey considers himself to be alienated from the world. Initially he sought only to be irritating in retaliation for his unhappiness. He told *Seventeen:* "I hated my childhood. I hated my teen years. I hated school. I hated everything about life." Morrissey stayed mostly at home while growing up, reading, writing poetry, and listening to music. "There was no sense of frivolity [fun] in my young life at all, ever," the singer revealed to *Spin* magazine.

Morrissey apparently still has little, if any, personal life. He is known for his celibacy and lack of intimate companions. He has reported people following him around just to see if his self-imposed isolation is a public relations gimmick, but it has always seemed genuine. Without binding relationships, Morrissey clings to his music. As he explained to *Seventeen* during an interview in 1994: "As I sit in this hotel room now, music is still all I have. It's all my fans have, too."

Despite the sad nature of his music and his apparent isolation, Morrissey is not unhappy. "I'd like to dispel the notion that I'm this foppish folk singer who is constantly miserable and would like nothing more than the end of the planet," Morrissey revealed to *Billboard*. "It's ridiculous, really.... Honestly, I'm not motivated by anything other than a great love of pop music, of songs that one can hum, which I'm afraid are sorely lacking in pop and rock music today."

Selected Awards

Record Industry Association of America, gold video certification, for "Hulmerist," 1991.

Record Industry Association of America, gold record certification, for *Viva Hate,* 1993.

Selected Discography

Viva Hate (Sire), 1988.
Bona Drag (Sire), 1990.

Kill Uncle (Sire), 1991.
Your Arsenal (Sire), 1992.
Beethoven Was Deaf (Sire), 1993.
Vauxhall and I (Sire), 1994.
World of Morrissey (Sire), 1995.
Southpaw Grammar (Sire), 1995.
Maladjusted (Mercury), 1997.

Further Reading

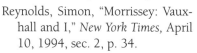

Farber, Jim, "Morrissey Gets Happy," *Seventeen,* August 1994, p. 151.

Reynolds, Simon, "Morrissey: Vauxhall and I," *New York Times,* April 10, 1994, sec. 2, p. 34.

Rogan, Johnny, *Morrissey and Marr: The Severed Alliance,* Omnibus Press, 1992.

Sprague, David, "Warner Leads Morrissey toward the Pop Spotlight," *Billboard,* February 19, 1994, p. 13.

Volk, Steven, "Morrissey: Vauxhall and I," *Rolling Stone,* April 7, 1994, pp. 73-74.

Contact Information

Sire Records
75 Rockefeller Plaza, 20th Floor
New York, NY 10019

Web Site

www.repriserec.com/morrissey

Oasis

British pop/rock band

Formed in
Manchester, England, in 1991

Pete Townshend's the only guy I can relate to because he wrote all the songs ... and he gave 'em to somebody else to sing 'em, and that's exactly what I do. And we particularly don't get on with our lead singers," said Oasis guitarist and songwriter Noel Gallagher in *Rolling Stone*. It's the eternal dilemma for Oasis. Noel is the artist and gifted songwriter, and his younger brother Liam is the cute one, the one that gets the attention as the singer. To top it off, like many brothers, the Gallaghers like to fight.

The Gallagher brothers are also known for other bad behavior, like mouthing off to the press and putting down other bands in public. This too makes for some good stories, but Oasis doesn't need the extra press coverage; they're already getting plenty.

Their three records *Definitely Maybe*, *(What's the Story) Morning Glory?*, and *Be Here Now* have had critics falling all over themselves with praise. *Newsweek* called *Definitely Maybe* "a fabulously cocky, shamelessly Beatlesy album that gave rock and roll a swift kick in

"You don't deserve us." –Noel Gallagher to an audience in Asbury Park, New Jersey, according to *Rolling Stone*

Noel Gallagher

music magazine *NME,* saying that "our kid's got 200 more (songs) just as good!"

Rough childhood

Noel and Liam grew up in Manchester, an industrial town in northern England. When Noel was 13, the boys' father, a country and western DJ, got him a guitar, and Noel figured out how to play the Beatles' "Ticket to Ride." Noel wrote a lot of songs but also got into a lot of trouble. He committed petty crimes and cut school. "There was just nothing there for the musician in me," Noel told *Rolling Stone.* When he was thirteen, he received a six-month probation for robbing a store. Brother Liam was troubled, too. He played soccer, but cut school a lot. In 1985, their parents got divorced and, since then, the brothers haven't had much contact with their father.

Madchester

In 1989, Manchester became the site of the "Madchester" music scene, where bands like the Stone Roses and the Happy Mondays were becoming famous. Noel signed up to be a roadie for the band Inspiral Carpets and Liam joined a band, Rain, with his friends—Paul "Bonehead" Arthurs (guitar), Paul "Guigs" McGuigan (bass), and Tony McCarroll (drums). They renamed the band Oasis in honor of a local club. In the meantime, Noel's experiences touring with Inspiral Carpets were inspiring him to try his own music. "They were just going through the motions for the money," said Noel in *Musician.* Noel thought, "If they can get away with it, I can."

the angst [anxiety]." The magazine liked *(What's the Story) Morning Glory?* even more, calling it "a richer showcase for Liam Gallagher's serrated [rough] John Lennon-ish voice and his brother Noel's increasingly ambitious songwriting."

In August 1997, eager fans in both the U.K. and the United States rushed out to buy the newly released *Be Here Now,* again in record breaking numbers.

Oasis's goal? "We want to be the biggest band in the world," said Noel in *Newsweek.* They do have the songs for it. After *Definitely Maybe* Liam bragged about Noel's songwriting in the British

Parents Aren't Supposed to Like It

The brothers together

Noel came back to England and saw an Oasis show. He was not impressed, but did like Liam's singing voice. He offered to join the band as guitarist and songwriter, but he told them he had one condition, "I can only do this one way: with me in complete control of it," he remembered in *Rolling Stone*. On the basis of Noel's demo for "Live Forever," Liam and the rest of Oasis accepted the strict conditions.

Two year overnight success

The band practiced intently and sent out demos for a year and a half, but didn't get anywhere until Alan McGee of Creation Records happened to catch one of their shows. He offered them a deal on the spot. While the band worked on new songs, Noel and Liam's fighting began to get more attention from the media, meaning more publicity for the band. By the time their 1994 record *Definitely Maybe* came out, it was the fastest-selling debut in U.S. history.

"We're singing about being young and wanting to escape from where you're from. We're not singing about how crap life is—we're singing about how great it could be."

Some in the media criticized Oasis for sounding too much like the Beatles or Rolling Stones, others defended the band. "The best rock and roll has come from people who grab someone else's style and say, 'Look what I can do with THIS,'" said *GQ*. Noel openly admits to being inspired by others. "The only thing

Liam Gallagher

that influences me when I write is other records. Which is why, I suppose, our record sounds like about ten other people's. I'm not making no bones about it. So what?" he said in *People*.

Big brother vs. little brother

The brothers continued to fight, often publicly, earning the nickname, "Bruise Brothers." At one point, they decided they wouldn't even do interviews together. "Too often in the course of disagreeing with each other orally they would end up writhing on the floor, fists flying, while the interviewer would take notes," noted *Rolling Stone*. The brothers do agree on

Blur vs. Oasis

Noel and Liam don't only fight with each other, they also fight with other bands. Their most famous rivalry is with the English band **Blur** (see entry). Some of the highlights (or lowlights): In June 1995, at the height of the feud, Blur's single "Country House" debuts in the UK at #1, beating out Oasis's "Roll With It" at #2; In October 1995, Noel is quoted in an English paper as saying that he hopes certain members of Blur get AIDS and die; In March 1996, Blur's Damon Albarn tells a British magazine, "The only thing we've got in common with Oasis is that we're both doing (terrible) in America."; In May 1996, Noel's management company issued a statement saying he turned down the Ivor Novello Songwriter of the Year award because it was being shared with Blur.

one thing—fighting is no big deal to them. "You argue and fight and call each other names, but you don't mean it. People think it's different and want to talk about the significance, but it's not a big deal really," said Noel in *People*. Liam agrees: "It's just me and my brother having arguments in a band. If we weren't in a band, we'd be havin' it in the house. If we had a greengrocers, Gallagher's Greengrocers, we'd argue over which way we set out the apples," he said in *Rolling Stone*.

Oasis gets huge

In 1995 Oasis got a new drummer, Alan White, and put out *(What's the Story) Morning Glory?* Critics loved it. "A bold leap forward that displays significant personal growth," said *Rolling Stone*. The public loved it too—it debuted at number one in England and in the U.S. went quadruple platinum, selling more than four million copies.

GQ praised the band's "vulnerability," suggesting "Liam brays out Noel's lyrics with such swaggering self-confidence that you could miss the fact that the songs veer from outrageous cockiness to I'm-a-phony-and-everybody's-gonna-find-out insecurity." *Rolling Stone* found part of Oasis's appeal to be the uplifting lyrics. "More than a few of Noel Gallagher's lyrics dwell on fantasy, escape and endless possibilities: 'I'd like to be somebody else'; 'tonight I'm a rock and roll star'; 'we'll find a way of chasing the sun'; and, of course, 'you and I are gonna live forever,'" said the magazine. Explained Noel: "We're singing about being young and wanting to escape from where you're from. We're not singing about how crap life is—we're singing about how great it could be."

More critics griping

Although Oasis's music got outstanding reviews from the press, their live performances did not. "Liam stands in front of his mike stand, usually with his hands behind his back, and that's about it. The rest of the band is even less animated, and this visual effect is completely at odds with the uplifting punch of the band's white-hot wall of noise," complained *Rolling Stone*. But the band members don't think their live show is a problem. "We wouldn't dare go on stage and prance around and preach to the audience," said Noel in a press release for

Definitely Maybe. Added Liam, "I've got no time for jumping about, do I? I'm too busy singing the songs."

Fame = good

Unlike many other bands, like **Pearl Jam** (see entry) or **Soundgarden** (see entry), the Gallagher brothers seek out fame and enjoy being rock stars immensely. "If you can't enjoy being in a job like this, then you've got big ... problems. You know what I mean? It's better than working in a carwash. What do these people want out of life if they don't want to travel the world, meeting loads of interesting people, playing music and getting paid *extremely* well for it?" said Noel in *Newsweek.*

What's next?

Noel has said that he pictures Oasis being a temporary thing. "There's other things I want to do. I'll probably run out of ideas, and I wouldn't just carry on forever, go through the motions for the next ten years. I'd rather be special than just another band who carried on," he said in *Rolling Stone.*

For now, though, the Gallagher brothers seem to be flourishing in the wake of the huge success of *Be Here Now.* American press and audiences are learning to accept the brothers' personal boisterousness and their tame onstage performances as Oasis trademarks. After touring in the United Kingdom for *Be Here Now,* Oasis will bring their show to the United States, where a great many ardent fans await them.

Awards

(What's The Story) Morning Glory? certified quadruple platinum.

Definitely Maybe, certified gold.

MTV European Music Awards, Best UK Band, 1994.

BRIT Awards, Best Newcomer, 1995.

BRIT Awards, Best Video, for "Wonderwall"; Best Group and Best Album, 1996.

Selected Discography

Definitely Maybe (Epic), 1994.

(What's The Story?) Morning Glory (Epic), 1995.

Be Here Now (Epic), 1997.

Further Reading

Cohen, Jason, "Oasis: The Trouble Boys," *Rolling Stone,* May 18, 1995.

Flanagan, Bill, "Lout Mouths," *GQ —Gentlemen's Quarterly,* July 1996, p. 31.

Giles, Jeff, "Next Stop, the Universe," *Newsweek,* February 5, 1996, p. 63.

Helliger, Jeremy, "Talking With.... Oasis's Noel Gallagher," *People,* February 12, 1996, p. 32.

Hendrickson, Matt, "Oasis," *Rolling Stone,* September 22, 1994.

Hewitt, Paolo, *Getting High: The Adventures of Oasis,* Hyperion, 1997.

Contact Information

Record company:

Epic
550 Madison Ave.
New York, NY 10022-3211

Fan club:

Trinity St.
3 Alveston Place
Leamingtom Spa, CV32 4SN
United Kingdom

Web Site

http://www.oasisinet.com/

SUEDE

(London Suede in the United States)

British alternative pop/rock band

Formed in 1989 in Haywards Heath, England (near London)

"Androgyny is something in the way you feel and behave. I know about five people who are 100 percent male or female, and they're the strangest people in the world." –Brett Anderson, lead singer and songwriter

Mat Osman, Richard Oakes, Simon Gilbert, Brett Anderson

Suede began in the 1980s when Brett Anderson (vocalist, songwriter) and Mat Osman (bass) were brought up in Haywards Heath, some forty miles from London. The two friends formed a band in 1989 with guitarist Bernard Butler, who answered a "Musician Wanted" ad in the British weekly, *New Musical Express*. Simon Gilbert soon replaced the drum machine they'd been using. For a while the band also included Justine Frischmann on second guitar and backing vocals. She stayed in the band for about eighteen months while dating lead singer Anderson before leaving to form her own band, **Elastica** (see entry).

Out of fashion, then in style

At first, Suede were hated by virtually everyone connected with the music business, including journalists, agents, and record companies. Audiences reacted disastrously to their performances. They even recorded a poorly received single, "Be My God/Art" that sounded peculiar in the context of the times. As Brett Anderson told Ginia

Bellafante of *Time*, "For quite a while we were a joke. We were out of step with the times."

In 1992, however, Suede suddenly became a sensation in England. First they started getting fantastic live reviews. Then in May the influential British weekly, *Melody Maker*, put them on its cover and proclaimed them "The Best New Band in England." In June they released their first single on the British independent label, Nude. Consecutive singles "Metal Mickey" and "Animal Nitrate" were hits in England, reaching the top twenty and the top ten, respectively. It seemed the public and the press were ready for Suede's glam and glitter rock stylishness. The band's songs addressed issues of sexuality head-on, confronting gender roles and stereotyping. Their sound appealed to the listener's sense of style and sophistication.

First album released in 1993

Suede released their self-titled debut album in England and the United States in 1993. In England, the album went straight to number one and became the fastest-selling debut album since 1984. The band spent the rest of 1993 playing to sell-out crowds in Europe, America, and Japan, receiving good reviews of their live performances. Although wildly popular in their home country of England, Suede didn't seem to go over as well with American audiences.

Suede's first album featured androgynous songs, a mixing of masculine and feminine points of view, that American critics called "gender-bending" or "polymorphous sexuality." Some songs touched on sexual themes such as bisexuality and masochism. Similarities were noted with with 1970s glam and glitter rockers like **David Bowie** (see entry) and T. Rex. "On their debut album, Suede alternates between lush melodrama and jangly hard pop," wrote Jeremy Helligar in *People Weekly*. "This trip has been taken before, but Suede puts fresh sparkle in the glitter."

American critics reacted differently to Suede than their British counterparts. Robert Christgau, writing about Suede's debut album in *Playboy,* noted that "Suede frontman Brett Anderson is everything Anglophobes can't stand—nasal, arch and flamboyant. Hetero in his private life, he flaunts an androgynous point of view in his desperately sexy songs."

Second album released in 1994

Early in 1994 Suede released the unusual single, "Stay Together," in England. It was an eight-minute piece that was written like a four-act play. The British music press went bonkers over it, with both *New Musical Express* and *Melody Maker* naming it "Single of the Week." The *NME* critic wrote, "Luxuriating in the ambitious, dramatic, exhausting spell of this makes everything else sound like so much ephemera. Like most great things, it leaves you utterly silent."

Two months later Suede was back in the studio recording their second album, *Dog Man Star.* Like "Stay Together," *Dog Man Star* was an extravaganza, with the music lasting about an hour. Similar in style to the first album but showing more songwriting talent, *Dog Man Star* again paid homage to 1970s glam rock. In some cases the sexuality of the songs was more overt, as when Anderson sang "I want the style of a woman/The kiss of a man" on the album's first cut, "Introducing the Band." The album also featured a selection of quieter songs with impressive production values, songs which Chuck Eddy described in *Entertainment Weekly* as "ornate gothic ballads."

Line-up changes and extensive touring

After *Dog Man Star* was recorded, guitarist Bernard Butler left the band and was replaced by 17-year-old Richard Oakes. The band toured extensively in Europe, America, and Japan in support of the album with this new line-up. Toward the end of 1995 Neil Codling, Simon Gilbert's cousin, joined the band on keyboards and backing vocals.

Suede's third album, *Coming Up,* was recorded between December 1995 and May 1996 at different London studios under the guidance of producer Ed Buller. With Suede's public eagerly anticipating the band's next release, the album entered the British sales charts at number one in the first week of its release. Most of the songs were written by Anderson, some with help from the new young guitarist, Richard Oakes. The album opens with "Trash," a hit single in England that sports such lines as, "We're the litter from

the breeze/We're the lovers on the streets." "Filmstar," a song about the nature of fame, pays tribute to glitter rockers Marc Bolan and T. Rex, with added references to famous British actors Michael Caine and Terence Stamp. Other notable songs on the album include a seven-minute "The Chemistry Between Us," the violent "Starcrazy," and the lush ballad "By the Sea."

While Suede continued to be extremely popular in England, it remained to be seen whether American audiences would fall in love with this stylish British band.

Selected Discography

Suede (Columbia), 1993.

Dog Man Star (Nude/Columbia), 1994 (as by London Suede).

Coming Up (Nude) 1996, United Kingdom; (Nude/Columbia), 1997 (as by London Suede).

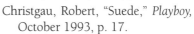

Further Reading

Bellafante, Ginia, "Ultra Suede," *Time,* May 24, 1993, p. 87.

Christgau, Robert, "Suede," *Playboy,* October 1993, p. 17.

Daly, Steven, "Suede: All Tat Gitters," *Rolling Stone,* May 27, 1993, p. 15.

Eddy, Chuck, "Dog Man Star," *Entertainment Weekly,* November 4, 1994, p.77.

Helligar, Jeremy, "Dog Man Star," *People Weekly,* November 14, 1994, p. 23.

Helligar, Jeremy, "Suede," *People Weekly,* May 3, 1993, p. 25.

Musto, Michael, "A Crabbier Shade of Suede," *Entertainment Weekly,* June 25, 1993, p. 100.

Thompson, Dave, "Suede," *Alternative Press,* May 1997, p. 34.

Contact Information

Suede Information Service
PO Box 3431
London N1 7LW
United Kingdom
London Suede

c/o Columbia Records
PO Box 4450
New York, NY 10101-4450

Web Site

http://www.suede.co.uk/
http://www.thelondonsuede.com

Dance music

When it began, rock and roll was dance music. Its listeners—mostly teenagers—gathered to swing each other around the dance floor as their favorite bands laid down steady rhythms. "It's got a backbeat, you can't lose it," sang Chuck Berry, one of the style's founders, in his classic song "Rock and Roll Music," which was covered by the Beatles and countless other bands. That constant, pounding backbeat was what it was all about; it made the body move, allowed its listeners to get lost in the excitement of the moment and each other. Song lyrics tended to be about dancing and the joy of love and the agony of a broken heart.

Rock gets serious

Then, sometime in the 1960s, rock music—like its ancestor, jazz—got serious. This development didn't happen overnight, and it took place for several reasons. Big political issues, like the war in Vietnam, the Civil Rights movement, and the assassination of leaders like President John F. Kennedy, got idealistic youngsters interested in larger matters. Folk-rock pioneers like Bob Dylan

Disco dancers in New York's Studio 54

were singing exciting songs about social change that made rocking around the clock look like hiding your head in the sand. And, for some, drugs—especially marijuana and LSD—made listeners more inclined to stare into their own minds than get up and dance. Rock music reflected these developments.

Soul, funk, and disco

Rock listeners who did want to dance turned to soul music, which exploded in the 1960s. A mix of the emotion of gospel with the drive of rhythm and blues, soul matured into one of the era's most exciting forms. Detroit's Motown label pioneered a smooth blend of sophisticated pop and funky rhythms, and scored huge hits with such acts as The Supremes (featuring Diana Ross), Smokey Robinson and the Miracles, Stevie Wonder, the Four Tops, The Temptations, and many more. The Memphis-based company Stax/Volt, meanwhile, got kids grooving to earthier soul hits by Wilson Pickett, Otis Redding, Rufus Thomas, Booker T. and the MGs, and others. Singer/bandleader James Brown, meanwhile, helped develop "funk" music as a form with a harder, more relentless groove; his songs began to move away from the brief, catchy form of pop hits into longer workouts. Funk became hugely influential during the 1970s under Brown, George Clinton's Parliament-Funkadelic, Earth, Wind & Fire, The Ohio Players, and others.

During the late 1960s, the California group Sly and the Family Stone tried to break the color walls of pop music—and for a while, they succeeded. With musicians black and white, male and female, they celebrated the ideals of the hippie generation, in songs like "Everybody Is a Star," "Everyday People" and "You Can Make It If You Try," while blending psychedelic rock and catchy pop with the hard funk grooves pioneered by James Brown. Their hit "Dance to the Music" is considered one of the greatest singles in pop music history by many critics, and represents the end of an era in dance-rock. During most of the 1970s, dancing was simply not as important to most rock listeners. Sly and the Family Stone moved away from rock into the genre of funk, which was hugely popular among African American listeners, but while elements of rock remained—as they did in the music of hard-grooving bands like Funkadelic—this was basically the last gasp of rock as dance music for several years.

The mid-1970s saw the rise of disco, a lighter, more pop-oriented groove music than funk. Often utilizing orchestras, disco records had a pounding, insistent beat and singable melodies. The most successful artists in this genre—singer Donna Summer, The Bee Gees with their massively successful "Saturday Night Fever" movie soundtrack—rode the wave to megastardom. But disco was also filled with one-hit wonders. Audiences were black and white, straight and gay, united in a celebration of "Good Times," as the smash by the group Chic had it. Disco was so successful that some rock groups, notably the Rolling Stones, dabbled in it. The Stones' "Miss You" was one of several hits they scored in the disco mode.

Parents Aren't Supposed to Like It

Overshadowed by disco, funk ventured further into electronics, and "electro-funk" and other styles depending on drum machines began to pave the way for hip-hop. The earliest rap records were the soundtrack for the period's underground dance clubs and parties, and a new kind of solo dance, breakdancing, became hugely popular during the late 1970s and early 1980s.

The New Wave

The late 1970s saw not only the "punk" revolution against the blues-based sameness of radio rock, but another, more commercial revolution, "New Wave." Catchier and more radio-friendly than punk, New Wave offered futuristic (and sometimes "nerdy") fashion and short, danceable pop songs, frequently laced with bleeping synthesizer sounds. Influenced by classic pop, disco, and electronic groups like **Kraftwerk** (see entry), this style got rock listeners onto dancefloors again. Groups as varied as chart-toppers The Cars and Cheap Trick, the eclectic New York rockers Blondie, British synth-popsters Soft Cell, ska-oriented groups like The Specials and the English Beat, herky-jerky smart-rock American bands like Talking Heads and Devo and Australian hitmakers Men At Work are all associated with this movement. While punk rockers were "slam dancing" (or "moshing," as it came to be called), New Wave audiences did the "pogo"—jumping up and down as if on a pogo stick—to the music's choppy rhythms.

After disco faded away, other dance forms began to emerge, depending on

Dee-lite's Lady Miss Kier

drum machines for their huge, hard beats. Prince carried the funk tradition on, but also ventured into newer styles, like rap and hip-hop, which developed together during this time. Hip-hop was a whole culture, not just a musical form, but such styles as "New Jack Swing" and other modernized forms of R & B music grew up during the 1980s. New hitmakers like Whitney Houston, Mariah Carey, Madonna, New Edition, and the many groups discovered by such producers as Jimmy Jam and Terry Lewis, L.A. Reid and **Babyface** (see entry) and (later) R. Kelly rocked the clubs—as well as the radio—with their new forms of soul.

Deee-Lite (see entry) arrived on the scene in the 1980s when alternative was the main music news. With their wild 1970s costumes, light-hearted attitude, and catchy pop/dance songs, Deee-Lite was kind of a musical misfit. It didn't matter though. "Groove Is in the Heart" became a hit for the band. On their follow-up record *Infinity Within,* the band added a strong political message to the mix and the record sold poorly. It proved again that most people like their dance music light and fun.

Electronica and techno

House music, which usually consisted of singers wailing soulfully over thumping rhythms and repetitive keyboards, was one of the earliest examples of what came to be known as "electronica." Depending on sampling technology (which lets producers play pieces of recorded music like instruments) for drum "loops" and other sounds, this form exploded in the late 1980s and early 1990s—first in England, later in the U.S. and elsewhere—spawning such styles as techno, jungle, and drum 'n' bass. Huge electronic-music dance parties, or "raves," attracted crowds on both sides of the Atlantic.

The mainstream music world sat up and took notice with the success of such "electronica" acts as Prodigy, **The Chemical Brothers** (see entry) and the Crystal Method in the late 1990s. Adopting the in-your-face attitude of alternative rock and psychedelic images inspired by drugs like Ecstasy, the new electronica was tougher, harder, more threatening than dance music had ever been—and it began to win a big chunk of the rock audience. The Chemical Brothers use computers and sampling to create a strong, beat-heavy sound. Not everybody was receptive to this band. At a festival show that the band played in Irvine, California, in 1997, nearly three quarters of the audience stood staring dumbfounded as the band stood on stage fiddling with computers and blaring out a very loud, thumping set.

Tricky (see entry) is another emerging artist. He came from the early British techno outfit Massive Attack and formed his own band in 1992. His music has been called "trip-hop" because it combines Tricky's hip-hop singing style with trippy dance beats. Tricky's music has received a lot of critical acclaim and is starting to get attention from the mainstream. Trip-hop was practiced by other U.K. acts like Portishead. U.S. experimenters such as Forest for the Trees explored the psychedelic side even more, often using more delicate beats and sounds.

Kraftwerk (see entry) is the old-timer of the techno field. The German band came out in the early 1970s with a new sound—harsh, computerized, and mechanical sounding. In 1974, the band had a hit with the song "Autobahn." Although the band hasn't had a lot of hits in their long career, they've had a big influence on the next generation of industrial and techno artists. (Music videos of techno songs frequently contain images of expressways and fast driving, a tribute to "Autobahn" and this pioneering techno outfit.)

One of the bands influenced by Kraftwerk is **The Orb** (see entry) who have expanded upon the music by softening the sound. The Orb specializes in a more ambient kind of techno, meaning it's the kind of music that's soothing yet danceable. The band creates their sound by repeating sampled noises over and over again to make an almost hypnotic beat.

There's a broad array of influences in **Moby's** (see entry) music. He combines just about everything in his sound, including hip-hop, dance, rock, reggae, and punk (he used to play in a punk band). Moby, a born-again Christian, is used to working against popular trends. In 1997, he started moving away from his trademark techno sound and started experimenting with musical instruments.

With the wane of "grunge" and second-wave punk, alternative rock audiences rediscovered ska, the Caribbean-born dance music that began in the 1960s and was revived during the early punk era. The 1990s generation of ska-influenced bands included platinum-sellers **No Doubt, Sublime** (see entries) and many others. Some punk bands, such as **Rancid** (see entry), explored the style in their music. Ska audiences "moshed" to the music, as well as "skanking," a slightly less aggressive dance style.

The rise of electronica and other dance forms during the 1990s caused some critics to predict that rock—or guitar rock, at least—would soon be dead. Of course, the same prediction had been made for decades. The more likely truth was that audiences refused to choose between rocking and dancing. They wanted to do both. For all of its changes over the years, dance music is still about moving the body and getting lost in the "Good Times."

CHEMICAL BROTHERS

British techno/dance band

Formed in Manchester, England, in 1992

♪ "It's about making new sounds. Sounds that people haven't heard before, new beats, new ways of doing things. That's what we do." —Ed Simons

DJs Tom Rowlands and Ed Simons began their music career as the Dust Brothers. They deliberately named themselves after the famous American hip-hop producers of the same name. Rowlands and Simons met at college in Manchester. "We used to go to clubs together and stuff," Simons recalls. Then the pair started DJing together. "DJing now, we think of as just a hobby. But I think the energy we used to get from music, was from DJing. What brought us together was rave culture, and being DJs in college. Now I think DJing is just something we do for a laugh. But it definitely gave us the energy." Rave culture was largely based on dance parties held at different underground clubs, with the music provided by the DJs.

Cutting Rhythms

At a bit of a loss for what to do after leaving school, the Dust Brothers decided to record a single. "We just made it as something to do," Simons explains. Although Simons and Rowlands both loved hip-hop, they equally loved the Manchester Sound bands.

Those groups made pop records with lots of swirling sounding guitars. They came from Manchester, thus the genre's name, and included bands like the Happy Mondays and Stone Roses.

What the Dust Brothers created on their first single, 1993's "Song to the Siren," was a sound apart from other club music of the day. Great beats collide with power chords, snatches of melody, and sampled vocals.

Chemical beats

The single got the duo lots of attention. Their *14th Century Sky* EP was an even bigger delight for club DJs. The Dust Brothers were becoming a dance sensation. The kids loved their mix-and-match styles, made up of off-the-wall sounds and ear-shattering rhythms. "Chemical Beats" was a great dance-floor favorite, with its pounding beats and totally different weird sounds.

Then came 1994's *My Mother Mercury* EP. The Dust Brothers were now so popular that they were asked to remix songs for famous indie bands like Primal Scream, techno bands like the Prodigy, and electro bands like St. Etienne.

Exit planet dust

Then, in 1995, the duo signed to Virgin Records. They were asked to change their name, because they couldn't continue on a major label with the same name as somebody else. From now on, they'd be known as the Chemical Brothers.

And so came their first album, *Exit Planet Dust,* where fans mourned the death of Dust and celebrated the arrival of the Chemicals. It was that album that introduced many Americans to the techno scene. *Rolling Stone* said the Chemical Brothers "fuse the precision pulse of hard-core techno and the sloppy flailing of underground rock." More accurately, *Exit Planet Dust* mixed techno grooves with hip-hop beats, then tossed in guitars and melodies. The album sold very well in America and was a hit in Britain. In early 1996, the band's "Loops of Fury" single furthered their fame.

Setting sun

What really broke the band was their next single, "Setting Sun." The song was cowritten by Noel Gallagher, guitarist with the Brit Pop band **Oasis** (see entry). "Noel is just someone we know," explained Simons. "He's a friend of ours really. We were going to remix the track 'Wonderwall' off their album (*What's the Story) Morning Glory?,* but that fell apart. He rang us up one day and said, 'I want to sing a track with you.' So he sent us quite a scaled down version of 'Setting Sun.' He wrote that song, and then off we went. He just came down to the studio and was there for about four hours. And we just took it from there."

The result was the biggest crossover hit of 1996. It's also one of the few Brothers' songs with lyrics. "You're part of the of the life I never had, I'll tell you that's just too bad." With Gallagher's distinctive vocals and the song's dark and threatening aura, "Setting Sun" set alight America's dance scene.

Don't stop the rock

Now that the country was aware of them, the Chemical Brothers dug in for the long haul. Most of the songs on 1997's *Dig Your Own Hole* were very different from "Setting Sun." The sound was much more hip-hop for starters. "We wanted to be different," Simons explained. "It's about making new sounds. Sounds that people haven't heard before, new beats, new ways of doing things. That's what we do." On *Dig Your Own Hole* they did it brilliantly. The album is filled with totally freaked-out sounds, strange beats, and cool samples. Stretching the bounds of dance is what the Chemical Brothers set out to do, and that's what they've done.

Selected Discography

As the Dust Brothers:

14th Century Sky EP, 1993.

My Mother Mercury EP, 1994.

As the Chemical Brothers:

Exit Planet Dust (Astralwerks), 1995.

Dig Your Own Hole (Astralwerks), 1997.

Further Reading

Aaron, Charles, "Chemical Brothers," *Spin,* February 1996, p. 32.

Ali, Lorraine, "Chemical Brothers," *Rolling Stone,* August 22, 1996, p. 36.

Chaplin, Julia, Spin Online, April 7, 1997.

Fricke, David, "Dig Your Own Hole," Rolling Stone Online, April 7, 1997.

Contact Information

Astralwerks
104 W. 29th St, 4th Floor
New York, NY 10001

Web Sites

http://www.geocities.com/SiliconValley/Heights/1275/Chemical.html

http://www.algonet.se/~inftryck/chemical/index.htm

Deee-Lite

American dance/pop band

Formed 1988 in New York City; disbanded 1996

Fusing the modern dance rhythms of hip-hop and house with 1970s-inspired disco and psychedelic P-Funk, Deee-Lite detonated dance floors in 1990 with their first album, *World Clique*. Their upbeat music and retro look led to instant success. *World Clique* gathered rave reviews, and lead singer The Lady Miss Kier (Kier Kirby) became a fashion icon. With subsequent albums failing to keep the group in the spotlight, they disbanded in November 1996.

"As a group, they're a festival of individuality; as a band, they're a party anyone can attend." –critic Christian Logan Wright in *Mademoiselle*

International origins

Deee-Lite originated with the meeting of two apparently different artists, Kier Kirby (later adopting the stage name of The Lady Miss Kier) and Dmitry Brill in New York City's Washington Square Park in the summer of 1982. They were eventually joined by Towa Tei (stage name Towa Towa), a DJ and computer expert from Tokyo, Japan, and the trio merged their musical abilities into Deee-Lite's sub-cultural groove.

The Lady Miss Kier

The Lady Miss Kier was born Kier Kirby in Pittsburgh, Pennsylvania. She grew up with the political awareness instilled by her activist mother, even accompanying her mother to political rallies. Later The Lady Miss Kier worked odd jobs as a waitress, a coat check, and a textile designer.

Dmitry Brill immigrated to the United States from the Ukraine in the former Soviet Union, where he played in a rock cover band. Brill arrived in New York expecting instant gratification, but he was unable to obtain immediate fortune as a cover musician. Brill then found work as a DJ in some of New York's large dance clubs.

Between 1982 and 1986 Kier and Brill cultivated their friendship and collaborated on writing songs. In 1986 they made their debut appearance at Siberia, a New York dance club. Soon after their first appearance, Kirby and Brill received a demo tape from Towa Tei, a Japanese computer sound specialist. Tei adopted the stage name Towa Towa and became the band's "DJ," but he mostly produced sounds from a computer. Towa Tei, like Brill, was a new arrival in the United States. He came from a cultural climate he considered oppressive. "When I was in high school, everyone listened to [commercial hard rockers] Whitesnake, or Japanese versions of Whitesnake," he related in *Rolling Stone*.

Kirby, Brill, and Tei formed Deee-Lite and continued playing gigs. They soon began presenting a homemade demo tape to record labels. An article in *Details* noted that apart from vague rejections, the group received only one formal reply: "Sorry, we can't use your stuff. It's completely unoriginal." Nonetheless, the group gathered crowds as a live act, drawing a cross-section of the various New York City dance scenes. As Jeff Giles described in *Rolling Stone,* "They were drawing vivid, multiracial, pan-sexual crowds that were often a thousand strong, and Kier was throwing daisies from the stage."

Recording dream realized, 1990

With such a large following, several record companies began courting Deee-Lite. "We turned down a lot of offers waiting for someone who understood our art. At a lot of the labels, the only people in power were white men. There were no minorities working in high positions. And you could see what was coming. You could *smell* it. They'd say: 'You're a Top Forty band. You could be the next.' And we'd way, 'Sorry, but you miss what we're about,'" Giles related in *Rolling Stone*.

"It's funk, soul, curly, wiggly music."

Deee-Lite liked to believe they were about the sense of freedom and diversity their audience embodied. Envisioning themselves as politically progressive and stylish, they were convinced that the groove of Deee-Lite was the sound of liberation on several levels.

Deee-Lite signed with Elektra and released their first album, *World Clique,* in 1990. The single, "Groove Is in the Heart," dominated dance-oriented radio stations and clubs. *People Weekly*'s Craig Tomashoff, admittedly not usually a fan of dance music, suggested that "Deee-Lite is the aspirin of dance music. Maybe it's because they actually use some real instruments and real musicians, instead of just sampling them. Whatever the reason, *World Clique* bubbles with energy."

Entertainment Weekly referred to the album as "one of the major musical happenings of 1990." As Kier told *Mademoiselle,* "It's funk, soul, curly, wiggly music." Cementing Deee-Lite's connection with 1970s funk, the group enlisted bassist-guitarist-vocalist Bootsy Collins along with several other Parliament-Funkadelic alumni to play on some tracks.

The trio's first album was met with enthusiastic success and Deee-Lite's Lady Miss Kier became the diva of dance. The band ushered in the retro-1970s look with their "Groove Is in the Heart" video. Their look, along with their music, was fun. Christian Logan Wright described Deee-Lite in *Mademoiselle,* "As a group, they're a festival of individuality; as a band, they're a party anyone can attend."

Tei did not join Deee-Lite on the tour promoting *World Clique,* opting to co-produce an album by Japanese artist Hajime Tachibana instead. So Deee-Lite went on the road without Tei. They were, however, accompanied by a nine-piece band. The highlight of the tour came when Deee-Lite played the prestigious Montreux Jazz Festival in Switzerland, where Deee-Lite was invited to share the stage with P-Funk pioneer George Clinton.

Kirby used her fame as a vehicle for expressing her political views. She filmed a pro-choice public service announcement with other female musicians. She protested the war in the Persian Gulf, recording the anti-war song "Riding on Through," but the song ended up backing a single and did not appear on *World Clique.* She also helped to raise money for AIDS relief.

Brill and Kirby were married in 1991, then returned to the studio to record their second album.

Second album released, 1992

Deee-Lite's second album, *Infinity Within,* embodied the political and social messages they always believed their audiences embraced. Including songs such as the environmental ode, "I Had a Dream I Was Falling Through a Hole in the Ozone Layer"; the safe sex anthem, "Rubber Lover"; and the brief ditty, "Vote Baby Vote," the music had been forfeited for the political message. Deee-Lite guessed wrong. Without the danceable nonsense of "Groove Is in the Heart," Deee-Lite's second release failed to chart like *World Clique*. Jeremy Hellingar observed in *People Weekly*, "Deee-Lite, those neo-disco darlings, have succumbed to the fashion for politically correct dance music."

A new member and a new album, 1994

D.J. On-e replaced Tei on Deee-Lite's third album, *Dew Drops in the Garden*. Response to the third album was disappointing. Like *Infinity Within, Dew Drops in the Garden* bombed. In 1996, Elektra released an album of remixes, *Sampladelic Relics and Dancefloor Oddities,* to poor reviews. Jeremy Helligar complained in *Entertainment Weekly,* "The electronic debris and jungle rhythms drown out their most deee-liteful assets: the sing-along melodies and social awareness that made 'Groove Is in the Heart' such transcendent strobe stuff." Later that year, the band announced its breakup.

Selected Discography

World Clique (Elektra), 1990.

Infinity Within (Elektra), 1992.

Dew Drops in the Garden (Elektra), 1994.

Sampladelic Relics and Dancefloor Oddities (Elektra), 1996.

Further Reading

Details, July 1992.

Entertainment Weekly, June 26, 1992.

Helligar, Jeremy, "Sampladelic Relics and Dancefloor Oddities," *Entertainment Weekly,* December 20, 1996, p. 76.

Helligar, Jeremy, "Dewdrops in the Garden," *People Weekly,* August 1, 1994, p. 2.

People Weekly, July 29, 1991; July 13, 1992.

Rolling Stone, July 9, 1992; September 17, 1992.

Wright, Christian Logan, "Deee-Lite," *Mademoiselle,* December 1990.

Contact Information

Elektra Records
75 Rockefeller Plaza
New York, NY, 10019

Fan club:

DeLovely Fan Club
528 Cedar Street, N.W.
Washington, D.C. 20012-1934

Web Sites

http:www.elektra.com/ambient_club/deeelite/index.html

http://www.vudu.com/deeelite

Kraftwerk

German techno/pop band

Formed in Dusseldorf, Germany, in 1970

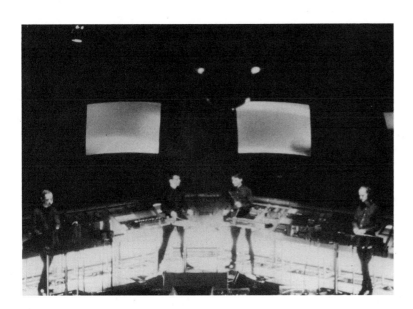

Responding to the mighty sound of industry, Kraftwerk (which means "power station" in English) created music that fused the human and the mechanical, man and machine. Founding members Ralf Hutter and Florian Schneider found inspiration in the nonstop, mechanical whir of industry. Their records laid the foundation for future generations of techno artists. In their most widely acclaimed release, *Autobahn,* (Vertigo/Mercury, 1974) Kraftwerk delivered a machine-like response to driving: repetitive, exact, and endless. Kraftwerk stayed busy and created more than a dozen records in ten years. Though the band has not recorded anything new since 1991, rumor has it that something may be in the works for the late 1990s. Kraftwerk, who allow no visitors or interviews and answer no mail, are keeping quiet.

Band formed in 1970

Ralf Hutter (born in 1946 in Krefeld, Germany) and Florian Schneider (born in 1947 in Dusseldorf, Germany) met in the late 1960s while studying classical music at the Dusseldorf Conservato-

"I think that people are beginning to learn to have a good relationship to technology, and even if we sometimes hit dead-ends I believe that it is a good development. And unavoidable." –Ralf Hutter

ry. Both majored in improvisational music. Dissatisfied with the constraints of classical music, the two bought electronic keyboards and amplifiers. In 1970, they put together their own recording studio, Kling Klang, in an oil refinery. Hutter said to rock critic Lester Bangs of *Creem,* "After the war, German entertainment was destroyed. The German people were robbed of their culture, putting an American head on it. I think we are the first generation born after the war to shake this off." Releasing *Tone Float* (recorded at Kling Klang) in 1970, with a band called Organisation, Hutter and Schneider soon left to form Kraftwerk.

"Kraftwerk is not a band. It's a concept. We call it 'Die Menschmaschine,' which means 'the human machine' ... Kraftwerk is a vehicle for our ideas."

Bringing aboard Klaus Dinger and Thomas Hohman, Kraftwerk released *Highrail* (1970), on the German Philips label. Well-received critically, it was not a commercial success. Dinger and Hohman left to form Neu. In 1971, Hutter and Schneider released *Var* in Germany, called *Kraftwerk* (Vertigo) in the United Kingdom. *Ralf and Florian* (Vertigo, 1973) was their initial foray into blending the modern (techno) with the traditional (strings).

Neu faces

With both Hutter and Schneider doing vocals and electronics, they added Wolfgang Flur on electronic percussion and Klaus Roeder on violin and guitar in 1974. Kraftwerk was now primed to re-lease *Autobahn. Autobahn* reached number five on the *Billboard* charts. The title track is a twenty-two minute ode to driving on what was then the world's super highway, the German Autobahn, which literally had no speed limit. The German Autobahn was known for its severe, electronic, and mind-freezing drive. Also influencing the band during this period was Emil Schult, an artist and musician. He was credited with leading the band to its ultimate synthetic destination, a band consisting solely of electronic instruments.

The machine plays itself

Hutter began toying with the notion of electronic instruments touring on their own. Furthering this idea was Kraftwerk's newest member, Karl Bartos, a percussionist who joined the band in 1975. Bartos's replacement of violin- and guitar-playing Roeder further emphasized the band's movement toward pure synthetic sound. *Radio Activity,* released in 1975, at times featured nothing more than radio interference and static. Kraftwerk also began using synthetic vocals. Even though it won an "album of the year" award in France, the album was not well received because of a rumor that Kraftwerk supported nuclear power.

The human machine

The next two releases, *Trans Europe Express* (1977) and *The Man Machine* (1978), continued Kraftwerk's artistic philosophy of human and machine as a single unit. "Kraftwerk is not a band," Florian Schneider told Ray Townley in *Rolling Stone.* "It's a concept. We call it

Parents Aren't Supposed to Like It

'Die Menschmaschine,' which means 'the human machine' ... Kraftwerk is a vehicle for our ideas." The only track from *The Man Machine* that refers to a human is significantly called "The Model." Live shows at this time routinely featured robots on stage and music apparently played without humans. Two tracks from *Trans-Europe Express*, "Trans-Europe Express" and "Showroom Dummies," were popular disco hits around the world.

Running out of steam

Kraftwerk's next release, *Computer World* (1981), did not enjoy the same success as the previous two. Critics called it tired and the ideas worn out. A single in 1983, "Tour De France," was taken from an album that was eventually shelved. *Electric Cafe,* released in 1986, was equally dismal in that the same old ground was covered. Mark Peel said of *Electric Cafe* in *Stereo Review,* "Maybe it's some kind of ... statement about the domination of technology, or maybe the group's machines really did take over the recording session." Another critic found their work cold and lifeless. Writing about *The Man Machine* in *Rolling Stone,* critic Mitchell Schneider said "Kraftwerk strikingly creates a sound so antiseptic that germs would die there."

Kraftwerk last appeared onstage in May 1993, in Osnabruck, Germany. They also appeared in 1992 with U2 at the "Greenpeace Stop Sellafield" benefit concert.

Lasting Impression

Kraftwerk's sound continues to be heard in today's electronic dance rhythms. It echoed in the 1980s in the music of such groups as The Human League and Ultravox. House deejays continued to mix Kraftwerk records into their creations. One might think of them as a necessary and vital link in the chain of musical evolution: the transition from the traditional to the mechanized to the electronic. More than simply a form of music, it's become a way of life.

Selected Awards

Album of the Year in France, for *Radio Activity,* 1976.

Grammy Award nomination for best rock instrumental performance, for "Computer World," 1982.

Selected Discography

Var (Vertigo), 1971

Kraftwerk (Vertigo), 1972

Ralf and Florian (Vertigo), 1973

Autobahn (Vertigo/Mercury), 1974, reissued, Elektra, 1988

Radio Activity (Capitol), 1976, reissued, Elektra, 1986

Trans-Europe Express (Capitol), 1977

Computer World (Warner Bros.), 1981, reissued, Elektra, 1988

Electric Cafe (EMI), 1986, reissued, Elektra, 1988

The Mix (The Best of) (Elektra), 1991

Further Reading

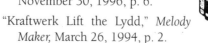

Clark, Carol, "News," *Melody Maker,* November 30, 1996, p. 6.

"Kraftwerk Lift the Lydd," *Melody Maker,* March 26, 1994, p. 2.

New York Times, June 16, 1991.

Roland, Mark, "Bike Boys," *Melody Maker,* July 20, 1996, p. 56.

Web Sites

http://www.cs.umu.se/studenter/kraftwerk/
mm91.html

http://www.geocities.com/SunsetStrip/8880

Parents Aren't Supposed to Like It

MOBY

Techno/dance composer and DJ

Born Richard Melville Hall on
September 11, 1965, in Darien, Connecticut

P raised for investing an impersonal genre with soul and spirit, Moby has received wide critical acclaim for rising above the cold, electronic bump and bleep of techno dance music. No small wonder for an artist who embraces Christ, vegetarianism, philosophy, and a mission to save the planet. Moby's electronic dance music throbs and pulsates, coolly moving and meandering in a distinct weave of funk, punk, hip-hop, gospel, reggae, and classical. His onstage antics mimic his diversity and flare for communication. Often diving into the audience, climbing atop sound boxes, or smashing equipment, he told *Interview:* "It's fun. It's about release and trust. When you make up your mind to jump, you just hope something's going to happen."

Solitary figure

Born Richard Melville Hall, he was given the nickname Moby from the literary classic, *Moby Dick,* written by his great-great granduncle, Herman Melville. Like the great white whale of Melville's novel, Moby is a solitary figure who refuses to be caught

"The meaning of life is to be loving and open-minded and full of spunk." –Moby

in any constraints. "I like working by myself," Moby said in *Musician*. "Engineers make me too self-conscious." Growing up a single child in a single-parent home—his father died when he was two—Moby told *Spin*, "I spent a lot of time by myself. I wasn't good looking. I wasn't good at sports." The contrast between his musician mother (who played keyboards at night and worked as a secretary nine-to-five) and his traditional grandparents, with whom he sometimes stayed, colored Moby's early years. He told *Rolling Stone*, "I wasn't brought up with this paradigm of how to live. So now I'm like 'Anything goes.'"

Anything goes

Moby started playing classical guitar at age ten. He moved on to post-punk in his late teens, briefly encountered drugs and alcohol, studied philosophy in college, discovered the teachings of Christ, was a New York DJ, and finally went solo. What developed Moby as an artist was the early hurt and chaos of growing up; what continues to fuel him is, as he revealed in *Spin*, "a feeling of inadequacy."

"I never felt like I fit in. I didn't know how to dress. I didn't even know where to buy my records."

In the 1970s, Moby played in and/or recorded with British influenced post-punk bands: AWOL, Vatican Commandos, the Pork Guys, and Flipper (while their lead singer was in jail). At this point in his life he discovered Christ. "I try to live up to his teachings but fail all

the time," Moby told *Rolling Stone*. "It's this yardstick that I hold up to my life but can never, never live up to." He also insists that he is no religious fanatic. In *Interview* he told Andrew Essex, "The only thing I worry about in being so open is being associated with the religious right, especially guys like Ralph Reed. I just don't get them." Avoiding the Christian Right (a conservative political movement), killing animals for food, and destroying the environment are predominant themes in Moby's life and his music.

Underground DJ

The next phase of Moby's career brought him to New York City and the ultra-hip world of underground dance clubs. Spinning records for various rap artists in New York's club Mars, he used a variety of nicknames: Barracuda, Mindstorm, and Voodoo Child. Still feeling the outsider, he said in *Spin*, "I never felt like I fit in. I didn't know how to dress. I didn't even know where to buy my records."

So in 1990, he began recording his own tracks with the independent Instinct label. His most popular releases included the singles "Go!" and "Voodoo Child." He soon gained notoriety for his off-base, varied sound and was hit with requests from industry big hitters—Michael Jackson, the Pet Shop Boys, the B52s, to name a few—to help with remixes of their material. His 1991 single, "Go!," was based on the theme for television's *Twin Peaks*. It became a Top Ten hit, and Moby found himself being labeled as techno's first star.

The beat goes on

With the 1993 release of his major label debut, *Move,* on Elektra Records, Moby emerged from the elite circle of underground artists. Fans who had previously blown-off techno dance were immediately won over. "Juxtaposition [placing different elements next to each other] and hybridization [mixing together elements of different origins]," he theorized in *Spin,* "is where newness comes from. It's where jazz came from, it's how rock 'n' roll was invented." Moby is very much opposed to any concept that seeks to limit and label. He told *Rolling Stone,* "Defining yourself as a white supremacist and saying 'I hate techno' are—in very broad terms—the same thing to me. It's exclusionary and it's wrong."

"Everything Is Wrong"

Moby is at odds with many aspects of modern life, which is what inspired his most critically acclaimed and commercially successful record to date. Released in 1995 on Elektra Records, *Everything Is Wrong* "throbs with all the kick and courage of his contradictions," proclaimed *Rolling Stone.* Lorraine Ali, reviewing the disk for the *Los Angeles Times,* called it "one of the most gripping collections of the year." But Moby has more to say than his music might communicate. Enfolded within the disc is a small booklet that criticizes the ecological wasteland we are creating and the unreasonableness of the Christian Right. "Christ preached love and humility and compassion, not hate and judgementalism," he writes. He also quotes American writer Henry David Thoreau, atomic scientist Albert Einstein, German medical missionary and author Albert Schweitzer, and Saint Francis of Assisi.

New release

Moby's latest disc, *Animal Rights,* was released in September 1996 in the United Kingdom and Europe, then in the United States in February 1997. A departure from his previous work, *Animal Rights* was inspired by heavy metal, headbanging guitar-driven rock. Jeremy Helligar in *People Weekly* wrote that there are "some moments of jaw dropping beauty," but some cuts "give one the feeling of being bludgeoned [heavily hit] by Tool and pummeled [pounded] with Nine Inch Nails." Critic David Browne noted in *Entertainment Weekly* that on the album, Moby "forsakes computers for metallic guitars, punky ravings, and prog-rock instrumentals." As a result, "much of the album feels arid, extra dry," according to Browne.

The album includes hardcore punk songs as well as instrumentals. Describing the album in *Alternative Press,* Moby said, "It's just a reflection of the two things that I'm interested in right now, which are really gentle expression and hard, heavy, nasty expression. That's my own listening diet."

For the first time, Moby sang all of his own vocals. In the studio, he first sang them off the top of his head for rehearsals, then recorded them knowing only half the words. Later he wrote them down, surprised "how unliterate [unpolished] and primitive they were," as he told *Alternative Press.*

Summing up *Animal Rights,* Moby said, "This record is dark and heavy, and there's not a lot of incentive for most people to get into it." That's Moby, an artist who by his own actions and creations, is free of constraints. Alternately serious and fun, he's a punker, rocker, and self-contained techno wiz who continues to confound and confuse.

Selected Discography

Moby (Instinct), 1992.

Ambient (Instinct), 1993.

Everything Is Wrong (Elektra), 1995.

Animal Rights (Elektra), 1997.

I Like to Score (Elektra), 1997.

Further Reading

Ali, Lorraine, "Animal Rights," *Rolling Stone,* February 20, 1997, p. 70.

Browne, David, "Animal Rights," *Entertainment Weekly,* February 21, 1997, p. 125.

"Danzig vs. Moby," *Alternative Press,* May 1997, p. 42.

Flick, Larry, "Moby Rocks Out on Electra's 'Animal Rights,'" *Billboard,* February 1, 1997, p. 9.

Gulle, Bob, "Animal Rights," *Audio,* February, 1997, p. 80.

Helligar, Jeremy, "Animal Rights," *People Weekly,* March 10, 1997, p. 24.

Rolling Stone, November 17, 1994, p. 102; March 23, 1995; May 4, 1995, p. 58; December 28, 1995.

Contact Information

Elektra Records
75 Rockefeller Plaza
New York, NY 10019

Moby
c/o D. E. F.
PO Box 2477
London NM6 6NQ
United Kingdom

Moby
c/o MCT Management
333 W. 52nd St., #1003
New York, NY 10019

Web Sites

http://www.moby.org

http://www.hyperreal.com/music/artists/moby

THE ORB

British ambient/dance group

Formed in London, England, in 1988

Back in the mid 1980s, Alex Patterson was DJing at a hip London club. Like most creative DJs, he soon realized that he'd rather make his own music instead of playing other people's. So in 1988, Patterson hooked up with Jimmy Cauty, who played in a popular electro-dance band called the Justified Ancients of Mu Mu (JAMS). JAMS was inspired by hip-hop and built around sampled bits of rock songs. In contrast, The Orb would be almost the exact opposite.

"I'm taking the Orb back to earth. The place is industrial, noisy, and definitely not ambient." –Alex Patterson

Ever-growing song titles

Patterson and Cauty released their first record in 1989, *A Huge Ever Growing Pulsating Brain That Rules from the Centre of the Ultraworld.* This EP (extended play) was unlike anything anyone had ever heard before; it eventually became a club hit. The Orb had founded a whole new genre of music: ambient/house. It was called this because although the music was slow and calm, it was fueled by beats that kids wanted to dance to.

However, Cauty's own band, now re-named KLF, were already stars in their own right. He saw The Orb as just a side project. When remixes that Patterson considered to be The Orb's were credited to KLF, a showdown occurred. The fight ended with Patterson leaving the KLF camp and taking The Orb name with him.

Adventures beyond the underworld

Patterson released the band's next single, the breezy "Fluffy Little Clouds," in 1990. Working as engineer on this record was a teenager called Thrash (a.k.a. Kris Weston), who was soon to become a permanent Orb member.

The following year, the pair released their debut album, *Adventures Beyond the Underworld*. Across two discs, The Orb sailed into the outer reaches of the universe. Many reviewers were already comparing the band to 1960s spacerock group Pink Floyd. That's why *Underworld*'s cover is almost the same as Floyd's *Animals*.

The Orb does have a spaced-out feeling to their music, but unlike groups like Pink Floyd, they never noodle in sounds just for the fun of it. Spacerock was a show-off kind of music, whereas The Orb's goal was to create a rhythm and mood that people could both dance and relax to.

Room at the top

The Orb next released the "Blue Room" single. It was a huge hit, going straight into the Top Ten. The song was almost forty minutes long and still holds the record for the longest single to ever

chart. A bit mystical, a bit Oriental, "Blue Room" further cemented The Orb's genius. As if to emphasize the song's listening appeal, the band was shown playing chess when the song was aired on British television's *Top of the Pops*.

It was no wonder, then, that the band's next album, *U.F.Orb* immediately entered the British charts at Number One when it was released in 1992. The record was more ambient, and thus not so danceable as their last, but that didn't make it any less great. Listening to *U.F.Orb* is like taking a journey into outer space. The music flows all around you, in the distance stars twinkle, and comets whiz by. And that's just what the album sounds like!

Introducing the band

The Orb mothership now included a host of musicians: mix master and famed producer Youth; guitarist Steve Hillage (former guitarist with the underground spacerock band Gong and with his own band System 7); and Jah Wobble, who had joined ex-Sex Pistols Johnny Rotten in the post-punk, experimental band PIL (Public Image Ltd.).

The Orb began playing live shows in 1989, and seeing them was an unforgettable experience. Because the band stay mostly behind synthesizers, they created a phenomenal light and slide show to help create a mood for the music. Their double live album, *Live '93* couldn't include that, but it does capture the grooves and atmospheres of their stage show, and allows the listener to imagine the rest. After the double live album was released, The Orb developed a more elaborate live show that began with several warm-up acts and finished with a set that included various musicians on guitars, keyboards, and electronics.

Unfocused noises and other cool sounds

In 1994, The Orb returned with new songs on the *Pomme Fritz* album. At the time, Patterson said, "The fans wanted an Orb greatest hits, I gave them *Pomme Fritz.*" It was much darker than the band's past records, and more experimental. A lot of people didn't like it, including *Rolling Stone.* "The group inspires awe with its mix of unfocused noises, samples, and textured synth lines. None of the songs contain an easily discernible melody, and the entire work feels incomplete."

Mother Earth

Apparently, some people wanted The Orb to stay the same, but Patterson refused to do that. Their next album was to see even greater changes. On 1995's *Orb vs Terrarvm,* the Orbship headed back home.

"I'm taking the Orb back to earth," Patterson said. "The place is industrial, noisy, and definitely not ambient in the [Brian] Eno/Harold Budd [noted ambient producers] sense of the word." What Patterson meant was that instead of moving towards the peaceful Muzak-esque ambience of producers Eno and Budd, *Orbvs Terrarvm* would be alive with sounds and rhythms.

On the album, The Orb explores Mother Earth, her valleys, lakes, rivers, and mountains. The music, in a way, follows Earth's geographical contours. The sounds of water dripping, flowing, burbling, run across much of the record. And this time, the music is driven by tribal and dub beats, while the electronic effects are almost harsh in places as well.

Orblivion

Thrash left soon after and was replaced by FMGQ (a.k.a. Andrew Hughes), the engineer on *Orbvs Terrarvm.* Even with this change, The Orb continued down the path begun with *Orbvs Terrarvm.* 1997's *Orblivion* was more repetitive and trancey than their previous albums, and a bit darker. It's also much more experimental in places. All and all, this album was much more danceable than their last two.

The Orb's music has taken on a life of its own over time. It changes, grows and breathes, and with every album it explores new territories.

Selected Discography

Adventures Beyond the Underworld (Big Life), 1991, United Kingdom.

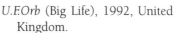

U.F.Orb (Big Life), 1992, United Kingdom.

Live '93 (Island), 1993.

Pomme Fritz (Island), 1994.

Orbvs Terrarvm (Island), 1995.

Orblivion (Island), 1997.

Further Reading

Cohen, Howard, "Ambient-rave Group Orb," Knight-Ridder/Tribune News Service, June 1, 1995.

Prendergast, Mark, "House with All Mod Cons," *New Statesman & Society,* April 9, 1993, p. 49.

Prince, David, "Interstellar Overdrive Reaching Escape Velocity," *Option,* January/February, 1995, p. 75.

Weiderhorn, Jon, "Obrus Terrerum," *Rolling Stone,* April 20, 1995, p. 69.

Weiderhorn, Jon, "Pomme Fritz," *Rolling Stone,* October 20, 1994, p. 146.

Contact Information

Island Records
400 Lafayette St, 5th Floor
New York, NY 10003

Web Site

http://bebe.uv.es/~vortex/music/chillout/orb.html

Tricky

British electro/dance artist

Born in 1964 in Bristol, England

When I was younger," Tricky says, "I wanted to be the best MC in the world, and now I want to be the best musician." Once it seemed Tricky just wanted to be a gangsta. He was arrested several times, and he could have spent his life in and out of jail for petty crimes.

Thankfully, Tricky was saved from such a useless life by the Wild Bunch. The Wild Bunch were a crew of local DJs and musicians that put on shows around the Bristol area in England. They gave Tricky his start to stardom by letting him rap during shows.

Together now

That was back in the late 1980s, and slowly the Wild Bunch began turning into the band Massive Attack. When the group finally went into the studio to record their first album, *Blue Lines*, Tricky went with them. He sang on several of the record's songs. Massive Attack's music was a stunning blend of reggae, hiphop,

"When I was younger, I wanted to be the best MC in the world, and now I want to be the best musician."

and electronics. The album received much attention in Britain and actually went into the music charts.

Keep your mouth shut

But Tricky was also writing his own songs, none of which Massive Attack wanted to use. So, the singer recorded his own "Nothing's Clear" for *The Hard Sell*, a compilation album which raised money for local charities. Still, Tricky continued working with Massive Attack. On their second album, *Protection*, he wrote lyrics for some of the songs, and also produced several of the tracks.

Make a change

A whole new sound and style was developing, which was tagged the Bristol Sound. It was based around Dub, a type of reggae that features slow, pounding bass and drum lines. Dub tends to be very repetitive and sparse, without vocals. But the Bristol Sound added melodies, vocals, and lots of electronics for atmosphere. Tricky began working with other musicians in creating this new sound. The band Portishead came out of this scene, along with solo artist Mark Stewart.

Massive Attack didn't want to move in this direction. Things came to a head when the band refused to use Tricky's latest song, "Aftermath." He'd already made a recording of it with Stewart and singer Martina Topley Bird. Now, he decided to put it out himself. Island Records heard it and was so impressed that they immediately signed him. When they re-released the single later in 1994, it immediately went into the charts. So did Massive Attack's *Protection,* and Tricky had arrived.

In 1995, Tricky's debut album, *Maxinquaye* went into the shops and soared up the chart to #3. The record features both Topley Bird and Tricky dueting together. The music is slow, hypnotic, soulful, and full of smokey atmospheres. The songs themselves were as dark as the music, filled with fear, paranoia, and unhappy relationships. "Awesome," is how the British music paper *NME* perfectly summed it up.

Brand new, your retro

Tricky now began producing many other artists including alternative star **Bjork's** (see entry) *Post* album and gangsta rap band **The Gravediggaz** (see entry). Then he began work on an EP, *Tricky Presents Grassroots*. On this record, Tricky literally returned to his roots. The record was totally rhythm and blues (R & B) although it was still Trickified. This wasn't the R & B of the 1960s, but R & B with a hiphop twist.

Tricky's second album, *Nearly God,* was also very different from *Maxinquaye*. Half of the songs on the record featured guest vocalists. Bjork appears on two tracks, and other guests include pophop star Nenah Cherry, Terry Hall (the former singer with British ska band The Specials), and singing star Alison Moyet. Topley Bird also sings on several of the tracks.

Musically, the album was still based on the Bristol Sound. But the songs were co-written by the guest vocalists, and that gives each song it's own unique sound.

Suffocated love

In a way neither *Grassroots* nor *Nearly God* were follow-ups to *Maxinquaye*. That arrived in 1996 in the shape of *Pre-Millennium Tension*. This album brought together many of the musical threads of Tricky's last three records. The atmosphere is pure smokey Bristol Sound, but there are bits of R & B, soul, blues, and even acid psychedelia within. Unlike *Maxinquaye*, the sound is stripped down to the bone. The beat pulses across the record, but the melody is carried by a flash of a guitar riff, a bit of bass, or a few keyboard chords. The lyrics are filled with frustration, and the music squirms with this emotion as well. "Can't hardly breathe," Topley Bird intones over and over again on "Vent." And the album is a bit like suffocating, but it's meant to be, that's why "tension" is in the title.

Aftermath

Since then, Tricky continued to work with other artists, write songs for movie soundtracks (including *The Crow*), and tour. Seeing Tricky live is like entering another world. The stage remains dark, so you can barely see the stage. Tricky wants the music to be the focus, not him. Slow, trance-like beats fill the air, the guitars and keyboards fill in the gaps, and below it all, Tricky and a female vocalist mutter, whisper, and softly sing. The band slowly weaves a spell, and the audience is caught up in the music, unaware of the group, the room, and the surrounding people. The music becomes all, and that has always been what Tricky has wanted to achieve.

Selected Discography

Maxinquaye (Island), 1995.

Ricky Presents Grassroots (Island), 1996.

Nearly God (Island), 1996.

Pre-Millennium Tension (Island), 1996.

Further Reading

Ali, Lorraine, "Wicked. It's Tricky," *Option*, September/October, 1996, p. 77.

Daly, Steven, "Tricky," *Rolling Stone*, November 14, 1996, p. 47.

Norris, Chris, "Brother From Another Planet," *Spin*, December 1996.

Reighley, Kurt, "Very Tricky," *Detour*, p. 119.

Contact Information

Island Records

400 Lafayette St., 5th Floor

New York, NY 10003

Website

http://www.primenet.com/~aboo/tricky/index.html

Hip-Hop and Rap

Like jazz, soul, and much early rock music, hip-hop and rap are African-American art forms. This doesn't simply mean that they're made by black artists—musicians of many colors and backgrounds have made important contributions—but that traditions African people brought to America during the slave period survived and became unique art forms in this country. In music, these African-based traditions, including the drumming that was a central part of cultures in different parts of the African continent, developed into much-beloved American standards over the years.

In the twentieth century these traditions gave birth to the joyous rhythms of ragtime, dixieland, swing, be-bop, free jazz, rhythm & blues, rock, disco, and rap. The sounds of African music ran through the gospel songs that shook the rafters of Southern churches—particularly its rich vocal harmonies—and in the earthy blues songs plucked on guitars on sharecroppers' porches.

When higher-paying factory jobs became available in Northern cities during World War II, Southern blacks moved North in

LL Cool J

droves. As a result, black southern musical forms—especially the blues—grew up. The "Chicago blues" sound would become a huge influence on rock music. Meanwhile, jazz composers like Duke Ellington merged traditional African forms with classical composition; the result was a uniquely American art form.

Jazz proved that the voice could be used as a horn or other instrument, with singers like Ella Fitzgerald and Sarah Vaughn "scatting," or singing sounds instead of lyrics. Rap proved the voice could be used like a drum, not only with the "human beatbox" approach, but in the rhythmic "flow" of rapping lyrics.

The birth of rap

Rap was born in New York, and first grabbed attention as practiced in the South Bronx area. It developed along two basic lines. Disco DJs" like Eddie Cheeba, Pete "DJ" Jones, DJ Hollywood, and Lovebug Starski appealed to older audiences, stressing crowd response over real rhyming. Their influences were 1960s-era pioneers like Grandmaster Flowers—whose crowning achievement came in supporting "funk-rock godfather" James Brown at New York City's Yankee Stadium—and obscurer names like M'Boya, and Plummer.

"B-Boy DJs," on the other hand, aimed their more aggressive delivery at younger listeners. Their disdain for dress codes and their elders cleared the way for them to dominate rap by the later 1970s. (B-Boy refers to "break boy," meaning a DJ who plays off the breaks in the music.)

Major B-boys included Afrika Bambaataa, a former Black Spades gang leader known for his twenty-five-crate record collection, and the Zulu Nation, an organization he founded to offset criminal activity. Not far behind came Grandmaster Flash (Joseph Saddler), credited with perfecting a technique called "scratching." Scratching is a way of manipulating the turntable needle while playing a record, so that the needle creates a rhythmic sound. (Some say thirteen-year-old Grand Wizard Theodore got the idea for scratching first.) When applied against two turntables, DJs could continually rearrange parts of songs to create recognizable grooves. "To see Flash on the turntables, you'd be in awe," recalled Rahiem, the last to join Flash's Furious Five in 1978. "He'd catch it [a record] in the air all the time, and he'd never miss. Handcuffed! He'd kick his shoe off, and move the cross-fader with his foot—the name [Flash] suited him well."

Flash and his fellow B-Boys' tricks expanded to "backspinning," which let DJs (disc jockeys) repeat important beats and phrases while a record "spun" backwards. For much of the 1970s, rap was a live medium. Tapes of shows were played on "boomboxes" or "ghetto blasters" toted around; these tapes helped spread rap music outside the confines of the South Bronx.

Rap's prime venue was "the park," with electrical power pirated from a nearby street light, as KRS-One's late partner in **Boogie Down Productions** (see entry), Scott LaRock (Scott Monroe Stirling), told the *New Musical Express*: "They were wild times. Throughout the

The Last Poets: Rap's Originators?

The Last Poets were an underground group who have sometimes been credited with founding rap music. Performing in and around New York City in the late 1960s, they read poetry addressing some of society's most pressing ills over pulsating African rhythms supplied by a conga drum. Essentially a black militant group, the Last Poets appeared in 1970 in their only movie, Right On. An album of the same name was also released on the Douglas label. They disbanded over personal and artistic differences later that year. The group consisted of David Jordan Nelson, Jr., Gylan Kain, Abiodun Oyawole, and Felipe Luciano.

Nelson told the Michigan Chronicle in 1992, "When the Last Poets began, their purpose was to create a way of saying things succinctly and strikingly. We wanted to bring poetry to the people through choreography and music to communicate significant truths to African Americans." The Last Poets were a far cry from rap in the 1990s, which Nelson feels the music industry gears more toward entertainment than education or art.

In 1990 The Last Poets got together again for a thirteen-city reunion tour that began in Detroit, Michigan. Then in 1992 Nelson sued the gangsta rap group NWA for sampling—and distorting—a poem on the Last Poet's 1970 album, Right On. At the time, Nelson announced that he would forego the suit if NWA would agree to record with him. Nelson has been quoted as saying that gangsta rap was a dangerous development, because it glorified gangster life. He told the Michigan Chronicle, "A gangster doesn't care who he takes advantage of as long as he makes money."

In 1993, Abiodun Oyawole and Umar Bin Hassan re-formed The Last Poets with drummer Don "Babtunde" Eaton. In 1995 they released an album, Holy Terror, on Rykodisc, that featured guest rappers (such as Melle Mel from the original Furious Five) and musicians (such as Bootsy Collins) doing politically conscious rap. Their fourth album since coming back, 1997's Time Has Come, featured Public Enemy's Chuck D on the song, "Down to Now."

Selected Discography

The Last Poets (Restless), 1971.

This Is Madness (Restless), 1971.

Retro Fit (Celluloid), 1992.

Holy Terror (Rykodisc), 1995.

Prime Time Rhyme of the Last Poets (On the One), 1995.

Prime Time Rhyme, Volume 2, (On the One), 1996.

The Legend: The Best of the Last Poets (M.I.L. Multimedia), 1996.

Time Has Come (Mouth Almighty), 1997.

Queen Latifah

considered the first true hip-hop group. By 1974-75, they'd emerged as the South Bronx's leading B-boys and most consistent live draw.

By 1979, several independent labels and rap entrepreneurs had emerged to record rap, including Paul Winley, who released two Afrika Bambaataa twelve-inch records, and Enjoy (1979-82), run by veteran record man Bobby Robinson, who'd found blues guitarist Elmore James and soul singer Gladys Knight, among others. By his own count, Robinson released nine twelve-inch rap records, including the first efforts from the Funky Four Plus One and Grandmaster Flash on "We Rock More Mellow" and "Superrrapin'." But Robinson lacked the desire to compete, as he told *Goldmine*: "About every third day, they [Grandmaster Flash & The Furious Five] wanted $500. They were tellin' me all kinds of lies—they ran me crazy!"

"Rapper's Delight" changed genre's profile

The business savvy of 1950s rhythm and blues (R&B) singer Sylvia Robinson, who had a 1973 hit single in "Pillow Talk," changed the nature of the rap music business. Assisted by her husband, Joe, Sr., and son Joey, Jr., she launched rap's most important label, Sugar Hill Records, when an aspiring artist, Big Bank Hank (Henry Jackson), handed her a tape of rhymes meant for someone else.

That tape yielded The Sugarhill Gang's "Rapper's Delight" (sung by rap trio Michael "Wonder Mike" Wright, Guy "Master Gee" O'Brien, and Henry "Big

summer the park would be jam-packed. People would be hanging off the trees."

By the mid-1970s, MCs (microphone controllers or masters of ceremonies) had begun assisting the DJs in rap shows, although they were usually limited to an occasional announcement or chant ("Freak, freak, y'all," or "What's your sign?"). In time, however, DJs realized more active MCs could heighten the entertainment and distinguish them from their competitors. The late Keith "Cowboy" Wiggins is regarded as the first MC, while Grandmaster Flash and the Furious Three, Four, Five, or Seven—depending on who was in the lineup—are

Rap and the Grammys

The first rappers to win a Grammy for Best Rap Performance were **DJ Jazzy Jeff and the Fresh Prince** (see entry), for their 1988 record, "Parents Just Don't Understand." The judges, always fairly conservative, chose to recognize a non-controversial party rap record that celebrated good times and fun. The next year Young MC beat out political rappers Public Enemy, whose hit "Fight the Power" was featured in Spike Lee's movie, Do the Right Thing. Also nominated were Tone Loc ("Funky Cold Medina"), Long Island-based rappers De La Soul ("Me Myself and I"), and DJ Jazzy Jeff and the Fresh Prince.

In 1991 two separate categories were established for rap performances, Best Rap Solo and Best Rap Duo or Group. MC **Hammer** (see entry) won in the solo category for his 1990 hit, "U Can't Touch This," taken from what was then the best-selling rap album of all time, Please Hammer Don't Hurt 'Em. Hammer's style of party rap appealed to black and white audiences alike. The Grammy for Best Rap Duo or Group went to four rappers for a track from the Quincy Jones album, Back on the Block. The four rappers—Ice-T, Melle Mel, Big Daddy Kane, and **Kool Moe Dee** (see entry)—represented hard-core and gangsta rap.

The next year, **LL Cool J** (see entry) picked up his first Grammy for his hit single, "Mama Said Knock You Out," in the Best Rap Solo Performance category; DJ Jazzy Jeff and Fresh Prince won their second Grammy with "Summertime." In 1993 Seattle's **Sir Mix-A-Lot** (see entry) won the Rap Solo Grammy for "Baby Got Back," while Southern rap group **Arrested Development** (see entry) won for Best Rap Duo or Group with "Tennessee."

West Coast gangsta rapper **Dr. Dre** (see entry) won the rap solo artist category for "Let Me Ride" in 1994. Incorporating jazz rhythms in their rap, the Digable Planets were rewarded with a Grammy in the Best Rap Duo or Group category for "Rebirth of Slick (Cool Like Dat)."

In 1995 women rappers took top honors at the Grammys. **Queen Latifah** (see entry), one of the most respected of all women rappers, won Best Rap Solo Performance for "UNITY." The popular trio, **Salt-N-Pepa** (see entry), won for Best Rap Duo or Group Perforance with "None of Your Business."

In 1996 the Grammys added a third rap category, Best Rap Album, won by hard-core New Jersey rappers, **Naughty by Nature** (see entry), for Poverty's Paradise. **Coolio's** (see entry) "Gangsta's Paradise," a somewhat melodic song about the gangsta lifestyle but not performed as gangsta rap, won for Best Rap Solo, while Method Man featuring Mary J. Blige won Best Rap Duo or Group with "I'll Be There for You/You're All I Need to Get By."

In 1997 rap veteran LL Cool J won his second Grammy for "Hey Lover" in the Best Rap Solo Performance category. West Coast rap group, Bones Thugs-N-Harmony won the Best Rap Duo or Group award for "Tha Crossroads," from the album E.1999 Eternal, which was produced by the late **Eazy-E** (see entry). The Best Rap Album award went to East Coast rap (and reggae) artists, **The Fugees** (see entry), for The Score.

Bank Hank" Jackson), which became a number four R & B and number thirty-six U.S. pop hit in 1979-80. Its fifteen-minute description (later edited to half that length) of a young man's daily life also reached number one in Canada and the Top Five in Europe, Israel, and South Africa. It was the first commercially successful rap single. One of the earliest plagarism fights in rap history arose when R & B-disco group Chic settled over the Sugar Hill label's use of its own 1979 disco smash, "Good Times," for the backing track.

With the commercial success of "Rapper's Delight," rap changed from novelty to contender overnight. Sugar Hill followed its early success with The Funky Four Plus One ("That's The Joint"), the all-female Sequence ("Funk You Up"), Spoonie Gee ("Spoonin' Rap," "Spoonie's Back") and The Treacherous Three ("Body Rock").

Sugar Hill's biggest successes came with The Furious Five, whose 1980 hit "Freedom" went gold, while its 1982 single, "The Message," achieved the group's highest R & B chart position at number four. Its oft-repeated hook ("It's like a jungle, / Sometimes it makes me wonder, / How I keep from goin' under") showed that rap could be more than just party music. "It made us dig deeper into our surroundings and look at ourselves," recalled the Furious Five's Rahiem.

Enter the new breed

The Furious Five experienced more success with "New York, New York," a number seventeen R&B hit in 1983, and the anti-cocaine "White Lines" that same year. By then, however, Flash, Rahiem,

and Kid Creole (Nathaniel Glover) found themselves pitted against fellow rappers Melle Mel (Melvin Glover), Scorpio (Eddie Morris), and Cowboy in a battle over their name and contract. The Furious Five would split after a court battle permitted Flash to leave Sugar Hill, while Mel—who'd written most of the group's raps—kept the name.

By then, however, rap's "old school" had begun dropping out, casualties of bad record deals and, often, cocaine, as Lovebug Starski told *Rolling Stone:* "All I knew was I was gettin' paid. Coked out of my mind. They [business associates] took advantage of me. Put that in bold." Spoonie Gee wound up in prison for drug use, and Flash told *Rolling Stone* "[I] walked away from my equipment for almost a year." "I lost touch with what I loved."

By the early 1980s, rap had smashed out of its South Bronx confines. White rock acts like Blondie ("Rapture") and The Clash ("This Is Radio Clash," "The Magnificent Seven") had embraced the style. So did films like *Wild Style* (1982), *Breakin'* (1984), and *Krush Groove*, all of which spread rap into middle America.

A new word is born

A host of new labels arose to challenge Sugar Hill's earlier dominance of rap, such as Tommy Boy, where Afrika Bambaataa's 1982 hit "Planet Rock" — which relied on drum machines and electronic keyboards—launched a new style of techno-rap. New York-based Profile Records, then known as a white rock label, signed **Run-DMC** (see entry) in

1983 for $2,500. Run-DMC's terse, tough descriptions of urban life on "It's Like That," "Rock Box," and "Sucker MCs" created another style often called hardcore rap. While Sugar Hill artists had been "more into their outfits," as promoter Van Silk related to *Goldmine*, Run-DMC dressed like its fans, in sneakers and jeans.

But the biggest successes belonged to the Def Jam label, with its roster of The Beastie Boys, **LL Cool J** (see entry), **Public Enemy** (see entry), and Slick Rick. The Def Jam record label was born in the dorm room of Rick Rubin, a white, Jewish student and rap fan/producer at New York University, who teamed up with black entrepreneur Russell Simmons to form a very influential team. Rubin brought a punk-rock energy and enthusiasm to his work with white rap pranksters the Beastie Boys and such important black rappers as LL Cool J and Run-DMC (see entries), throwing rock samples into the mix and expanding the music's audience. Run-DMC's collaboration with rock vets Aerosmith on a rap remake of Aerosmith's "Walk This Way" was a national smash, and signalled that mainstream listeners were ready for rap's brash, funky style.

To describe the harder, faster, and more aggressive rhythmic styles of these new rap groups, writers—and the performers—used a newer term, "hip-hop," which suited the new style's impatience.

The drummer bows out

Also during this period, Kurtis Blow's onstage DJ, Davey DMX (Dave Reeves),

helped create sampling, which directly took loops of other records. By doing this, DJs could mix two records simultaneously and not worry about the perils of "skipping" records and dropped needles, as Blow often recounted. Sampling also eliminated the need for a live drummer, permitting crazier beats a musician couldn't try. Others, like Doug E. Fresh, The Fat Boys, UTFO and Whodini used their vocal chords to imitate drum machine sounds, becoming a "human beatbox," as they called it.

Rap's new era began in the mid-1980s

Hip-hop entered a new era in 1986, with Run-DMC's monstrously successful "Walk This Way." "Rap It Up" emerged as television's first syndicated hip-hop showcase in 1988, followed by "Yo! MTV Raps," hosted by Andre "Dr. Dre" Brown (not to be confused with Death Row Records' Dr. Dre of NWA).

The arrival of political rappers like KRS-One of **Boogie Down Productions** and the group **Public Enemy** (see entries) in the early 1980s was one of the first signs that rap was growing up. With their own security force wearing military uniforms and carrying plastic machine guns onstage during performances, Public Enemy developed a reputation as the Black Panthers of rap (after the militant black organization formed during the civil rights struggle of the 1960s). Public Enemy recorded its first platinum album in 1988, *It Takes a Nation of Millions to Hold Us Back*. Public Enemy's "Fight the Power" appeared on the soundtrack to

Ice-T appearing on the Arsenio Hall Show in 1992.

murder, drugs, pimping, and theft, but which was criticized for glamorizing these things—and causing violence itself. Nonetheless, groups like N.W.A. (featuring future rap solo superstars **Ice Cube, Dr. Dre** and **Eazy-E**) and the Geto Boys became hugely successful. N.W.A.'s famous anti-police track was attacked by politicians and other public figures, but was also an anthem for a large—and multi-colored—audience. Ice-T ignited even greater controversy with "Cop Killer," which was considered a rap song even though he recorded it with his rock band Body Count. The song was incendiary enough to be condemned by then Vice-President Dan Quayle and other political figures and commentators.

Dr. Dre (see entry) emerged in the early 1990s as hip-hop's most influential producer, thanks to his P-Funk-influenced West Coast style, with its phat grooves and sampled synthesizers. His work with rapper **Snoop Doggy Dogg** (see entry) and Snoop's cousin, singer-rapper Warren G., scored massively, as did Dre's own smash album "The Chronic." But the rap audience has always been fickle, and soon such artists as **Tupac Shakur** and **Notorious B.I.G.** (see entries) seized the spotlight, though both were gunned down in separate (but possibly related) incidents in the late 1990s. B.I.G.'s producer, Sean "Puffy" Combs, emerged as one of the most influential figures in the hip-hop world with his Bad Boy Entertainment label, production efforts, and his own recordings.

the popular Spike Lee movie *Do the Right Thing,* and set the standard for "consciousness-raising" rap in the late 1980s, which attacked racism, police brutality, and other injustices with intelligence and seriousness. Female rappers like **Queen Latifah, Salt-N-Pepa** (see entries) and Monie Love began to find an audience in the following years, as righteous rap politics opened up a form that had been dominated by men.

Gangsta rap

The end of the 1980s and the beginning of the 1990s saw the rise of so-called "Gangsta" rap, which claimed to be expressing ghetto reality in its stories of

Other hardcore rap acts, such as Cypress Hill, Wu-Tang Clan (and the solo

Parents Aren't Supposed to Like It

efforts of its many members) and Master P—who sold hundreds of thousands of records and videotapes on his own No Limit label out of his car until a major-label deal brought him into the mainstream—also captured the imagination of hip-hop fans. A new wave of female artists, from experimental singer-songwriter Missy Elliott to sultry Lil' Kim, Foxy Brown and Mia X, also leapt onto the charts in the late 1990s.

That hip-hop not only survived, but has thrived, testifies to its importance. Despite bad business deals, constant media criticism, and an unstable touring climate—in which promoters must carry $1 million in liability insurance—hip-hop has had little trouble staying relevant. The science of beats, boasts, and "breaks," born almost three decades ago in New York City's South Bronx area, is now its own multibillion-dollar industry (accounting for $3 billion annually, or one-third of all record sales each year).

As hip-hop enters its third decade, no one trend seemed predominant—though some expected gangsta rap to fade following the 1996 and 1997 shooting deaths of Tupac Shakur and The Notorious B.I.G. Whatever happens, rap artists will always feel a duty to describe their lifestyles in terms critics refuse to understand. As rap historian Ronin Ro reminded listeners of the Sugar Hill boxed set: "As our government unleashes new crime bills, toys with civil rights, and threatens wide-scale welfare reform, the lyrics shine with even more immediacy."

Further Reading

Berman, Eric, "The Godfathers of Rap," *Rolling Stone*, December 23, 1993-January 6, 1994.

Considine, J. D., "Fear of a Rap Planet: The Biggest Style of the Last Decade Has a Problem with Attitudes," *Musician*, February 1992.

Costello, Mark, *Signifying Rappers*, Ecco Press, 1997.

Greenberg, Steve, "Sugar Hill and the Rise of Hip-Hop," essay for *The Sugar Hill Records Story*, 5-CD boxed set, Rhino Entertainment, 1997.

Heibutzki, Ralph, "What's the Deal?: Rappin' & Rockin' the House That Sugar Hill Built," essay for *The Sugar Hill Records Story*, 5-CD boxed set, Rhino Entertainment, 1997.

Heibutzki, Ralph, "Time Enough for the Old School: The Hip-hop Revolution, 1970-1990," *Goldmine*, May 1996.

Owen, Frank, "Wasted In The Zoo," (interview with the late Scott LaRock), *New Musical Express*, August 26, 1987.

Ro, Ronin, "Sugar Hill: Birth of an Industry," essay for *The Sugar Hill Records Story*, Rhino Entertainment, 1997.

Rose, Tricia, *Black Noise: Rap Music and Black Culture in Contemporary America*, University Press of New England, 1994.

Stancell, Steven, *The Encyclopedia of Rap and Hip Hop*, Schirmer Books, 1996.

Toure, "Only One Star in the Two Schools of Rap," *New York Times*, August 13, 1995, p. 21, section 2.

Arrested Development

American rap group

Formed in southern rural Georgia,
1988; disbanded, 1995

"Brothers and sisters keep messing up, / Why does it have to be so damn tough?" –from "Tennessee"

While Arrested Development stayed together as a group for only about seven years, its Afrocentric politics, righteous optimism, and stripped-down sound nudged listeners from a steady diet of "gangsta" rap. In that style's place, Arrested Development offered positive looks at struggle and redemption. The music reflects the outlook of the group's frontman, Speech. Nothing in Speech's world came easy. Yet, through his own and his group's ups and downs, Speech urged listeners to uphold basic values and not be distracted by ambition.

Maintaining a focus on the group's basic values was a constant struggle for Arrested Development amid critical praise and multiplatinum sales, Speech confided to *Rolling Stone*'s Chris Mundy: "We came to the conclusion that the first 500,000 people who bought our [first] record understood it. They were people who were touched personally. The rest of the people just bought it because of hype."

From gangster to messenger

Although his band won considerable attention for its southern rural style, Speech first hailed from Milwaukee, Wisconsin, where he was born Todd Thomas in 1968—the same year that civil rights leader Martin Luther King, Jr., was assassinated. His parents divorced, and Speech's mother sent him to Ripley, Tennessee, where he spent summers with his paternal grandmother. Exploring a country environment affected Speech deeply, as he made clear to *Musician's* Bill Flanagan: "Up north I was playing with video games, down south I had the grass and the fields. It gave me a whole new appreciation and it gave me a warmth."

Speech also found his social consciousness shaped in other important ways. His mother ran a newspaper, the *Milwaukee Community Journal,* where years later he'd write an occasional column, "20th Century African." Speech's mother also took him and his brother Terry on trips to Africa, which would inspire tracks like "Africa Inside Me."

"How can anybody want to change the situation they're living in if they don't want to live?"

An erratic high school student by his own admission, Speech's path changed for good in 1987, when he enrolled in music at the Art Institute of Atlanta, Georgia. His nickname was already in place, he informed *The Source*; already called "Peach" for his light complexion, Speech added the "s" to give him more authority as a DJ.

Arrested Development kick-started when Speech met Timothy Barnwell, who as Headliner would become the group's DJ and co-rapper. Influenced by the prevailing "gangsta" style, the duo worked along those lines until they realized its limits. To Speech, it boiled down to one simple question, he told *Musician* readers: "How can anybody want to change the situation they're living in if they don't want to live?" This inspired the group's name, since it amounted to a comment on the black community's need for inspiration, as Speech saw it.

Others understood Speech's vision

Speech and Headliner soon discovered others who felt as they did, starting with an old man they'd met on campus, Baba Oje, who became the group's "spiritual advisor." Next came Speech's cousin, Montsho Eshe, who was a teenage dancer, and drummer Rasa Don, who fell into the fold with his fiancee, singer Dionne Farris, after meeting Speech backstage.

Arrested Development's aims were modest, Speech told the Associated Press's David Bauder. Having been signed by Chrysalis Records for a single, he simply hoped to sell 100,000 copies of an album to avoid losing the group's contract. The years spent chasing that dream inspired the 1992 debut album's title, *Three Years, Five Months and Two Days in the Life Of...*

Critical praise followed almost immediately. *Rolling Stone* called the debut "an incredible sprawling journey across

Arrested Development delivered upbeat hip-hop

time, cultures and musical styles." Besides upbeat blues and funk sampling, the single featured Farris's soulful wailing, a prominent feature of "Tennessee"'s middle break, and sounds of daily life. (To keep those sounds of daily life in mind, Speech and Headliner listened solely to cassettes of chicken noises during their days off on the group's first European tour.)

"Tennessee," which uses a snippet of funk-rock pioneer Prince's song "Alphabet Street," was inspired by the loss of Speech's brother and grandmother, who died only a few days apart in 1991. It was Speech's testimony of how far he'd come, and the distance to go, as he told

Rolling Stone: "Sometimes I tear during 'Tennessee,' thinking, 'Here I am in front of a big audience, and I wonder if my brother Terry can see me.'"

Throughout 1992, Arrested Development could do nothing wrong. MTV quickly began airing "Tennessee"'s black and white video, while two more singles became hits. "Mr. Wendal" praised a homeless man's wisdom, while "People Everyday" reworked a late-1960s anthem by Sly & the Family Stone. The group also won two Grammy Awards, including the first-ever Best New Artist for a hip-hop group, and more honors for Best Rap Video from MTV, as well as a "Soul Train" Music Award.

Parents Aren't Supposed to Like It

Beatniks with boomboxes?

When Arrested Development played President Bill Clinton's inaugural festivites in January 1993, many took it as a sign of hope, a feeling cemented by the group's appearance that summer as part of the alternative-rock festival Lollapalooza. At the same time, the band was developing an image as "beatniks with boomboxes." To hardcore rap fans, Arrested Development's bright clothing, cheery tempos, and promotion of rural lifestyles made them nothing but "hip-hop hippies." A live MTV *Unplugged* album, and the contribution of a more aggressive track, "Revolution," for director Spike Lee's film, *Malcolm X*, aimed to change the group's new image.

> **"This business has no avenue for feelings. It's money, money, money, let's make money. If you're not making money, let's move on."**

Speech did not like being stereotyped because of the values expressed in Arrested Development's music. "We do talk about a lot of issues," he informed *Rolling Stone*, "but in order for us to think on a higher level, we don't have to smoke a joint or do coke or heroin." The one-off *Malcolm X* contribution, "Revolution," combined traditional African drumming with a thumping bass line to come off as "a grittier, harder-edge single than anything on the group's debut album," *Rolling Stone's* year-end issue noted.

No rest for Arrested Development

But such distinctions made no impression on the backlash that followed, starting with 1993's *Unplugged*, an album most critics considered unnecessary. Nonstop attention took its toll on Speech, who still hoped to "just get deeper into what we did music for in the first place," he told the Associated Press.

Behind the scenes, Speech had acquired a reputation for being domineering, and major changes occured in the original line-up of the band. Farris quit to pursue her own career after an alleged altercation with soul-popsters **En Vogue** (see entry), and after that Headliner was apparently demoted from DJ to co-rapper. "This business has no avenue for feelings," Headliner complained to *Vibe*. "It's money, money, money, let's make money. If you're not making money, let's move on." Kewsi Asuo took over the turntables, while funk/jazz bassist Foley, singer Nadirah and dancer Ajile entered the fold, too.

Third album released in 1994

Zingalamaduni, the group's mid-1994 album, borrowed its title from a Swahili phrase, "beehive of culture," and kept its focus positive. Speech showed he'd broadened as a lyricist, addressing property issues in "Achen' for Acres" ("If you've got land to stand on, you can stand up") and "Mister Landlord," which urged that person to "step off my yard!"

Rolling Stone gave the album a four-star rating, suggesting its reception may rest on "how much finger snapping and head bobbing the new songs inspire." But other critics and audiences were cooler, leading to slower sales. *Entertainment Weekly's* Michael Walker lamented Arrested Development's bid to shove "peace, love and understanding (and a nearly unpronounceable album title) [down their] audience's throat."

Group disbanded in 1995

For many, the novelty of Arrested Development's upbeat hip-hop had worn off. Its last major moment came in late 1994, when the group played in South Africa for the recently-freed new president, Nelson Mandela's inauguration. After a long silence, the group disbanded in 1995, an event almost ignored amid the new dominance of "gangsta rap" at the cash register.

Since the breakup, Dionne Farris has released an acclaimed solo album, while Speech's long-awaited solo efforts in 1996 won only lukewarm reviews. However, while hardcore supporters may consider him left over from an early 1990s trend that didn't stick, Speech has always taken the long-term view. "In the future," he told *Musician,* "I hope that when people look back on the late '80s and '90s, they'll know that the gangsta reality and the glamorous women reality wasn't the only reality. There was another side."

Selected Awards

Quadruple-platinum award for debut album, 1993.

Grammy Awards for Best New Artist and Best Rap Album, 1993.

Soul Train Music Award, 1993.

Best Rap Video of the Year, MTV, 1993.

Band of the Year, *Rolling Stone,* 1993.

Album of the Year, *Musician* and *The Village Voice,* 1993.

Selected Discography

Three Years, Five Months and 2 Days in the Life Of... (Chrysalis), 1992.

MTV Unplugged (Chrysalis), 1993.

Zingalamaduni (Chrysalis), 1994.

Further Reading

Bauder, David, Associated Press interview, reprinted in *The Herald-Palladium,* June 30, 1994.

Flanagan, Bill, "Speech Meets Superfly" (joint cover story/interview with Curtis Mayfield), *Musician,* 1993.

Mundy, Chris, "Speech Therapy: Arrested Development Calls for a Revolution of the Mind," *Rolling Stone,* January 7, 1993.

White, Armond, "AfroEccentric," (*Zingalamaduni* album review), *Rolling Stone,* June 30, 1994.

Contact Information

Chrysalis Records
8730 Sunset Blvd., 5th Fl.
Hollywood, CA 90069

BOOGIE DOWN PRODUCTIONS

American hip-hop group

Formed in South Bronx, New York City, 1986

No hip-hoppers have seen more ups and downs than KRS-One, the co-founder of Boogie Down Productions (BDP), who went from homeless shelter-dweller to self-styled "Blastmaster" and "Teacher." It all comes down to timing, as he told *Rolling Stone:* "Rap is always out of time. Hip-hop is always on time."

As a New York City teenager, Laurence Parker had already seen more than most people do in a lifetime. By age thirteen, family problems pushed Parker onto streets, subways, and libraries, where he gradually educated himself. While staying at the Franklin Avenue Shelter on 166th Street in the South Bronx, he met a social worker, Scott Monroe Stirling, who became Scott LaRock, after the old school DJ Coke LaRock. Parker became KRS-One: Knowledge Reigns Supreme Over Almost Everyone. Suitably inspired, they formed a duo: Boogie Down Productions (BDP).

Early road proved rocky

BDP's earliest recording attempts were plagued by problems. For instance, one of their early tracks sat on Zakia Records' shelf

"Rap music is the voice of the people—the *last* voice of the people. It's not confined with notes, or bars, or what you say, or what record company you come out on, or having to win any Grammy Awards or anything." –KRS-One

KRS-One

when police arrested the owner on drug charges. Their next label, Sleeping Bag Records, where they cut "Success Is the Word," went bankrupt. Spring Records, who enjoyed Polygram's major-label distribution, passed on BDP altogether. Promoter Van Silk—then working for Spring—recalled his frustration in being unable to convince his bosses to sign the two, who he felt had something special. "You could see the determination to blow up in their eyes," said Van Silk.

Tired of the runaround, BDP issued a single, "Crack Attack," followed a year later by the album *Criminal-Minded* on their own B-Boy label. When asked to explain the title, LaRock responded: "Because everyone is [criminal-minded]; it's just that some are more naked about it than others."

"You don't stop the violence with cookies. You don't stop the violence with flowers."

One of the album's tracks, "My 9mm [millimeter] Goes Bang," which bluntly described what happens to somebody caught on the wrong side of an automatic weapon, was a terrible foreshadowing of LaRock's August 1987 murder, when two men shot him for breaking up an argument. He left behind a son, Scott, Jr., and KRS-One—who continued with brother Kenny, and D-Nice (Derek Jones) as DJs. The new BDP trio cut *By All Means Necessary*, whose best-known track, "Stop the Violence," begged hip-hoppers to pull together and stop the disruptions then plaguing their concerts. "Real bad boys," thundered KRS-One, "move in silence."

Striking out against self-destruction

Some questioned the cover of *By All Means Necessary*, which showed KRS-One posing with a rifle. He argued it only borrowed from a similar photo, and stance, taken by murdered civil rights leader Malcolm X. "You don't stop the violence with cookies. You don't stop the violence with flowers," he told *Option*.

KRS-One followed that message with a twelve-inch single, "Self-Destruction," targeting black-on-black violence. Its sales helped to raise $250,000 for the National Urban League. In 1989 he introduced—and co-produced—companion Miss Melodie's *Diva* album, began lecturing at colleges, and contributed "Jack of Spades" to Keenan Ivory Wayans's film, *I'm Gonna Get You Sucker*, a spoof of the "blaxploitation" movies of the 1970s.

"Jack of Spades" appeared on the next BDP album, *Ghetto Music*. The album displayed traces of reggae, something KRS-One attributed to his Jamaican father who always had the hottest records in that style. Like previous albums, *Ghetto Music* tackled serious topics, including police brutality in "Who Protects Us From You?," and more concerns about violence in "You Must Learn."

Boogie Down became a letdown

As the 1990s opened, KRS-One kept up the heat with the record *Edutainment*, which emphasized words over beats. Writers like Q's Paul Davies praised this style, calling the album "as powerful, and as uncompromising, as Public Enemy's

Parents Aren't Supposed to Like It

call to arms." Others found KRS-One taking his "Teacher" role too seriously.

"I am the embodiment of what a lot of MCs are trying to do. I'm not doing hip-hop, I *am* hip-hop."

KRS-One was coming under fire for his attitude in other areas than his music. On tour at Westcliff Pavilion, KRS-One walked offstage after just fifteen minutes, calling the sound system "wack" and angering crowds and critics alike. These outbursts weren't recorded on BDP's live album, *Live Hardcore Worldwide,* but KRS-One's public image did nothing to boost sales of 1992's *Sex and Violence.* Although critics felt the album showcased an angrier, stronger KRS-One, the public passed it up.

In 1993, KRS-One took a solo plunge on *Return of the Boom Bap,* which reviewers considered as good as *Criminal-Minded.* KRS-One told *Rolling Stone* he had no doubts about what kind of album he'd made. He had lived out the dream of any hip-hopper: to come out swinging off the streets, making socially conscious music that people wanted to hear. "I am the embodiment of what a lot of MCs are trying to do," he told Toure. "I'm not doing hip-hop, I *am* hip-hop."

But KRS-One's aggressive public displays (like shoving PM Dawn's Prince Be off a New York stage) were catching up to him. In KRS-One's view, those actions amounted to "hip-hop throwing commercial rap off the stage." Such reasoning failed to rescue *Boom Bap,* which had already fallen off the R & B charts by early 1994.

Despite that setback, KRS-One has continued to pursue his search of hip-hop culture on recent albums like *KRS-One* (1995), as shown by "MCs Act Like They Don't Know," "Rappaz R N Dainja," and "Represent the Real." This trend continued on *I Got Next* (1997), which features a remake of Blondie's 1981 crossover hit, "Rapture," retitled "Step Into a World (Rapture's Delight)."

In *USA Today's* view, songs like "The MC," "Blowe," and "Can't Stop, Won't Stop" find KRS-One "at the top of his game." *I Got Next* shows KRS-One refusing to slow down, whatever the public may think. For them, he offers a simple message about hip-hop: "Attitude is all it is."

Selected Discography

As Boogie Down Productions:

Criminal-Minded (B-Boy), 1987.

By All Means Necessary (Jive), 1988.

Ghetto Music: The Blueprint of Hip-Hop (Jive), 1989.

As KRS-One:

Edutainment (Jive), 1990.

Return of the Boom-Bap (Jive), 1994.

KRS-One (Jive), 1995.

I Got Next (Jive), 1997.

Further Reading

Brown, Russel, "Family Entertainment," *Sounds,* April 7, 1990.

Davies, Paul, "*Edutainment* album review," *Q,* March 1990.

Ehrlich, Dimitri, *"Return of the Boom-Bap* album review," *Rolling Stone,* November 25, 1993.

James, Mandi, "Boogie Nights" (concert review), *New Musical Express,* March 17, 1990.

Owen, Frank, "Wasted in the Zoo," *New Musical Express,* September 26, 1987.

Toure, "KRS-One Interview," *Rolling Stone,* December 23, 1993-January 6, 1994.

Contact Information

Jive Records
137-139 W. 25th St.
New York, NY 10001

Web Site

http://www.cduniverse.com/

COOLiO

American rap artist (West Coast and gangsta rap styles)
Born Antis Ivey, Jr., August 1, 1963, in Los Angeles, California

oolio's hobbies of reading Anne McCaffrey's "Pern" fantasy novels and spending nights fishing off the pier in his hometown of Los Angeles, California, do not seem in keeping with the image of a hip-hopper or the ambition that fueled his fifteen-year struggle to start a hip-hop career. The road was not always pleasant for Coolio, but in 1994, his struggles to make it in hip-hop paid off. That year "Fantastic Voyage," Coolio's single based on Lakeside's 1981 funk hit of the same name, went Top Ten with little apparent effort. A year later his song "Gangsta's Paradise" was 1995's hottest single. Overnight, anyone who watched MTV knew Coolio by his tangled braids—the style was even parodied in the hip-hop spoof film, *Don't be a Menace to Society While Drinkin' Your Juice in the Hood.*

Yet success barely seems to have impacted Coolio, who still insists that he'll retire to write novels in the McCaffery mode he so enjoys. "Some people think I'm hard, crazy, a wild-style gangsta," he told *Details'* Gavin Edwards. "Some people know that really I'm just a good person. I don't play the hard role no more."

"Tell me, why are we
so blind to see /
That the ones we
hurt are you and me?"–from
Coolio's "Gangsta's Paradise"

Coolio dreams of retiring from hip-hop one day to write fantasy novels

Coolio has little patience for anyone claiming that he glamorizes crime. His cautionary "message raps" advocate safe sex, denounce violence, and praise strong black mother and father figures—something that his early life lacked.

A difficult childhood

Coolio was born Antis Ivey, Jr., on August 1, 1963, in South Central Los Angeles—one of America's most troubled, violent areas. (Coolio has often given differing birthdays—and recollections of his early life.) His childhood and teen years were troubled. When he was two, Ivey's mother, a factory worker, left his father, a carpenter, who later moved to San Jose, California. Ivey and his sister Venita stayed behind with their mother and her new husband, a postal worker. As a young boy, Ivey was bullied for his small size and asthma.

The family moved to Compton, a dangerous and decaying industrial center near Los Angeles. When Ivey was eleven, his mother, suspicious that her husband was cheating, ended her marriage with a shotgun blast that shattered her husband's arm. Out went the Disneyland outings supported by the step-father's salary. Life grew harder when Ivey's mother began drinking up what income remained. By junior high, Ivey had changed from a shy "bookworm" into a fixture of the streets: "I started acting crazy, bring a knife to school, hit you on the head with a bottle, whatever."

Never an official member of Los Angeles's murderous Crips gang, Ivey took to wearing their "colors" and clip-on earrings for survival's sake. He told *Details'* Edwards, "You got to be down so you don't get beaten down." He even robbed houses when older youths made him. Although he'd dreamed of attending Harvard—and had gotten straight A's—by his tenth-grade year Coolio was showing up in school just enough to avoid being expelled.

Took refuge in books, rap

Throughout these troubles, Ivey read for inspiration; besides McCaffrey, he often consulted John D. Fitzgerald's Great Brain series. "The idea of a triumphant boy genius appealed strongly to Coolio, even though the books were set in turn-of-the-century Utah," a *Details* article observed.

By 1979, Ivey had made his hip-hop debut at an eleventh-grade dance, having been introduced to the style by neighbors who'd moved from New York, the birthplace of hip-hop. His nickname, he recalled, stuck when a friend poked fun by asking: "Who do you think you are, Coolio Iglesias?" Coolio's used it ever since.

While he did not share the Crips' bloodthirsty nature (he once saw them beat someone dead with a hammer), Coolio still had scrapes with the law. Around the age of twenty, he spent six to ten months in jail for trying to cash a friend's stolen money order, apparently as a favor. Upon release he fell back into crime, but managed to cut a twelve-inch record, "Whacha Gonna Do?," on an independent label sometime between 1983 and 1985. It made him one of the first West Coast rap stylists to record. He was a promising artist, too, until crack cocaine intervened.

Beating his addiction

Ironically, Coolio's longest-lasting job—scanning passengers and luggage at Los Angeles International Airport (LAX)—came during his crack addiction. Starting there in 1985, Coolio eventually transferred to luggage duty so he could steal unclaimed suitcases. By 1987 Coolio had managed to stop using crack, but he felt his neighborhood's temptations might be too difficult to ignore. He moved to San Jose, where he stayed with his father and joined the state's Department of Forestry in Sacramento. The combination of disciplined teamwork and hard physical labor kept Coolio off drugs when he returned to Los Angeles in 1989, and he dove headfirst back into the music business.

Coolio's first half-year there was difficult. He played house parties, skating rinks, and any place else that would hire him. In 1991 Coolio joined WC and the MAAD Circle, whose greatest success came with its *Ain't a Damn Thing Changed* album, which sold 150,000 copies. From that experience, Coolio hooked up with his rap partner, DJ Wino.

The old temper resurfaced in 1992 when he reportedly planned to stab Bronx artist Tim Dog for releasing an anti-gangsta single. As *Details* reported it, **Naughty by Nature's** (see entry) Treach intervened, though Coolio declares to this day: "If you dis me on a record, when I see you, we gotta fight."

Coolio gets his break

Coolio's break came in 1993, when manager Paul Stewart passed on his demo tape to rap label Tommy Boy—which yielded a record deal. Coolio's debut album, *It Takes a Thief,* came across as a straight autobiography. Besides the self-evident title track, Coolio talked about surviving on welfare ("County Line"), starving ("Can-O-Corn"), and drugs ("'N Da Closet"). Its topics also dealt in humor and optimism, especially in "Fantastic Voyage"—whose lyrics express the dream of escaping to where "It really don't matter if you're white or black."

The video's multicultural beach party played an important part, too, as *Rolling Stone* noted: "Coolio uses soul music and funk from the Seventies and early Eighties for its power to evoke a time of greater innocence and optimism." By the fall of 1994, Coolio had toured with the sweet throated R & B singer R. Kelly and sold one million copies of *It Takes a Thief*.

Became 1995's hottest news

If anything, Coolio became bigger with his second album, *Gangsta's Paradise,* whose title track addressed his old Compton neighborhood's dwindling prospects. Its lush string section, pulsing bass, and co-rap with L. V. gave "Gangsta's Paradise" a number-one slot, where it stayed four weeks in July 1995. Coolio won Grammy and American Music Awards for Best Rap performance; overnight, its two million sales made him 1995's hottest news.

The song's appearance on the *Dangerous Minds* soundtrack made the top of the charts, too. On the Internet, Coolio claimed the inspiration came from Stevie Wonder's "Pastime Paradise": "Actually it wasn't so easy to get a clearing [to use material from the song] at the beginning, but I think what it was he had not heard it…. He signed the release form the same day he heard it." Other tracks, like "Too Hot," "Cruisin'," and "A Thing Goin' On" updated funk classics by Kool and the Gang, Smokey Robinson, and Billy Paul's soul hit "Me and Mrs. Jones," respectively.

Since then Coolio has appeared in commercials—including one for Reebok—and the 1996 film *Phat Beach,* where he made a memorable impression during a party sequence. The role moved Coolio to pursue acting and writing when his hip-hop days ended. Judging from a questionnaire from the *Daily Iowan,* he hasn't lost his sense of humor. When asked how he'd react to seeing anti-hip-hop activist C. Delores Tucker on a Compton street, Coolio responded: "Nothing. [I would] Keep walking."

Selected Awards

American Music Award, Favorite Rap/Hip-hop Artist, for "Gangsta's Paradise," 1996.

Grammy Award, Best Rap Solo Performance, for "Gansta's Paradise," 1996.

Grammy nomination, Best Record of the Year, for "Gangsta's Paradise," 1996.

Selected Discography

It Takes a Thief (Tommy Boy), 1994.

Gangsta's Paradise (Tommy Boy), 1995.

My Soul (Tommy Boy), 1997.

Further Reading

Cooper, Carol, "The Big Payback" *Rolling Stone,* September 22, 1994.

Edwards, Gavin, "The Rebirth of Coolio," *Details,* March 1996.

"Five Questions For Coolio," interview "questionnaire" excerpted from *The Iowa State Daily Iowan,* February 22, 1996.

Hatt, Doug, "Gangsta In Paradise," *People Weekly,* January 29, 1996, p. 51.

Jackson, Devon, "Breaking the Sound Barrier," *Harper's Bazaar,* February 7, 1996.

Rubiner, Michael, "Old-School Cool," *Rolling Stone,* June 15, 1995.

Contact Information

Tommy Boy Music
1747 First Avenue
New York, NY 10128

Web Site

http://home1.swipnet.se/~w-10840/

DJ JAZZY JEFF & THE FRESH PRINCE

American rap duo

Duo formed 1986 in Philadelphia, Pennsylvania

🎼 "We like to give the audience a lesson in rap. It's not hard, anyone can do it. It's not about black or white, it's just about having fun." –Jazzy Jeff

"Rap music is a subculture: hip-hop. It's a style of dress, an attitude, a look, a language. It's more than just music." –The Fresh Prince

DJ Jazzy Jeff (Jeffrey Townes) and The Fresh Prince (Will Smith) must rank among hip-hop's unlikeliest success stories. Their clean-cut image —and avoidance of rap's angrier, more militant side —may not score points with "gangsta" fans, but it has gotten them into mainstream media, television, and shows where hardcore performers remain uninvited. The duo's humorous takes on monster movies, clueless parents, and parties have helped them survive, no matter what trend dominates hip-hop. Instead of carrying across messages, Jazzy Jeff and The Fresh Prince poke fun at every day problems, notably in their 1989 Grammy-winning single, "Parents Just Don't Understand." While less active in recent years due to Smith's acting career, they continue to hold their own, thanks to their broad appeal.

Duo met at a party

Unlike many hip-hoppers, Smith and Townes come from stable, middle-class backgrounds. Will Smith was born in Philadelphia, Pennsylvania, on September 25, 1968, the second of four children to Willard Smith, Sr., an engineer. The boy began rapping at age twelve; his "Fresh Prince" nickname came from being able to charm his way out of trouble.

"I can just keep talking," Smith laughed to *Vibe*'s Amy J. Cohen in the 1990s. "The other person will never win. Even if the other person knows that he is right, I'll just keep talking and talking until the other person gives up." Such charm earned Smith his "Fresh Prince" nickname by persuading teachers to look past shortcomings like unfinished homework.

Born Jeffrey Townes in Philadelphia (around 1969, although some sources say 1965), Jazzy Jeff also began perfecting his craft from an early age—in this case, ten. His parents' basement made a suitable training ground for sharpening his mixing and scratching skills. In time, Townes became a celebrated local DJ.

While Smith excelled academically at Overbrook High School, he opted for a hip-hop career after meeting Townes at a party in 1986. Since Townes had already cut a solo album (1985's *On Fire*), they had little difficulty in signing with Jive Records that same year —and getting a hit single, "Girls Ain't Nothing but Trouble." It set the tone for what followed: light party music that anyone could appreciate.

Parents didn't know; MTV did

Not surprisingly, this pop/rap approach—and clean-cut image—hardly impressed socially conscious or "hardcore"-styled artists. But their first album,

Rock the House, sold 600,000 copies, for which Jazzy Jeff made no apology to the *Philadelphia Inquirer*: "We don't approach the music with the idea of getting a message across. We just sing about our experiences, and the audience finds it funny, or can relate to it."

The big breakthrough came with 1988's double-platinum *He's the DJ, I'm the Rapper,* which yielded a smash single in "Parents Just Don't Understand." It made fun of parents who didn't know what kind of school clothes their children really wanted. In the MTV video, the Fresh Prince pleads to "put the bell-bottom Brady Bunch trousers" back.

With their shows free of crowd problems, Jazzy Jeff and The Fresh Prince found themselves touring America and Canada with **Run-DMC** (see entry), "attempting to bring rap out of the ghetto by presenting songs that relate to everybody," noted *People Weekly* in October 1989. By then, however, the team faced greater mainstream competition from the likes of **MC Hammer** (see entry) and Tone-Loc. Their next album, *And in This Corner* (1989), sold one million copies, or half that of its predecessor. But that letdown still yielded another memorable single and video, "I Think I Can Beat Mike Tyson" — whose poke at overactive egos only cemented the pair's mainstream appeal.

Acting career interrupted recording

As 1990 began, Jazzy Jeff and his partner stayed hot with a Grammy Award nomination for "I Think I Can Beat Mike Tyson," which lost—amid stiff competition from **Public Enemy** ("Fight the Power"; see entry), Tone-Loc ("Funky Cold Medina") and the eventual winner, Young MC.

That year, Smith landed the acting role that changed his life: *The Fresh Prince of Bel-Air.* The show was created after Smith met Warner Brothers executive Benny Medina, who wanted a show based on his teen years of living with a rich Beverly Hills family. NBC bought the idea, casting Smith as a West Philadelphia teen living with the rich Banks family of Bel-Air. Initially dismissed as a 1990s-era *Beverly Hillbillies, The Fresh Prince of Bel-Air* quickly became a top show among teenagers.

"The people I work with are great and I like acting," Smith told *Vibe* as the show began. He hoped to keep both careers—even though Townes wouldn't move to Los Angeles—and didn't mind signing autographs, even if "there are times when I would like some privacy," he confessed.

In 1991, Jazzy Jeff & The Fresh Prince stormed back with a major pop and R & B hit, "Summertime," off their *Homebase* album. The single took Kool & The Gang's "Summer Madness" as its musical base, allowing Smith to rap about romance and community barbeques. It won a Grammy for Best Rap Duo/Group Performance in 1992. *Homebase* yielded a second Top 20 hit, "Ring My Bell," which updated Anita Ward's soul oldie of the same name.

Next album took a U-turn

After years of swearing off "gangsta" rap, Jazzy Jeff & The Fresh Prince sur-

prised fans by moving into a much harder-edged style with *Code Red.* Released in the fall of 1993, listeners wondered where all the good times went, while critics considered *Code Red* surprisingly effective—due to its production and the duo's hip-hop roots, which ran deeper than most admitted.

By that time, Smith's acting roles had inevitably taken priority. His starring movie roles began with *Six Degrees of Separation* (1993), in which he played a Boston con man, and 1995's *Bad Boys* with comic actor Martin Lawrence. The two played Miami police detectives trying to locate $100 million in stolen drug money. *The Fresh Prince of Bel-Air* ended its run in 1996. That summer, Smith's role as alien enemy Captain Steven Hiller in *Independence Day* put him into superstar status, followed by the blockbuster *Men in Black* (1997), which cast him and Tommy Lee Jones as human superagents going after aliens.

"People love that government-conspiracy stuff—the black suits and sunglasses," Smith told the *New York Times's* Ian Spelling. While considering *Independence Day* and *Men in Black* sequels, Smith indicated a new album would be forthcoming. He and Townes were recording it at current girlfriend Jada Pinkett's Hollywood Hills home, though their Jazzy Jeff & The Fresh Prince name would no longer apply. The stylistic approaches in their next efforts remained to be seen.

Selected Awards

"Parents Just Don't Understand," Grammy Award for Best Rap Performance, 1989.

Parents Aren't Supposed to Like It

"I Think I Can Beat Mike Tyson," Grammy Award Nomination for Best Rap Performance, 1990.

"Summertime," Grammy Award for Best Rap Duo/Group Performance, 1992.

Selected Discography

Rock the House (Jive Records), 1987.

He's the DJ, I'm the Rapper (Jive Records), 1988.

And in this Corner... (Jive Records), 1989.

Homebase (Jive Records), 1991.

Code Red (Jive Records), 1993.

Solo Albums

On Fire (Jive Records), 1985. By DJ Jazzy Jeff.

Further Reading

Hoerburger, Rob, "DJ Jazzy Jeff & The Fresh Prince," *Seventeen,* May 1989, p. 47.

Philadelphia Inquirer interviews, March 18 and 26, 1990.

"Jazzy Jeff and Fresh Prince, Rap's More Mild Than Wild Guys," *People Weekly,* October 3, 1988, p. 81.

Ressner, Jeffrey, "No Nightmares for D.J. Jazzy Jeff and The Fresh Prince," *Rolling Stone,* December 1, 1988.

Spelling. Ian, "Will Smith Eagerly Awaits 'Men In Black' Release," *New York Times* interview, reprinted in *Chicago Tribune,* June 26, 1997, section five, p. 7.

Thompson, Melissa, "17 Questions: Will Smith Gets Fresh with Jazzy Jeff," *Seventeen,* December 1993, p. 85.

Contact Information

Jive Records
9000 Sunset Blvd., Suite 300
Los Angeles, CA 90069-5891

Web Sites

http://www.pureartmkt.com/purefilm/kensax/willsmith.html

http://www.wfe.edu/~bergqkj4/jjfp.html

http://metaverse.com/vibe/interviews/iview.will-smith.html

Dr. Dre

American rap artist, producer (West Coast, gangsta rap styles)

Born Andre Ramelle Young on February 18, 1965, in Compton, California

"People ask me how I come up with all these hits, and I can only say that I know what I like ... and what people like to play in their cars." –Dr. Dre

No producer has impacted 1990s hip-hop more than its most creative mixer, Dr. Dre, whose skills have lifted him from project resident to platinum performer and multi-media executive. As rap writer and historian Toure wrote in the *New York Times,* "Dr. Dre has been the single most important force behind L.A. hip-hop." As proof, Interscope Records owner Jimmy Iovine, whose label distributes Dre's work, cites his twelve-year-old nephew. "You couldn't get more white and suburban than him," Iovine told *Rolling Stone.* "But Dre's record is all the kid listens to. When you sell this many albums, they are not all going to the South Bronx."

Dre adds little to such explanations. "I can take anybody who reads this magazine and make a hit record on him," he added. "You don't have to rap. You can do anything. You can go into the studio and talk." The record-buying public agreed; by late 1994, Dre had either rapped on or produced albums selling 28 million copies.

Yet Dre's talents have been overshadowed by run-ins with peers and police, making him seem "less a hero than as a menace to soci-

The "Other" Dr. Dre

Yes, there are two rap personalities who go by the rap name of Dr. Dre.

When people hear the name "Dr. Dre," they immediately associate it with Andre Ramelle Young, Grammy-winning rap artist and producer of "gangsta" hip-hoppers NWA, Eazy-E, and others, and one-time house producer for rap labels Ruthless Records, Death Row Records, and Aftermath.

However, the name is also used by Andre Brown, a New York City DJ who started cutting "the wheels of steel" for old school rappers like Disco Dave, The Sugarhill Gang, and Woody Wood, when hip-hop began in the late 1970s.

This Dr. Dre (Andre Brown) was the original "Yo! MTV Raps" host. He also worked with The Beastie Boys, **LL Cool J** (see entry), and **Run-DMC** (see entry)—all staples of the mid-1980s hip-hop revolution, led by the New York-based Def Jam label. Dre was around when Def Jam began in Rick Rubin's New York University dorm room—and also knew the members of **Public Enemy** (see entry), its most controversial success story.

In 1993, Brown paired up with Ed Lover for a comedy, Who's the Man? When MTV canceled its rap show, Dr. Dre stayed in New York and became a DJ for the station HOT-97 FM. Dre still holds a fondness for the old days, as he told Request's Eric Lindblom in 1993: "I miss that dorm-room record company style of the old Def Jam. I want to get some of that energy back."

Further Reading

Lindblom, Eric, "MTV Rappers Cop a New Note," *Request,* May, 1993.

---

ety, [someone] who is lionized by those afraid or unwilling to call him on his lack of respect for women," noted *Request's* Amy Linder. As one critic has pointedly remarked, few performers have made as much of an impression on police blotters since 1970s funk godfather Sly Stone—and managed to stay so influential.

Compton gave roots, inspiration

Born Andre Ramelle Young in Compton, California (an urban-industrial area south of Los Angeles), Dre's first memories involve DJing his mother's parties at age four, "picking out certain songs and stacking them so this song would go after that song," he said in *Rolling Stone.* "I would go to sleep with headphones on, listening to music."

Dre needed such positive distractions in Compton, where never-ending gang warfare claimed his brother, who was beaten to death, and numerous friends. His mother's tastes—funk and soul singers such as James Brown, George Clinton, and Marvin Gaye—inspired Dre to become a full-time DJ at Compton Centennial High School. His nickname, Dr. Dre, which came from idolizing 1970s basketball star "Dr. J" (Julius Irving), fell into place there.

Dre's earliest public exposure as a DJ came at a Los Angeles nightclub, Eve After Dark, where he manned the turntables on weekends and its four-track recording studio during the week. This moved him past scratching and sampling (DJ techniques) into recording vocal and keyboard patterns, all of which prepared Dre to join his first real group, World Class Wreckin' Cru.

From World Class to NWA

Dre formed the Wreckin' Cru with Antoine Carraby (DJ Yella), who managed Eve After Dark, in 1982. Their style ran closer to funk-rockers like **Prince** (see entry), with flashy costumes to match. A Dre-produced demo, "Surgery," sold 50,000 copies as the group's first independent single. Its success persuaded Dre to reject Northrop Aircraft's offer of a job there, following his 1983 graduation from Compton Centennial.

Just over a year later, Dre quit the Wreckin' Cru following disputes over material. He fell into playing live shows with O'Shea Jackson (**Ice Cube**; see entry), and founded Ruthless Records in 1985 with a local drug dealer, Eric Wright (**Eazy-E**; see entry), who needed an outlet for his profits.

Originally plotted as a more mainstream label, Dre and Eazy-E nudged Ruthless to a tougher approach when New York-based group HBO wouldn't record "Boyz in the Hood," a song that later inspired John Singleton's film of the same name. Eazy-E, who'd never dreamed of rapping, fell into the featured artist slot. The duo wound up selling 10,000 singles from their own car trunks.

> **"I'm not trying to send out a message or to be a role model, or anything like that. I go into the studio to make records to entertain people, and if you don't like it, then don't buy it. It's as simple as that."**

Ruthless soared in 1987 when JJ Fad's "Supersonic" single sold half a million copies. That led to a distribution deal with Atlantic Records and a six-figure check that allowed Dre to produce other artists. They included The D.O.C., his girlfriend Michel'le, and what would become hip-hop's most notorious outfit, NWA (Niggaz With Attitude).

Run-ins rocketed Dre to success

Consisting of Dre, Ice Cube, Eazy-E, MC Ren (Lorenzo Patterson), and DJ Yella (Antoine Carraby), NWA began with its 1987 album, *NWA and the Posse* (Macola Records), and its first single, "Dopeman," which Dre wrote and produced. Its lean and mean beats married to blunt comments on drug use ("If you smoke 'cane [cocaine], you're a stupid [expletive]") set the tone for NWA's career, which would resemble one long run-in with authorities.

When NWA followed with *Straight Outta Compton* in 1989, however, they sold two million copies and ripped open the envelope of acceptability. The thudding title track made NWA's intentions clear ("Here's a murder rap to keep ya dancin' / With a crime record like Charles Manson"), as did the graphic detail of "Gangsta Gangsta." So did "I Ain't the 1," whose lyrics upset women. But no track raised more fury than NWA's anti-police anthem. Its lyrics, about getting revenge on police provoked a protest letter from the FBI to Ruthless's parent company, Priority Records, and local police pressure to cancel NWA concerts. NWA said its music only documented a reality of 3,000 gang-related murders and 15,000 woundings since 1980. Of course, Dre admitted to *Melody Maker* that the group realized what it was doing, starting with the name: "We knew people would say, 'I can't believe they even said that!'"

Disputes pushed Dre elsewhere

NWA continued to upset with *100 Miles and Running*, a 1990 EP whose title track discussed their police run-ins, and their 1991 album, both of which sold more than one million copies and raised new howls of outrage. Women's groups blasted tracks that demeaned women, while critics questioned what they saw as mindless anger in "Appetite for Destruction." By then, members had begun quitting over money disputes, starting with Ice Cube in 1990, then Dre a year later.

Dre in trouble, then launched Death Row Records

After leaving NWA, Dre found himself in and out of the courtroom and in trouble with the law. First he fended off assault charges and a $22.75 million lawsuit filed against him by Fox-TV talkshow host Dee Barnes. She alleged Dre hit her and broke her jaw in 1992, after he'd seen a profile on the NWA split that he thought made them look bad. Dre settled the case out of court. In June 1992, Dre surrendered to charges of assaulting producer Damon Thomas; in October, he pleaded to battering a police officer during a brawl earlier that year. He served house arrest time on both charges, wearing an electronic monitoring bracelet.

At the same time, Dre launched Death Row Records with Marion "Suge" Knight, after concluding NWA—and Eazy-E in particular—had cheated him out of royalties and payments. Dre never forgave Eazy for the suits that dragged on into 1993, "because Ruthless spent the year trying to figure out ways not to pay me so that I'd come back on my hands and knees," he claimed in *Rolling Stone*. "If I had to go back home living with my mom, *that* wasn't going to happen."

Back in touch (and on top)

Dre's life seemed back on track when the suits finally ended. His solo debut, *The Chronic*, launched Death Row Records in 1993. It sold three million copies and spent eight months in *Billboard*'s Top Ten.

The Chronic's lead single, "Ain't Nothin' But a 'G' [Gangsta] Thang," sold a million copies, while its follow-up went gold. To some listeners, however, Dre's personal redemption wasn't evident on some of the more violent and sexist

Death Row Records: The Rise and Fall of a Gangsta Rap Label

Gangsta rap label based in Los Angeles, California

Formed in 1992 by Dr. Dre (Andre Ramelle Young) and Marion Hugh "Suge" Knight

Dr. Dre had one simple reason for founding his Death Row Records label in 1992—to gain greater prominence, and profits, than he'd seen as a producer. Until then, Dre's production skills had supported Ruthless, the label he'd founded with rapper Eazy-E. But when Dre and Marion "Suge" Knight reviewed the Ruthless contract, they claimed major irregularities in back payments and royalties. Although seven of eight Dre-produced albums had reaped platinum, Knight felt they could do better for themselves.

Two sides to every story

At Knight's urging, Dre left Ruthless. Its president, Eazy-E, claimed he'd only released Dre after being threatened by men carrying baseball bats and pipes. Naming Knight among them, Eazy filed racketeering and conspiracy lawsuits against Dre, which were all dismissed by August 1993. Dre claimed in his first Death Row biography, that while Eazy-E owned Ruthless, "I was never supposed to be signed to him, or owned by him." No matter; he had $14 million in startup capital, thanks to Knight's ownership of the publishing rights to white hip-hopper Vanilla Ice's only platinum album.

That bounty convinced Jimmy Iovine, head of Interscope Records, to distribute Death Row's albums. While nobody wanted the business, "I just knew they had great music," Iovine told Rolling Stone, "and that they ...

wanted to make it out of the ghetto. That's something I can understand."

Death Row walks the "Dogg"

The public agreed after Dre's solo debut, The Chronic, sold three million records and introduced a lanky six-footer who'd appeared on over half its songs: **Snoop Doggy Dogg** (see entry). If anything, Snoop's solo debut, Doggystyle, surpassed Dre, selling five million copies in just two months following its August 1993 release. Rolling Stone gave Doggystyle a four-star review, citing Dre's production as the primary reason for listening to "the unacceptable face of contemporary rap." Snoop's success nearly crashed for good in August 1993, following his arrest on murder charges. Police contended Snoop helped two friends escape after the shooting death of 20-year-old Philip Woldermariam. A jury eventually acquitted Death Row's newest star of murder in February 1996 after a mistrial was declared.

The label kept rolling ahead, despite Knight's reputation for physical violence and unsavory business practices. Dre's contributions to Helter Skelter, a reunion with **Ice Cube** (see entry), and the Above the Rim soundtrack, ensured a high profile for Death Row in 1995.

So did Tha Dogg Pound, who won critic's praise. An even bigger star emerged in **Tupac Shakur** (see entry), who'd contributed "Pour Out a Little Liquor" on Above the Rim. His lengthy string of hit albums did much to establish the "gangsta rap" character who found himself "Thuggin' against society / Thuggin' against the system that made me."

Death Row on the rocks?

Pressure against the violent images of gangsta rap began building from all sides, like Republican William Bennet and black civil rights leader Jesse Jackson, who told Newsweek's John Leland: "We're going to take away the market value of these attacks on our person." In response to these pressures, Time Warner sold Interscope, which distributed Death Row's product, only to see Iovine and Field find a new owner in Seagram's Gin. Seagram's owned 80 percent of MCA, which began distributing Death Row/Interscope.

After Tupac Shakur's September 1996 murder in Las Vegas, Nevada, Shakur's mother sued Death Row, claiming her son had been cheated of royalties from his final Makaveli: Don Killuminati album. Next, in February 1997, American Express sued Death Row's attorney, David Kenner, and his wife for allegedly charging $1.7 million in unpaid credit card bills. Kenner blamed former accountant Steve Cantrock. However, Cantrock said he'd been forced to sign a statement that he'd stolen $4.5 million from Death Row while fearing for

his life. Finally, producer Johnny The J (Johnny Jackson) filed suit to recover royalties from Don Killuminati tracks.

Facing the Music

Meanwhile, Knight had been jailed since October 1996 for probation violations. They stemmed from security video of his participation in a Las Vegas casino brawl, just minutes before Shakur's shooting. Knight put his problems down to white establishment persecution, especially after national media questioned why he hadn't been arrested: "A black brother from Compton creates a company that helps people in the ghetto. So what does the government try to do? They bring him down."

Federal officials replied they had a duty to investigate Knight's alleged gang ties, and to determine if Death Row qualified as a criminal enterprise. They cited claims by convicted drug dealer Michael Harris, who alleged he'd given $1.5 million in "seed money" to the label; ex-associates like Cantrock promised to cooperate with such efforts. By then Dre had distanced himself from Death Row, forming a new label in Aftermath.

Despite Knight's plea for understanding, Los Angeles Judge Stepehen Czuleger sentenced him to a nine-year term on February 28, 1997. Czuelger said the defendant didn't understand how much he'd abused his position: "You blew it. I hate to say it, but you really did."

Since California law bans convicted criminals from running businesses in prison, Knight's relatives vowed to take over—even as new lawsuits, and bankruptcy rumors, loomed. To most observers, the high-profile "gangsta rap" era appeared over—along with Knight's participation in it.

tracks. Dre made his position clear enough to *Request*: "I'm not trying to send out a message or to be a role model, or anything like that. I go into the studio to make records to entertain people, and if you don't like it, then don't buy it. It's as simple as that."

The Chronic also launched several other budding hip-hoppers, most notably **Snoop Doggy Dogg** (see entry), who rapped on more than half of the album's tracks; his Dre-produced *Doggystyle* (Death Row, 1993) sold 800,000 copies in its first week. Other tracks introduced rappers that included Daz, D Ruff (David Ruffin, Jr., son of the late Temptations singer), Kurupt, Rage, and RBX.

"People in the suburbs, they can't go to the ghetto, so they like to hear about what's goin' on.... Everybody wants to be down."

To critics, Dre's employment of world-class bassists like Tony Green did much to push *The Chronic* and *Doggystyle* above standard hip-hop fare, which relied more on production tricks than on live musicians. The resulting tour with rappers Boss, Geto Boys, Onyx, and **Run-DMC** (see entry) proved somewhat less successful, suffering from hit-and-miss organization and canceled gigs.

Back in trouble again?

Dre faced new legal problems in January 1994, when Los Angeles police arrested him for drunken driving after a high-speed chase. Since he'd already broken his 1993 probation, Dre received an eight-month jail sentence, a $1,053 fine, and orders to finish a ninety-day alcohol education program.

Musically, Dre stayed busy as ever. He won his first Grammy Award in 1994 when "Let Me Ride" won for Best Solo Rap Performance. He then produced younger brother Warren G.'s debut single for Death Row's own *Above the Rim* compilation. In between those efforts, Dre reunited with Ice Cube on Death Row's *Murder Was the Case,* for which he directed an eighteen-minute video starring Snoop Doggy Dogg.

Dre and Ice Cube collaborated in a larger way on their *Helter Skelter* album (Death Row, 1995), an event postponed by Dre's eight-month jail sentence, which began on January 10, 1995. In 1995 Dre also contributed "Keep Their Heads Ringin'" to the film *Friday,* in which Ice Cube starred. The song's video won Dre an MTV Video Music Award for Best Rap Video.

By 1996, however, Dre had left the Death Row fold over the same issue that drove him from Ruthless: money. True to form, he kept busy, founding Aftermath Entertainment to explore new sounds. Its first release, *Dr. Dre Presents ... The Aftermath* included his recording, "Been There, Done That," which critics took as his comment on the decline of gangsta rap. In Dre's eyes, Aftermath was also part of a commitment to explore other styles, such as heavy rock. That posed no problem for Iovine, whose Interscope Records distributed Aftermath's product. "He can rap, he can produce ... he can direct a video with humor. Do you know how hard that is?" the Interscope head asked *Rolling Stone.* "Famous movie directors can't do that."

Dre has no doubts about his longevity. It all comes down to what people enjoy, he asserts: "People in the suburbs, they can't go to the ghetto, so they like to hear about what's goin' on.... Everybody wants to be down."

In the end, *Rolling Stone* concluded that Dre's lasting contribution may lie in making gangsta rap "a viable pop genre for thousands of white twelve-year-olds who may not even know what a 'G' thang is."

Selected Awards

"Nothin' But a `G' Thang," certified platinum, 1993.

"Dre Day," certified gold, 1993.

The Chronic, certified triple platinum, 1993.

Grammy Award, Best Rap Solo Performance, for "Let Me Ride," 1994.

American Music Awards: 1) Best Artist (Rap/Hip-Hop), and 2) Best New Artist (Rap/Hip-Hop), 1994.

MTV Video Music Award, Best Rap Video, for "Keep Their Heads Ringin'," 1995.

"Keep Their Heads Ringin'," certified gold, 1995.

Grammy Award Nomination, Best Rap Solo Performance, for "Keep Their Heads Ringin'," 1996.

Selected Discography

With NWA:

NWA and the Posse (Macola), 1987.

Straight Outta Compton (Ruthless), 1989.

100 Miles and Runnin' EP (Ruthless), 1990.

Efil4zaggin (Ruthless), 1991.

Greatest Hits (Priority), 1996.

Solo Albums:

The Chronic (Death Row), 1993.

Murder Was the Case (Death Row), 1994 (contributor).

Helter Skelter (Death Row), 1995 (with Ice Cube).

Friday Soundtrack (Priority Records), 1995. Includes Dr. Dre's "Keep Their Heads Ringin'."

Dr. Dre Presents ... The Aftermath (Aftermath), 1996.

Further Reading

Garcia, Jane, "Telling It Like It Is," *New Musical Express,* August 18, 1989.

Gold, Jonathan, "Day of the Dre," *Rolling Stone,* September 30, 1993, p. 38.

Linder, Amy, "Ain't Nothing but a Gender Thing," *Request,* May 1993.

Nelson, Havelock, "Get Down—And Never Mind When Dr. Dre Did," *Rolling Stone,* March 18, 1993, p. 40.

Powell, Kevin, "Hot Dogg," *Vibe,* September 1993.

Samuels, Allison, and David Gates, "Last Tango in Compton," *Newsweek,* November 25, 1996, p. 74.

Toure, "Only One Star in the Two Schools of Rap," *New York Times,* p. 21, section 2.

Toure, "Snoop & Cube," *Rolling Stone,* January 27, 1994.

Contact Information

Aftermath Entertainment
10900 Wilshire Blvd., Ste. 1230
Los Angeles, CA 90024

Web Sites

http://www.aswellas.se/drdre.html

http://www.aftermath.com/

Eazy-E

American rap singer, producer, record company executive
(West Coast, gangsta, hardcore rap styles)

Born Eric Wright on September 7, 1963, in Compton, California;
died March 26, 1995, in Los Angeles, California

"He was the most Machiavellian guy I ever met. He instinctively knew power and how to control people. And his musical instincts were infallible." –Music business manager Jerry Heller, on his late client

What Eric Wright lacked in physical size, he more than compensated for in brute business sense. He was one of hip-hop's most notorious and provocative artists. One of the 1990s most successful black capitalists, the man called Eazy-E made no bones about the game he played. "Listen, man," Eazy snapped to *Melody Maker*'s Michael Odell, "I used to be a drug dealer. I was making more money when I was seventeen than I am now. I made and spent a million dollars. If I was really smart, I'd go back to drug dealing and be even richer that way."

Yet Eazy successfully graduated from Compton's narcotics wars to become the tough, seasoned head of his own Ruthless Records label, whose records typically hit platinum. Other music business pros remember a less aggressive figure who wanted attention, as *Rap It Up* radio syndicator Glenn Ford recalled to *Goldmine* about Eazy's first chart-topper, "On The Radio": "He was so glad to be on the radio. It didn't really make much difference to him [how he got there]."

More than any other performer, Eazy changed hip-hop's focus, language, and subject matter. His work as part of NWA challenged politicians to confront inner-city realities as never before, especially on tracks such as "Dopeman" and "Gangsta, Gangsta." Eazy-E made headlines to the end of his short life, when he became the first major hip-hopper to admit he had AIDS (Acquired Immune Deficiency Syndrome), which killed him at age thirty-one. He left behind seven children, fathered by six different women, and a confusing, contradictory legacy that fans argue about to this day.

Accidental rapping yielded gold

Like his partners in NWA, Eazy grew up around drugs, gangs, and violence in Compton, California, a decaying industrial area south of Los Angeles. There, Eazy profitted as a cocaine dealer who soon needed an outlet for his swelling profits. Years later, he jokingly described that problem to a British TV crew as "opening my own pharmacy" —except it was illegal.

A chance 1986 meeting with rapper **Dr. Dre** and **Ice Cube** (see entries) convinced Eazy to help them found Ruthless Records. Its first success, the "Boyz-in-the-Hood" single, inspired John Singleton's film of the same name. It was recorded by Eazy after New York rap group HBO declined to record the track.

Boosted by the single's 10,000 sales, Ruthless swooped into the big leagues with JJ Fad's 1987 novelty smash single, "Supersonic," which convinced Atlantic Records to sign a six-figure deal with Eazy. At the same time, lawyer Jerry Heller, who'd managed 1970s hard rockers like Styx, became his informal business adviser. Heller wound up managing Eazy's first real group with Cube and Dre—NWA.

NWA's Reputation Built Slowly

NWA's first album, *NWA and the Posse* (Macola Records, 1987), was later cited as an early example of "gangsta" rap, a style that married hard beats to equally hard rhymes that were often filled with curses, profanity, and violent images. The album attracted little attention beyond its core inner-city audience. At this time a small-time rap label, Ruthless's earliest records came from a pressing plant where the machinery was run by hand.

Ruthless's small-time days were over when Eazy's solo debut, *Eazy-Duz-It* (1988), went platinum, aided by a major-label distribution contract with Island Records. Eazy divided his record between straight party jams ("We Want Eazy") and more graphic fare like "Nobody Move," a blow-by-blow description of an armed robbery. British music periodical *Melody Maker* called Eazy's album "another highly colorful compendium of brutal stories from the war zone, from the darkened streets of Compton." *Eazy-Duz-It* eventually went double platinum, selling more than two million copies in the United States.

NWA's second effort, the ground-breaking *Straight Outta Compton* (1989), pushed the envelope of acceptibility fur-

Eazy-E told "brutal stories from the war zone"

banned them from using plastic guns at a June 1990 gig there. Amid the free speech debates spawned by the recording, some listeners missed a personal tribute to Eazy's father, Charles Wright, on *Straight Outta Compton*'s "Express Yourself." The original had been cut by Charles Wright's Watts 103rd Street Rhythm Band in 1970. For his version, Eazy sampled the original chorus, building on a phrase used in black culture since the 1930s Harlem Renaissance.

Eazy proceeded to antagonize readers about a different issue when he claimed no interest in politics: "I bet there ain't anybody in South Africa wearing a button saying 'Free Compton,' or 'Free California.'"

Such controversy, critics noted, didn't hurt *Compton*'s platinum sales, nor that of its 1991 follow-up, *Efil4zaggin'*. The latter album survived an obscenity ban in England and debuted at number two on *Billboard*'s pop chart, the first album to do so since Michael Jackson's *Bad* in 1987.

NWA essentially disbanded when Dre himself quit over money issues, leading to suits and countersuits between himself and Ruthless. Eazy's own standing took a hit in March 1991, when he accepted an invitation to a luncheon hosted by President George Bush for Republican Senate candidates. With his presence there considered a sellout, or just downright foolish, Eazy noted his $2,500 contribution went to a Republican politician who'd spoken against censorship—an issue that cut across party lines, he said. Eazy told Alan Light of *Rolling Stone* with characteristic blunt-

ther. No track struck more nerves than the now-famous anti-police anthem. The song inspired an angry letter about its content from the FBI. But nothing would force NWA to moralize—not cops, lawsuits, nor obscenity tickets. "Our position is that we're neutral. We are not telling 'em [fans] to do it [violence], we not telling 'em not to," Eazy declared to Fab Five Freddy (*Yo! MTV Raps*' original cohost) in *Interview*.

Personal touches went unnoticed

Such bluntness didn't make NWA more acceptable to forces like the City Council of Birmingham, England, which

Parents Aren't Supposed to Like It

ness. "I ... ain't a Republican or Democrat. I didn't even vote."

A year later, Eazy again found himself pressed into service as a spokesperson, when Los Angeles erupted in riots after a jury acquitted four white policemen of beating black motorist Rodney King. "I'm not surprised by this at all," he told *Melody Maker*. "I knew it was coming. I really think this is just the start of things.... It was stupid to burn down our own neighborhoods, though." Later, Eazy talked about reissuing his anti-police anthem after the Rodney King incident. Then, in the spring of 1993, Eazy puzzled peers by appearing to support Theodore Briseno, one of the cops charged with beating King. That act, said *Rolling Stone*'s David Thigpen, "baffled" other hip-hoppers, who'd begun calling Eazy a "sell-out."

Solo career inconsistent

Eazy's slipping reputation had little impact on Ruthless, which continued to grow with the signings of all-Jewish "posse" Blood of Abraham and Bone, Thugs-N-Harmony, among others. Eazy's solo efforts, however, were less well-received by critics, who found them suffering in light of an ongoing feud with Dre.

When a full-length album, *Temporary Insanity*, failed to appear, Eazy responded with a strong-selling EP, *5150 Home For The Sick* (1992). The next year's *It's On (Dr. Dre) 187um Killa* debuted at number five on *Billboard*'s chart. Yet, the album puzzled fans by seeming too obsessed about Dre, including the title, which is street slang for a gang-style

murder. Without Dre mixing, mused *The Source*, "many people wouldn't be interested in hearing him [Eazy] drop lyrics for a whole record."

Dre's "Dre Day" video had almost certainly upset his rival, with its "Sleazy-E" lookalike toting a "Will Rap for Food" sign. But if Eazy had regrets, they didn't show in *Eternal E* (1995), and *Str8 off tha Streetz of* [expletive] *Compton* (1996), the latter issued after his death.

Eazy suffered from AIDS

Until those releases, Eazy's profile had been relatively quiet, due to his entering Los Angeles's Cedars-Sinai Hospital for a lung problem on February 24, 1995, due to AIDS. Less than a month later, Eazy had gotten married. He drafted his last message to fans, urging them to be cautious in their sexual behavior.

Eazy died on March 26, 1995—not from a fellow gangsta's bullet, but from a disease he'd never imagined facing. In his short life he was a leader in a new form of musical expression, if a controversial one. After his death, one fan wrote on Eazy's home page: "His voice was unique as that of **Nirvana**'s leader [singer/guitarist Kurt Cobain; see entry]. And his group, NWA, created 'gangsta rap.'"

Selected Discography

With NWA:

NWA and the Posse (Macola Records), 1987.

Straight Outta Compton (Priority/Ruthless Records), 1988.

100 Miles And Running EP (Ruthless), 1990.

Efil4zaggin' (Ruthless), 1991.

Greatest Hits (Priority), 1996.

Solo Recordings:

Eazy-Duz-It (Priority/Ruthless), 1988.

5150 Home for the Sick EP (Ruthless), 1992.

It's On (Dr. Dre) 187um Killa EP (Ruthless), 1993.

Eternal E (Ruthless), 1995.

Str8 off tha Streetz of [expletive] Compton (Ruthless), 1996.

Further Reading

Browne, David, "Efil4zaggin'," *New York Times,* June 23, 1991.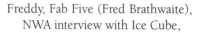

Freddy, Fab Five (Fred Brathwaite), NWA interview with Ice Cube,

Dr. Dre, Eazy-E, MC Ren, *Interview,* 1990.

Garcia, Jane, "Telling It Like It Is," *New Musical Express,* August 18, 1989.

Light, Alan, "Eazy-E Interview," *Rolling Stone,* August 8, 1991.

Owen, Frank, "Hanging Tough" (interview with Ice Cube and Eazy-E), *Spin,* March 1990.

Powell, Kevin, *Vibe,* December 1993.

Thigpen, David, *Rolling Stone,* May 27, 1993.

Wild, David, and Jon Wiederhorn, "Eazy-E, 1963-1995," *Rolling Stone,* May 4, 1995, p. 25.

Web Site

http://home1.swipnet.se/~w-10437/eazy.htm

Fugees

American rap group
(reggae and rhythm and blues-flavored rap styles)

Formed late 1980s in West Orange, New Jersey

The Fugees (short for "refugees") are a New Jersey-based hip-hop trio who came to prominence in 1996 with a new reggae-flavored rap sound. Released early in the year, the group's second album, *The Score,* was propelled to double-platinum status (for selling more than two million copies) on the strength of such cuts as the Grammy-winning remake of Roberta Flack's 1973 hit, "Killing Me Softly with His Song" (Flack's original version also won a Grammy) and the band's theme song, "Fu-Gee-La." Other notable songs on the album included a new version of Bob Marley's classic reggae ballad, "No Woman, No Cry," and "Ready or Not," which samples 1960s soul group The Delfonics' "Ready or Not Here I Come (Can't Hide from Love)."

The Fugees spent most of 1996 touring in support of *The Score,* building a reputation as a stunning and surprising live act. One of the band's performing innovations was to use live instruments (rather than recorded samples) on stage, something unusual in the rap scene. Wyclef Jean plays guitar, and the full touring band included a live rhythm section and an onstage DJ. As Chris Schwartz,

"Our whole thing is that we want to show there's much more to hip-hop than what people think." –Wyclef Jean

Fugees at 1997 "Coming Home Concert" in Port-au-Prince, Haiti. From left to right: Wyclef Jean, Prakazrel Michel, Lauryn Hill

the head of RuffHouse (the Fugees' label) told *Rolling Stone,* "Clef is the first cat I've ever seen to be able to come onstage and play guitar in front of an entire hip-hop crowd and win them over."

Band members met in New Jersey

The core trio that are the Fugees consist of Wyclef "Clef" Jean, a native Haitian who emigrated to Brooklyn, New York, with his family when he was nine; Lauryn "L" Hill, the group's female vocal-

ist, who grew up in South Orange, New Jersey; and Prakazrel (pronounced PRAZ-well) "Pras" Michel, born in Brooklyn to Haitian parents who later moved to New Jersey.

The Fugees grew out of a rap group called the Tranzlator Crew (so-called because they were trying to rhyme in different languages) while Michel, a senior, and Hill, a sophomore, were still attending the same high school in the late 1980s. Tranzlator Crew, a trio consisting of Michel,

Hill, and another woman, worked out of a West Orange recording studio. One day Michel's cousin Jean, who was a guitarist in a reggae band, stopped by and improvised some raps over tracks the group had recorded. Under the guidance of Khalis Bayyan (born Ronald Bell), who's known as the saxophonist and producer for 1970s funk band Kool and the Gang, the trio commenced playing local gigs as the Fugees, with the other woman leaving the group for college. In the beginning, Hill recalled in *Rolling Stone,* "We sang, we rapped, we danced. As a matter of fact, we were a circus troupe."

Blunted on reality

The Fugees auditioned for label representatives in their manager's office. Although their performances were impressive, none of the labels seemed interested. Then they auditioned for RuffHouse, a Pennsylvania-based independent label affiliated with Columbia that had some success with Latino rap group Cypress Hill. RuffHouse co-founder Chris Schwartz liked the fact that the Fugees couldn't be pigeonholed into any one category or style of music.

The Fugees' debut album, *Blunted on Reality,* was released in 1993. Nearly all of the songs were determined by the album's producers, who wanted faster mixes and more forceful rhymes from the group. The producers were trying the get the Fugees to sound more like other hardcore rappers, which wasn't exactly why the label signed them in the first place. Naturally, the album received poor reviews in the hip-hop community.

Jean was allowed to produce one track on the album, "Vocab." Unlike the other tracks, this one featured the group rapping over a simple acoustic guitar. The album didn't sell well, but the Fugees got a break when one of the tracks, "Nappy Heads," was released as a single with a slower remix and became a popular dance track. Jean then remixed "Vocab" and "Boof Baf" for the next two singles, giving them an earthier sound. After those two singles did well, Jean became an in-demand mixer.

Fugees even the score

With more control over their material, the Fugees set to work on their second album. Making use of a homemade recording studio that Jean had constructed in his uncle's basement, the band recorded all of *The Score* there (with the exception of "Fu-Gee-La"). They were trying to get a Tuff Gong feel, a reference to reggae legend Bob Marley's recording studio in Kingston, Jamaica. They named the studio Booga Basement. "It's not chic," Jean told *Rolling Stone,* "but it comes out good quality, because you feel like you're at home."

The first indication that the record-buying public also thought the music was good quality came when album-oriented radio stations began playing the track, "Killing Me Softly with His Song." Featuring Hill's soulful voice, the song drew attention to the album, helping it debut at number twelve on *Billboard's* album chart. In February 1997, the song won the group its first Grammy Award.

Critics generally gave the album good reviews. *Time*'s music critic, Christopher John Farley, praised the Fugees for "cross[ing] cultural and musical boundaries to create a sound that is bold and fresh." Looking back on the album after it had been out for a while, *Rolling Stone* writer Alec Foege described *The Score* as "an hour-long opus on which no single track paints the whole picture. Slower and more textured than its predecessor, *The Score* drifts effortlessly from up-to-the-moment hardcore to reggae to old-school rap to '70s-style easy listening to Haitian-flavored acoustic folk."

With music industry recognition and a double-platinum album under their belts, the Fugees are facing high expectations from critics as well as listeners. Drawing on the rich musical traditions of rap, reggae, and rhythm and blues, the Fugees are positioned to become one of the leaders in the movement to reinvent rap, to clean it up and refresh its sound with new combinations of musical styles.

Selected Awards

The Score certified double platinum, 1996.

"Killing Me Softly with His Song," (track from *The Score*), Grammy Award for Best R & B Performance by a Duo or Group with Vocal, 1997.

The Score, Grammy Award for Best Rap Album, 1997.

Selected Discography

Blunted on Reality (RuffHouse/Columbia), 1993.

The Score (RuffHouse/Columbia), 1996.

The Carnival (RuffHouse/Columbia), 1997. As Wyclef Jean and the Refugee Allstars.

Further Reading

Danticat, Edwidge, "Hanging with the Fugees," *Essence,* August 1996, p. 85.

Danticat, Edwidge, "The Fugees," *Harper's Bazaar,* June 1996, p. 62.

Farley, Christopher John, "The Score," *Time,* February 12, 1996, p. 79.

Foege, Alec, "Fugees: Leaders of the New Cool," *Rolling Stone,* September 5, 1996, p. 40.

Meyer, David N., "Remaking a 'Killing,'" *Entertainment Weekly,* March 22, 1996, p. 73.

Samuels, Allison, "Here's What's Going On: Fugees are the New Conscience of Rap," *Newsweek,* April 15, 1996, p. 70.

Contact Information

RuffHouse Records
129 Fayette St.
Conshohocen, PA 19428

Web Site

http://www.music.sony.com/Music/ArtistInfo/Fugees/

Gravediggaz

American rap group (East Coast, gangsta, hardcore, and horrorcore rap styles)

Formed in 1994 in New York City

Gravediggaz attack hip-hop from two angles: first, as an all-star "supergroup" of rap groups De La Soul, Stetsasonic, and Wu-Tang Clan members breaking from their regular projects; second, as exploiters of horror imagery. Such imagery isn't new to hip-hop, as shown by The Geto Boys' "Mind Playin' Tricks on Me"—or reggae tracks like Papa Michigan's and General Smiley's "Diseases." By and large, however, horror kept its distance from hip-hop, with exceptions like Whodini's "Haunted House of Rap." But such lighter efforts had nothing in common with Gravediggaz tracks "Two Cups of Blood," "1-800-Suicide," and "Deathtrap." The Gravediggaz' world is dark and downbeat, mixing jazz and soul samples with heavy metal.

When Gravediggaz surfaced with *6 Feet Deep* (Gee Street, 1994), the press quickly labeled it "horrorcore" since its Halloween-themed content was too obvious to ignore. Gravediggaz' members had lengthy resumes, too. Its apparent mastermind, Prince Paul (Paul Huston), is best known as Stetsasonic's DJ and the producer of **De La Soul's** (see entry) three albums. He's an in-

> "With songs that make metaphors out of gory talk, Gravediggaz delves into the dark side of life, addressing such topics as suicide, drug abuse, and mental illness." – critic S.H. Fernando, Jr., *Rolling Stone*

demand mixer and ran his own Dew Doo Man label for a time.

Close behind came Rzarector, or Wu-Tang Clan's RZA, who took an active co-production role in *Tricky Versus the Gravediggaz: The Hell EP.* So did Fruitkwan, another active Stetsasonic member, while The Grym Reaper (Anthony Berkley) ran his own label (Plasma) and group (The Brothers Grym) with his brother, Brainstorm.

The quartet's busy schedules didn't affect the quality of *6 Feet Deep,* which *Rolling Stone* considered "definitely worth checking out." Its sixteen tracks take listeners on a life-and-death trip, from "Just When You Thought It Was Over (Intro)" to "Rest In Peace (Outro)." The album's themes looked at mental illness ("Defective Mind [Trippin']"), self-destruction ("1-800-Suicide"), and death ("Six Feet Deep"). MC Serch (Third Bass), Biz Markie, and **Living Colour** (see entry) guitarist Vernon Reid were among the all-star contributors.

While horrorcore "didn't make the expected waves" in hip-hop, as *The All Music Guide to Rock* noted, its reviewer still gave *Six Feet Deep* a four-star rating. Calling Gravediggaz "more intelligent than their image," John Bush laid highest praises on its production: "Big beats and jazzy samples carry the album well."

Since then Gravediggaz have remained dormant, apparently working when its members grab enough time away from their own projects. They still managed to contribute songs for films such as Spike Lee's *Tales from the Hood*

(1995) and *The Crow: City of Angels* (1996). *Tales* seemed a juicy vehicle for Gravediggaz. It centers on three men visiting a funeral home trying to collect a drug "stash" they'd left there. The mortician, who's accidentally found the drugs, conducts them on a guided tour—telling horror stories along the way—only to spring an ugly surprise on his guests in their final destination, the basement.

In 1996, Fruitkwan, RZA, and Too Poetic joined forces with groundbreaking British "triphop" master **Tricky** (see entry) for *The Hell EP.* While Prince Paul did not appear, his remaining cohorts stood their ground for two tracks. RZA coproduced "Psychosis," on which Too Poetic rapped along, and "Tonite Is a Special Nite (Chaos Mass Confusion Mix)." All three remaining Gravediggaz shared the rapping on that track.

With two albums to their credit and contributions to several compilation CDs, the Gravediggaz' brand of "horrorcore" didn't achieve the same level of popularity as other rap styles. However, as rap music undergoes changes in the years to come, there will be room for the innovations of Gravediggaz.

Selected Discography

6 Feet Deep (Gee Street), 1994.

Tricky Versus the Gravediggaz: The Hell EP (Island Records), 1996.

Further Reading

Bernard, James, "6 Feet Deep," *Entertainment Weekly,* August 19, 1994, p. 62.

Fernando, Jr., S. H., "Gravediggaz: Six Feet Deep," *Rolling Stone,* October 6, 1994.

Contact Information

Gee Street Records
14 East 4th Street, 3rd Floor
New York, NY 10012-1155

Web Site

http://www.mnsinc.com/trixter/gravediggaz/

Hammer

American rap artist (West Coast, pop, and R&B rap styles; formerly M.C. Hammer)

Born Stanley Kirk Burrell, East Oakland, California, March 30, 1963

"I spent more than $7 million in legal fees. Contrary to popular belief, what got most crazy for me was the reality—the big price I paid for celebrity." –Hammer

At his 1990-91 peak, Hammer—hip-hop's most successful crossover artist—could celebrate $33 million in overall earnings (according to *Forbes* magazine). He owned seventeen cars, including a Ferrari, and several thoroughbred horses. His Bustin' Records label and production company employed 100 people, mostly friends from before he was successful. He mixed with celebrities like the Sultan of Brunei and baseball and football star Deion Sanders.

So what, asked the *San Francisco Examiner*'s Cynthia Robbins, had Hammer ever expected? "I just wanted some nice suits," he responded. "And some nice pairs of shoes. Seven suits, one for each day of the week ... and my own car. Paid off. Then I could live out of a shoebox." Despite having filed bankruptcy in 1996, Hammer had no regrets: "My thing is: I have a need to entertain and *that* makes money. I'll be happy in my next house. I am not defined by the material things around me.

"Holy Ghost Boy" found hip-hop

Born Stanley Kirk Burrell in East Oakland, California, on March 30, 1963, Hammer was the youngest of seven children. His father managed a legal gambling club; his mother worked in factories. When Hammer turned five his parents divorced, leaving him to be raised by his mother in a tough East Oakland neighborhood. He escaped by making up his own commercials, singing, and dancing—but Hammer's earliest love was baseball.

Legendary Oakland A's owner Charlie Finley reportedly spotted the boy, age 11, doing James Brown impressions in the Oakland Coliseum parking lot. He made Hammer an Oakland A's bat boy, who traveled with the team when he wasn't in school. He earned his nickname by his resemblance to famed slugger Henry "Hammerin' Hank" Aaron.

In 1981, Hammer graduated McClymonds High School, in West Oakland, and sought a communications degree while preparing for a major league baseball career. When he didn't make the San Francisco Giants, Hammer dropped out of college and enlisted in the U.S. Navy for three years. On leaving the Navy, Hammer's born-again Christianity sparked an interest in forming a Christian duo, the Holy Ghost Boys, who played local clubs. In 1987, his career got a boost from Oakland A's Mike Davis and Dwayne Murphy, who loaned Hammer $20,000 apiece to form Bustin' Records. This enabled him to sell his first single, "Ringin' 'Em," from his car trunk.

"Got it started" with $750,000

Suitably encouraged, Burrell became M.C. (after "Master of Ceremonies") Hammer. His early record-making led to an album, *Feel My Power,* with ex-Con Funk Shun (a late 1970s soul/disco group) member Felton Pilate producing. It sold 60,000 copies in the area, attracting a $750,000 advance from Capitol Records, who signed its new artist in May 1988.

Capitol reissued *Feel My Power* as *Let's Get It Started,* adding four new songs; it topped the R & B (rhythm and blues) chart, and reached number thirty on the pop charts. The album went platinum, with 1.5 million copies sold. From the start, noted *Time's* Jay Cocks, Hammer set out to establish himself as different: "His material lacks the violence, racism and sexism that rap lyrics have been criticized for, and his sound is up-to-date, and eminently danceable."

Unlike more radical hip-hoppers like **Public Enemy** (see entry), or NWA, Hammer made no secret of his mainstream political slant and his Christianity. His performances were accented by huge stage spectacles—where the audience saw as many as thirty performers jumping around. His bulging, baggy "balloon" pants became an MTV fixture, thanks to *Please Hammer Don't Hurt 'Em* (1990)—which became hip-hop's all-time best-seller.

Debuting at number one, *Please Hammer* stayed twenty-one weeks on the charts and went on to sell an astonishing 18 million copies. Its success was remarkable given the $10,000 recording costs. Hammer's good taste in sampling also powered his signature tune, "U Can't Touch This"—which freely borrowed the riff of Rick James's funk smash, "Super Freak"—to a number eight peak position.

"Have You Seen Her," which recalled The Chi-Lites' 1973 soul classic of that name, went to #4; and "Pray," a sampling of Prince's "When Doves Cry," did best of all at #2 in November 1990. While Hammer took lumps for using so many samples and a casual approach to rhyming, consumers didn't mind. As *People Weekly* noted: "With his clean image, nonpolitical lyrics and flashy performances, Hammer appeals to a broad spectrum of Americans."

Image began showing cracks

By 1991, Hammer seemed virtually unstoppable. British Knights shoes hired him in a series of "U Can't Touch This"-style commercials. Pepsi became a sponsor of his tours. Capitol agreed to fund Bustin' Records, run by brother Louis, Jr., with whom Hammer also acquired several thoroughbred racehorses. He even had a cartoon and a doll named "Hammerman."

The next album, *Too Legit to Quit* (1991), settled at number five on the charts, followed by his contribution to *The Addams Family* movie, "Addams Family Groove," which reached number seven. Behind the scenes, Hammer's image took knocks from his dancers and musicians, who accused him of imposing too many rules. They also complained of poor working conditions and twelve- to fourteen-hour rehearsals.

His *Rocky V* single, "Here Comes the Hammer," got no higher than #54, despite a $1 million video clip—an important problem, since the song had been Hammer's first to be written alone and without sampling. Lawsuits piled up; in February 1991, Davis and Murphy sued to recover their $40,000 loan, claiming they'd been promised 15 percent of Hammer's future income.

In June 1991, an employee claimed that Hammer stood by while several men—including two of his brothers—raped her. Hammer counter-sued for $30 million; he lost in 1993 when a jury ordered him to pay about $163,000 in damages to the alleged victim. In June 1992, another Navy buddy sued Hammer over a $5,000 loan that he claimed was promised against 2.7 percent of all future earnings. Finally, in October, James Earley sued, claiming that Hammer had promised 40 percent of *Please Hammer*'s profits, but only had given him $100,000.

Career profile began slipping

Amid these problems, *Too Legit to Quit*—which became a rallying cry in professional sports—appeared near the end of 1991 and went Top Ten. *Rolling Stone*'s Alan Light felt that "Hammer shows a broader range than in the past," but the critic faulted the album's production: "Unfortunately, the songs are too long, and the title track is tediously repetitious."

More problems plagued the tour, which kicked off in April 1992 supported by future hitmakers **Boyz II Men** (see entry) and Jodeci. The 150-show outing played to half-empty halls, while Hammer's massive musical and production "posse" guaranteed he'd have trouble making a profit. Light called Hammer's May 1992 Madison Square Garden gig in New York City "disappointing": "The activity on stage was excessive and unfocused, the numerous costume changes broke the concert's momentum, and Hammer hardly displayed his dancing skills." Suitably chastised, Hammer began keeping a lower profile, disrupted by the odd lawsuit. In January 1993, Muhammad Bilal Abdullah claimed his song had been stolen for "Here Comes the Hammer." He sought $16 million in damages.

On his next effort, *The Funky Headhunter* (1994), Hammer decided on some radical changes, dropping the "M.C." part of his name, and jumping from Capitol to Giant/Reprise Records. Critics found the album, which peaked at number twelve and faded quickly, well-meaning but unsuccessful. Michael Dyson of the *New York Times* called *Headhunter* "a sizzling rejoinder to critics who have accused him of selling out," but said "Hammer's staccato delivery reveals that he needs to improve his rhyming skills."

From legit to bankrupt

By then, it appeared Hammer's larger-than-life spending had caught up with him. While *Headhunter* had been a gold record, *Rolling Stone* reported he'd desperately sought to close a three-album,

$25 million deal. Labels expressed little interest, while Capitol, on Hammer's departure, had closed Bustin' Records for lack of success.

In 1995, Hammer raised eyebrows for signing with Marion "Suge" Knight's Death Row label. His choice of an executive renowned for his criminal activities seemed odd given Hammer's personal views, as did Hammer's adoption of a "gangsta" look, complete with knit cap. That did not help *MC Hammer V: Inside Out,* which flopped, as Knight began serving a nine-year prison sentence for parole violations in 1996.

In April 1996, Hammer filed for a Chapter 11 bankruptcy protection, citing $9.6 million in assets against $13.7 million in debts—including a $28,650 American Express bill. Had he saved more wisely, the *New Yorker* concluded, Hammer might have counted on $3-5 million per year for life. Instead, Hammer found himself being forced to sell his sprawling "Hammer Time" estate for half its reported $12 million cost. He refused to concede, citing an upcoming HBO role and two other movie offers. "I'm not saying, 'I give up!' I'm saying, 'Enough,'" he told the *Examiner.* "Lawyers are $250 an hour. Just to answer these lawsuits costs you $10,000."

The man who'd once been ranked America's nineteenth most successful entertainer by *Forbes* had a philosophical reason for his downfall. Claiming that his fiscal carelessness "blessed me to see the big picture," Hammer vowed not to repeat his mistakes: "I had an up-close and personal conversation with God and he spanked me. I deserved it."

Selected Awards

Let's Get It Started, certified platinum,1989.

Please Hammer Don't Hurt 'Em, certified platinum, 1990.

American Music Awards, 1) Best Soul/R & B Album, 2) Best Rap Album, both for (*Please Hammer Don't Hurt 'Em*), 3) Best Soul/R&B Single, for "U Can't Touch This," 4) Best Soul/R&B Artist, and 5) Best Rap Artist, 1991.

Grammy Awards, 1) Best R & B Song/Best Rap Solo Performance, for "U Can't Touch This," and 2) Best Music Video, Long-form, for *Please Don't Hurt 'Em, The Movie,* 1991.

Rolling Stone Reader's Picks, 1) Best Male Rapper, 2) Best Dressed Male Artist, and 3) Worst Male Singer, 1991.

Too Legit to Quit, certified platinum, 1991.

American Music Awards, Favorite Artist (Rap Music), 1992.

Grammy Award nomination, "Addams Family Groove," 1993.

The Funky Headhunter, certified gold, 1994.

Soul Train Hall of Fame induction, 1995.

Selected Discography

Feel My Power (Bustin' Records), 1987.

Let's Get It Started (Capitol), 1988.

Please Hammer Don't Hurt 'Em (Capitol), 1990.

Too Legit to Quit (Capitol), 1991.

The Funky Headhunter (Giant/Reprise Records), 1994.

MC Hammer V: Inside Out (Death Row Records), 1995.

Further Reading

Cassidy, John, "Under the Hammer," *The New Yorker,* August 26-September 2, 1996, p. 62.

Cocks, Jay, "U Can't Touch Him," *Time,* August 13, 1990, p. 73.

Cohen, Charles E., "A Cry of 'Please, Hammer, Don't Stiff Us,' Brings Relief from M.C.," *People Weekly,* April 4, 1991, p. 81.

Dyson, Michael Eric, "Funky Headhunter," *New York Times,* April 17, 1994, p. 32, section 2.

Light, Alan, "Too Legit to Quit" (concert review), *Rolling Stone,* July 9-23, 1992.

Light, Alan, "Hammer: Too Legit to Quit," *Rolling Stone,* November 28, 1991.

Robbins, Cynthia, "Hammering Out a Life after Bankruptcy: Rap Star Forced to Sell Ostentatious Spread in Fremont," *The San Francisco Examiner,* May 4, 1997, p. 1.

Russell, Lisa, "M.C. Hammer Couldn't Make the Big Leagues in Baseball, So He Began Rapping Out Hits in a Different Field," *People Weekly,* August 6, 1990, p. 59.

Contact Information

Interscope Music Publishing
10940 Wilshire Blvd., 20th Fl.
Los Angeles, CA 90024

HEAVY D & THE BOYZ

American rap artist
(East Coast, rhythm and blues,
and soul rap styles)

Heavy D born Dwight Myers, near
Montego Bay, Jamaica, 1967; raised
in Mount Vernon, New York

While many hip-hop careers crash and burn after five years, Heavy D & The Boyz have stayed above the pack for a decade. To date, "The Overweight Lover of Hip-hop," as Heavy D calls himself (he's also known as "The Hevster"), has sold four million records, and had a long string of hit singles—by doing things his way.

When record labels only promoted lean teens as sex symbols, Heavy D made his 300-plus pounds a selling point. "When you buy my records," he told *The Source*'s Asondra Hunter, "you're getting me and I'm non-threatening." And when "keeping it real" means living out "gangsta" rap's violent image, Heavy D has sold records by focusing on good times, romance, and the odd social comment. He considers himself an all-American success story, raised by parents who stressed hard work as the key to success. Heavy D's mother and father spent "fifteen years passing each other in the night just to make ends meet," he reminded *USA Today*. "When you see that, how could you ever give up?"

"There's no need to focus on all that negative stuff. So I don't want to make records based on that. I want to make records based on what it (hip-hop) should be like. Or what I want it to be like." —Heavy D

Ten years after becoming rap label Uptown's biggest act, Heavy D has found himself coming full circle since being named the label's president. He took the job to show youths "that you don't have to be in front of a camera or on the radio to be successful; being behind the scenes and instrumental in the business side is just as important."

Non-threatening image succeeded

If one phrase describes Heavy D, it's "non-threatening," as he told Hunter: "I never pretend to be something I'm not." That philosophy has served him well in his mission of becoming an all-around entertainer.

Born the youngest of five siblings near Montego Bay, Jamaica, in 1967, Dwight A. Myers experienced life's hardships early. His father, Cliff, was a film technician, while his mother, Eulahlee, was a nurse. On emigrating from Jamaica, "they had to leave some of their children behind for a couple of years while my grandmother took care of me," Heavy D explained. The Myerses soon settled in Mount Vernon, New York, where Heavy got his earliest taste of American "old school" rap. By his teens, he'd begun a local performing career with DJ Eddie F (Eddie Farrell), G Wiz (Glen Parrish) and Trouble T-Roy (Troy Dixon) as Heavy D & the Boyz. G Wiz handled choreography, costumes, and sets (and later got involved on the video side, too).

As his press material admitted, Heavy D's story might have been different if not for the $1,500 he'd won gambling in Atlantic City, New Jersey. Heavy loaned it to Farrell, who bought a computer. "Before long he had traded the computer in for a drum machine," he said, "and that's how we got started making demos."

Demo led to deal

The first of those tapes caught Andre Harrell's attention, who quit Rick Rubin's Def Jam label to make the Boyz his first signing at his own Uptown Records label in 1986. "Mr. Big Stuff," the group's first single, rewarded Harrell with a radio smash. It also showed Heavy D could tackle more than basic hip-hop, having been based on a Gladys Knight song of the same title. The same elements worked well on *Livin' Large* (1987), whose funky beats and smart raps sold 500,000 copies. It also kicked off Heavy D's long tradition of poking fun at his size with "The Overweight Lover's in the House." Such efforts helped the album go platinum, selling more than one million copies.

"(My mother and father spent) fifteen years passing each other in the night just to make ends meet. When you see that, how could you ever give up?"

Heavy D's crossover potential became more pronounced with 1989's *Big Tyme* album, which also shipped platinum. While politically-oriented rap groups like **Public Enemy** (see entry) had trouble getting airplay, Heavy D used his cameo on Levert's smash, *Just Coolin'* to reach conservative listeners not usually interested in hip-hop. After *Just Coolin'* appeared, writer Deram Hampton noted, "everyone from [rhythm and blues/soul singer] Patti Labelle to [arranger] Quincy Jones began incorporating rap into their formulas for hits."

Love found itself a hit

In 1991 Heavy D & The Boyz released *Peaceful Journey*, which mixed strong message tracks with its blend of party and romance rhyming. It came out of a troubled period, beginning when childhood friend Trouble T-Roy died on January 15, 1990, of an apparent off-stage fall and continuing with his brothers' deaths. "Every day it hurts," Heavy recalled to *The Source* years later, "but the next day it hurts a little less... I had to accept their [Trouble T-Roy's and his brothers'] deaths or I'd walk around being dead too." On another alarming note, Heavy found himself caught in a disastrous charity event in late 1991. Meant to raise money for AIDS (Acquired Immune Deficiency Syndrome) education—using a basketball game featuring hip-hop's brightest lights, the City College of New York (CCNY) show drew 5,000, or twice as many people as expected. The resulting crush outside claimed nine lives, raising fresh accusations of hip-hop's "built-in" violence. Ironically, as Heavy pointed out to critics, his own style took strong stances against the drugs and guns decimating poor black neighborhoods.

On a brighter note, *Peaceful Journey*'s title track became a hit single, along with its remake of The O'Jays/Third World ballad, "Now That We Found Love," which went to number five on the *Billboard* charts. Alan Light's review of *Peaceful Journey* reflected critics' positive feelings toward Heavy D's music, calling it "a masterful display of pop's rap strengths". A Grammy Award nomination for "Now That We Found Love" followed.

Branched out as actor, executive

Heavy D began exploring acting and record label projects. He first broke into TV with roles on *A Different World, The Fresh Prince of Bel-Air,* and *In Living Color,* whose theme song he composed. Heavy's best-known role came in 1995's *Riff Raff,* a play written and directed by Laurence Fishburne. Set in a trashed-out apartment on New York's Lower East Side, Heavy D played Tony, an old crime partner of ex-con Mike (Fishburne), and Torch, a junkie (Titus Welliver), who've just botched a heist. The *Los Angeles Times*'s Scott Collins praised the "crisp, tough portrayals," while the *New York Times* singled out Heavy's recital of "a flashy, nearly epic prose poem" evoking "the lurid, cautionary barroom ballads of the gaslight era."

"I have love for anyone who's doing their thang on the screen," Heavy told *The Source*, "just as long as they're representin'. If they're not delivering on the screen, then that's just plain tacky, and I'm not gonna fall for that." By 1993, Heavy D had realized another dream in starting his own Music 4-Life label. He released two Jamaican hits ("Big & Broad", "Dem No Worry Me") with Super Cat and Frankie Paul on that label.

Next effort sounded more "streetwise"

Both singles reflected another change that served Heavy D well: dancehall, a style that combined hip-hop and reggae. It's smoother, funkier, and faster, or a natural extension of Heavy's Jamaican background. "In terms of the lyrics," he told *Spin*, "dancehall is even harder than rapping. They [DJs] talk much faster, and it's more skillful." Fans heard this trend on *Blue Funk* (1993), which went gold—despite having no hit single.

Heavy bounced back on 1994's *Nuttin' but Love,* whose title track went Top Ten and won a Grammy nomination. On "Black Coffee," Heavy D saluted his ideal woman (*"No sugar, no cream / That's the kind of girl I want down with my team"*). New Jack Swing wizard Teddy Riley, Heavy's main producer since his debut album, was back, along with Pete Rock and Marley Marl.

In 1996, Heavy D's executive dreams took a serious notch upward—when Uptown's parent label, MCA, named him to succeed Harrell (who'd left to run Motown). The reason, Heavy D guessed, came in his production of Soul For Real's album, which went gold.

Kept outlook positive, despite tragedies

The appointment signaled how far he'd come after quitting high school as a ninth grader (to later return for his GED, or General Equivalency Diploma). Nor did his recording lapse; his sixth album, *Waterbed Hev* (1997), again delved into his wild romantic side on "Big Daddy," "Shake It," and "Keep It Comin'," which lifted part of The Gap Band's own "Yearnin'", while "I'll Do Anything" reworked Hall & Oates's pop hit, "Can't Go For That."

"I wanted it so that if someone was driving cross-country from New York to Cali[fornia] or vice-versa," said Heavy in *Waterbed Hev*'s press material, "they wouldn't feel the need to take the tapes out." The public clearly wanted to keep playing those tapes. By March 3, 1997, *Billboard*'s Hot 100 chart for that week showed the single "Big Daddy" at number twenty-one, and number five on its R & B charts. That summer, *USA Today* reported Heavy had been signed to star in the Fox film *Blunt Force*.

As 1997 closes, Heavy D remains outspoken as ever for personal responsibility and against hip-hop violence—having been disturbed by the shootings of **Notorious B.I.G.** and **Tupac Shakur** (see entries), whom he considered friends. It's an attitude forged by losing one of his brothers to guns and another to a crack cocaine overdose.

"Crack came along and people lost their souls," Heavy D told Hunter, while remaining equally scathing toward marijuana smoking: "Half these cats [out] smoking weed ain't got no sense." If his tragedies hold a message, Heavy D believes, it's that where individuals go is up to them. "I got to taste life in a lot of different ways that people would never know about," he told *USA Today*. "But I keep God in my life."

Selected Awards

Platinum albums for *Living Large* (1987), *Big Tyme* (1989) and *Peaceful Journey* (1991); gold album for *Blue Funk* (1993).

"Now That We Found Love," Grammy Award Nomination, Best Rap Duo or Group Performance, 1991.

"Nuttin' but Love," Grammy Award Nomination, Best Rap Duo or Group Performance, 1994.

"Rock with You," (contribution to *Q's Jook Joint*, Quincy Jones) Grammy Award Nomination, Best Rap Duo or Group Performance, 1997.

Drama Desk Award, *Riff Raff*, 1995.

Selected Discography

Livin' Large (Uptown/MCA), 1987.

Big Tyme (Uptown/MCA), 1989.

Peaceful Journey (Uptown/MCA), 1991.

Blue Funk (Uptown/MCA), 1993.

Nuttin' but Love (Uptown/MCA), 1994.

Waterbed Hev (Uptown/MCA), 1997.

Further Reading

Collins, Scott, "Fishburne's Riff Raff: A Gritty Evolution," *Los Angeles Times*, November 23, 1994, p. F14.

Considine, J.D., "No Lightweight," *Baltimore Sun*, June 8, 1997, p. 1E.

Hunter, Asondra, "He Who Bears a Cross," *The Source,* April, 1997, p. 11.

Jones, Steve, "For Heavy D, Hard Work Is No Burden," *USA Today*, April 2, 1997, p. D9.

Patterson, Demetrius, "The Music Man: '90s Style," *Tarrytown Daily News*, January 13, 1996.

Samuels, Anita M., "Heavy D, the CEO: He Raps Like a Dream, But Can He Make It in the Corporate Boardroom?," *New York Times*, January 14, 1996.

Contact Information

Uptown Records
729 Seventh Avenue, 12th Floor
New York, NY 10019-6831

Web Site

http://www.mca.com/mca_records/library/bios/bios.heavyd.html

Ice Cube

American rap artist, producer
(West Coast, gangsta, and hardcore rap styles)

Born O'Shea Jackson, June 15, 1969, in Compton, California

"I don't have the answers, I just bring out what I see. If they [critics] can tell me I'm lying, I'll stop. But they can't."

Actor, activist, and rap artist Ice Cube has few peers among his hip-hop brethren. Few artists are as intensely personal, nor command as much respect; when riots tore apart his South Central Los Angeles neighborhood in 1992, Ice Cube's Street Knowledge production offices stayed untouched. That hands-off policy remains a source of pride, as Cube made clear to *Details*: "That was a mood that everybody had. We're ready for anything and everything. They say two wrongs don't make a right, but it damn sure makes it even." Ice Cube's releases have displayed a very dark side, such as his work on NWA's best-known anti-government and police anthem, or solo efforts like "Black Korea," in which he urges Asian grocers to "pay respect to the black fist," or see their stores burned down.

A child of his times

Born O'Shea Jackson in 1969, and named after his mother Doris's favorite football star, O. J. Simpson, Ice Cube's childhood years differed little from his classmates' at Hawthorne Christian

High in Compton, California, near Los Angeles. Although Cube dabbled in sports, that failed to capture his imagination. Nor did he follow in the footsteps of his father, Hosea, as a machinist.

Instead, Cube dove headfirst into hip-hop at age fifteen, scribbling his earliest rhymes during classes. After exposing them to a friend, Jinx, the pair cut a tape betraying little of Cube's future talent. Essentially, he informed *Rolling Stone,* "It was pathetic. The beat was going, and I was over in the left corner."

Cube's stage name occurred because "I was too cool for my age," he told *Details* writer William Shaw. That comment stuck after Cube's older brother caught him calling his own girlfriend for a date. It also seemed to fit Cube's personality; when a drugstore owner wouldn't serve him beer, he threw a brick through the store window. The experience left his legs permanently scarred after jumping a fence to escape.

By his own admission, Cube's earliest rhyming "wasn't no exciting type of mind-boggling [work]," as he told *Rolling Stone,* but persistence later paid off handsomely in other ways—beginning with mid-1980s performances with Jinx's cousin, **Dr. Dre (Andre Ramelle Young)** (see entry).

Hooked up with Ruthless empire

Needing an inspired lyricist, Dre introduced Cube to local drug dealer **Eazy-E** (Eric Wright; see entry), who'd recently formed Ruthless Records. Their label exploded in 1986, when New York-based group HBO rejected doing the song "Boyz in the Hood" (which inspired John Singleton's film of the same name) as being "too California [in style]." Ignoring the emerging East and West Coast style wars, Eazy-E became the featured artist. "Boyz in the Hood"'s nitty-gritty take on Compton life sold 10,000 independent singles, convincing the trio that a streetwise sound might succeed.

However, when they formed NWA, Cube's mother urged him to complete his education at Phoenix Institute of Technology, where her son, then eighteen, had studied drafting for a year. Cube's studies ended after police arrested him in a local drug dealer's company; assuming the worst, they locked him up with thirty-five other men for seventeen hours before sending him home.

On returning to the group, Cube's firebrand imagery pushed NWA into public noteriety on *NWA and the Posse* (Macola, 1987), and the platinum-selling *Straight Outta Compton* (Priority, 1989). He quickly became the group's spokesman, seeing no need to aplogize for its harshest tracks.

While he appreciated older blacks' resentment of using the "n" word in lyrics, Cube reasoned its provocative nature might finally make politicians listen to inner-city concerns. "They want to sweep it under the rug," he told *New Musical Express.* "They think as long as black kids are killing black kids, that's cool."

Ice Cube

He balked at re-signing with NWA, causing manager Jerry Heller to remark: "Eazy-E is a major star and a successful businessman. Ice Cube is not."

Cube proved otherwise on his fiery solo debut, *AmeriKKKa's Most Wanted* (Priority, 1990), which went platinum and convinced critics he'd been the force behind NWA. They praised his production collaboration with **Public Enemy's** (see entry) Chuck D, even as they groaned over Cube's excessive profanity and attitude toward women.

"They want to sweep it under the rug. They think as long as black kids are killing black kids, that's cool."

Yet not even Revolutionary Communist Party leaflets ("If You're Dissing the Sisters, You Ain't Fighting the Power") could persuade Cube to back down. "The people that wanna hold us down better hope to God that all so-called [black men] aren't like this one right here," he told *Spin.* "Now, that would be a problem, wouldn't it?"

Albums ran roughshod over criticism

Ice Cube's *Kill at Will* (Priority, 1991) EP won praise for "Dead Homiez," recalling the funeral of a friend lost to gang violence, where Ice Cube finds himself "dressed up, because society is messed up." Its theme of young black men seeming an "Endangered Species," as another EP track claimed, proved topical in Cube's film debut, *Boyz in the Hood* (1991).

Runaway NWA success turned sour

NWA's platinum success soon soured for Cube, who left in 1990 after finding he'd only earned $32,000 on tour, and little more for writing the group's lyrics.

Playing the haunted, violent Doughboy, Cube won praise for his acting, even as he confessed that crying on camera had been difficult. "It's really hard for me to show emotions," he told *Details,* "to pull emotions out of the sky. I haven't cried in eight years."

Cube's *Death Certificate* (Priority, 1991) album displayed a wider ambition with its "life" and "death" sides, while continuing his knack for upsetting different groups. He settled with grocers threatening to boycott St. Ide's Malt Liquor—which Cube endorsed at the time—over "Black Korea."

Yet no compromise seemed possible on "No Vaseline," an apparent jibe at NWA manager Jerry Heller. Its harshest line, "You can't be a n— for life crew / With a white Jew telling you what to do," drew fire for anti-Semitism, a charge Cube dismissed, pointing out that Street Knowledge employed whites and Asians. His drive to be called "pro-black" failed to wash in *Rolling Stone.* Ice Cube, the magazine's 1991 year-end issue urged, must know "that you don't put out a fire with gasoline."

Headlines made little impact

If Cube's peers disavowed his stances, that didn't show at the Lollapalooza II alternative rock festival in 1992. Inheriting its 1991 hip-hop slot from hardcore rapper **Ice-T** (see entry), Cube won praise from audiences and artists like the **Red Hot Chili Peppers** (see entry), who appeared in a video

("Wicked") for his next album, *The Predator.*

In the spring of 1992, Los Angeles erupted with arson, looting, and violence over a jury's acquittal of white policemen caught beating black motorist Rodney King on videotape. These events inspired some of the tracks on Cube's 1992 album, *The Predator.* Cube called the album a demand for understanding. Anybody who felt surprised by the riots' ferocity was woefully out of touch, he informed *New Musical Express's* Gavin Martin: "We don't own no stores no more, no hotels, nothing. Damn, y'know, we have to start talking about things that affect us." Priority publicist Pat Charbonnet put matters tersely in defending Cube's imagery: "People call them [hip-hoppers] rebels or radicals, but really they are voices that articulate the sentiment of their times."

Entertainment Weekly called *The Predator* Cube's "strongest, most cohesive work yet," while *Rolling Stone's* Darryl Smith waxed cooler about lyrics that continued to dis(respect) women. Awarding it a begrudging two out of four stars, Smith lamented the "musically muddy" results of what reads like "a gangsta's manifesto—common and tinny."

From hip-hop to multi-media

Despite the flack, *The Predator* debuted at number one on *Billboard's* pop and R & B charts simultaneously, the first record to do so since Stevie Wonder's *Songs in the Key of Life* (1976); by late November, it appeared headed for platinum.

Cube also squeezed in another movie role in *Trespass* with Ice-T; its original title, *Looters,* had been changed after the riots.

Critics found Cube stumbling on *Lethal Injection* (Priority, 1993); in *Rolling Stone's* eyes, it recycled the same South Central imagery too often, without any new insight. Slamming its "boring, predictable" rhymes ("Got this sewed up like Betsy Ross"), *Rolling Stone* writer Touré felt "Mr. Stay True to the Game has...chosen to become a multimedia hip-hopper at the expense of his music." The album received just two of four stars from *Rolling Stone.*

Cube rebounded in 1995 with Dr. Dre on their joint *Helter Skelter* album. He was also heard on the soundtrack to the 1995 film *Friday,* for which he wrote the script as well as appearing in the movie. The film was a positive affair, Cube told MTV's Bill Bellamy in May 1997; to his knowledge, it was "the most successful film of its type," when considering its budget.

Cube took a slightly different tack in the 1996 action film *Anaconda,* which pitted him against a giant snake. Nor did he show any signs of slowing down in Hollywood, with his role in 1997's *Dangerous Ground* (filmed in South Africa and co-starring Elizabeth Hurley) and his *Players Club* T-shirts announcing his forthcoming film. In keeping with his multi-media profile, Cube planned to act in, direct, and script the film.

An album release seemed farther away (Cube has mentioned a double-CD planned for early 1998), but Cube promised a series of one-off collaborations. He'd spoken to NWA's MC Ren (Lorenzo Patterson) about that possibility, as well as to Cypress Hill's B-Real, urging: "All the walls of division should come down."

Selected Discography

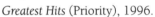

With NWA:

Straight Outta Compton (Priority), 1989.

Greatest Hits (Priority), 1996.

Solo Recordings:

AmeriKKKa's Most Wanted (Priority), 1990.

Kill at Will EP (Priority), 1991.

Death Certificate (Priority), 1991.

The Predator (Priority), 1992.

Lethal Injection (Priority), 1993.

Bootlegs & B-Sides (Priority), 1994.

Helter Skelter (Death Row), 1995 (with Dr. Dre).

Further Reading

Blackwell, Mark, "Ain't That a Bitch," *Spin,* May 1990.

Garcia, Jane, "Telling it Like it Is," *New Musical Express,* August 18, 1989.

Linden, Amy, "Targeting 'The Bigger Enemy,'" *People Weekly,* January 11, 1993, p. 21.

Martin, Gavin, "The Predator's Decision Is Final," *New Musical Express,* November 5, 1992.

Owen, Frank, "Hanging Tough," *Spin,* February 1990.

Rule, Sheila, "Generation Rap," *New York Times Magazine,* April 3, 1994, p. 42.

Sager, Mike, "The World According to AmeriKKKa's Most Wanted Rapper," *Rolling Stone,* October 4, 1990.

Shaw, William, "Fire and Ice: A Gangsta's Tale," *Details*, July 1993.

Smith, Darryl, "Ice Cube's Meltdown," *Rolling Stone,* January 7, 1993.

"The Year in Records," *Rolling Stone*, December 12-26, 1991.

Toure, "Snoop & Cube," *Rolling Stone,* January 27, 1994.

Contact Information

Priority Records
6430 Sunset Blvd., Ste. 900
Hollywood, CA 90028

Web Sites

http://www.galactica.it/101/black/accb.html

http://web.mit.edu/madmike/www/cube.html

Ice-T

American rap artist
(West Coast, gangsta, and hardcore rap styles)

Born Tracey Marrow (some accounts say Morrow), c. late 1950s
(date unknown), Newark, New Jersey

"Ice back on the streets? / You don't want that / 'Cause I'll break ill / And you'll really have to body count the cops I'll kill / It's on." –

from Ice-T's "It's On,"

He's been called a "foulmouthed moralist" (*Newsweek*), "a perennial winner on the Scare-O-Meter" (*Melody Maker*), a hip-hop capitalist, and a cynical hustler by his critics. Depending on who's talking, Ice-T is a brave, anti-establishment critic, or an irresponsible stone-thrower against American social norms. Throughout his 1980s and 1990s hip-hop career, Ice-T has been unable to avoid making a controversial move. When his heavy metal band Body Count released its furious anti-brutality anthem, "Cop Killer," police unions lobbied Warner Brothers Records to cancel its release and picketed Ice-T gigs.

Yet Ice-T remained unbowed, leaving Warner Brothers to release records independently. A product of the Los Angeles inner city, Ice-T hasn't stopped helping former associates—whether they work in his body shop, or win deals with his Rhyme Syndicate label. "To me that's the nature of someone who comes from the ghetto," he said to *New Musical Express*'s Sylvia Patterson. "Anybody who's ever been poor, if they get a chance they're gonna immediately help their family and their friends...." But Ice-T is clearly not on a quest for sainthood and self-sacrifice, as he explains clearly in his publicity packet: "The name of the game is capitalism, and I aim to win that game, too."

Early acting proved the ticket

Ice-T's journey from hustler to hip-hopper took a circular route, between the East and West Coasts. Born Tracey Marrow during the late 1950s in Newark, New Jersey—Ice-T has never given his actual birth date—he ended up in Los Angeles by the seventh grade, after both parents had died. There, Ice-T lived with an aunt. By his teenage years, Ice-T had already begun two parallel paths at Crenshaw High School. When not scribbling rhymes for local gangs, he was committing credit card fraud, robbery, and even arson with his friends.

When his high school girlfriend got pregnant, Ice-T enlisted in the U.S. Army to "get responsible." By his own admission, that didn't happen after serving a four-year hitch there. When Ice-T returned to Los Angeles, he returned to the criminal circuit—but not without making his first recording.

In 1982, Ice-T cut "The Coldest Rap," an independent effort that netted a mere twenty dollars—but opened doors to DJing mostly white crowds for $50 per week. Eventually, Ice-T decided he could do better rhyming than mixing. There were no obvious outlets for his talent: "the concept of actually getting paid for rapping was too farfetched to even think about," he told Time's Sally B. Donnelly.

In 1984, however, Ice-T found something that helped him escape the street life: a small part in the break-dancing film Breakin', which his friends wouldn't let him reject. That led to further roles and the odd record. While he dismisses those efforts today as "artistic prostitution" to pay rent, they saved Ice-T from what he saw happening to his friends. "You got a chance," Ice-T recalled his friends saying in Time. "White people like you, man. They've got their hand out; you should take it." Such advice, and the support of girlfriend Darlene Ortiz, helped Ice-T survive his earliest and leanest years.

"Crime rhyme" boosted career

Around the same period, in 1983, Ice-T acquired his most important ally in Jorge Hinojosa, his manager who's stayed with him without a contract. As Ice-T recalled in Creem, he needed whatever encouragement came. "The girls would jock me and we'd say, 'Yo, yo baby, we've got an album coming out and you just ain't never heard from us,'" he laughingly told the magazine in 1993.

"We lived in one little room and paid rent," Darlene Ortiz told Details's Scott Cohen in 1991. "We didn't have a car for two years." When Ice-T finally broke out of that life with his 1987 debut album, Rhyme Pays, hip-hop's commercial profile had changed drastically—thanks to smash-hit records like Run-DMC's remake of Aerosmith's "Walk This Way."

Although New York rappers had been dominant, Ice-T's graphic descriptions of

Ice-T appearing on the Arsenio Hall Show in 1992.

ors, which starred Sean Penn as a veteran cop battling Los Angeles gangs. Backed by a minimal bass-drum pattern, "Colors" described turf wars not being aired in the national press: "The gangs of L.A., we never die / Just multiply." It also offered no hope to reformers, black or white: "I don't need your persistence, social assistance / Any problem I got, I just put my fist in."

A lightning rod on free speech issues

With Ice-T's next album, *Freedom of Speech (Just Watch What You Say)* (1989), the artist became involved in arguments about censorship. Its opener, "Shut Up (Be Happy)" set the mood. Punk singer Jello Biafra ranted a dictatorship's mock address to Americans, while sampled guitars from heavy metal group Black Sabbath growled away behind him. Other tracks tackled Los Angeles street life, such as "The Hunted Child," who snarls, "What I call home, you call Hell ... / When I die, I'm going to Hell again," while "Peel Their Caps Back" offered one of the most startling descriptions of gang murder: "Then all of a sudden, a bullet came through my eye / My dome exploded, and I felt my other brothers die." Still other tracks, like "The Iceberg," raised familiar concerns about sexism. Ironically, Ice-T would later dismiss *Freedom of Speech* as too preoccupied with censorship: "People at the record company wanted me to do that and I'm sorry that I listened to them." The album still made the U.S. Top Forty.

street realities—which he called "crime rhymes"—pushed him into living rooms and record racks. Tracks like "Six in the Morning," that told of gang members battling police, opened a new approach only suggested by previous hip-hop groups.

When Ice-T returned with 1988's *Power,* the heat increased. It featured a cover of a scantily-clad Ortiz and two aggressive hits in "High Rollers" and "I'm Your Pusher," which jokingly compared records to favorite drugs. *Power's* million-plus sales also jump-started heated debates about Ice-T's aggressive stance on race, sex, and money.

Such concerns only escalated with Ice-T's title contribution to the film, *Col-*

Original Gangster dispelled laughter

With the sprawling, twenty-four-track *Original Gangster* (1991), Ice-T returned to familiar themes and a sparser sound. "Home of the Bodybag" pitted old song snippets against drumbeats and police sirens. The title track, "Original Gangster," set a defiant tone: "Point blank and twisted / No imagination needed, 'cause I lived it."

"Prepared to Die," "The Tower," and "Escape from the Killing Fields" again portrayed blacks caught up in violence beyond their understanding. Not every track struck such a grim tone, however. As he told *Melody Maker*: "I can't do that 'Oh so holy' thing." He didn't want politics or moralizing to dominate his music.

Original Gangster, which went Top Ten in America, received mostly positive notice. "It's his candor that really draws blood," *Musician* observed. His role as a cop in the film, *New Jack City* (1991), to which Ice-T contributed the soundtrack's title song, gained Ice-T positive attention as well. The title song's pounding lyrics summarized the life of a drug dealer: "Jammed into a paradox / Every dollar I eat / another brother drops."

That same year, Ice-T played the first alternative Lollapalooza rock festival, sharing the stage with black rockers **Living Colour** (see entry) and industrial noisemakers **Nine Inch Nails** (see entry). He also signed friends like Donald-D, Everlast, and British hip-hoppers Hijack to his new Rhyme Syndicate label.

Declared independence after "Cop Killer" furor

Ice-T's fortunes changed in 1992, when authorities blasted "Cop Killer," a song he'd done on Lollapalooza stages with his metal band, Body Count. The song's chorus, "I'm about to bust some shots off / I'm about to dust some cops off," drew fire like few songs had ever done. Ice-T pulled the song from Body Count's self-titled debut album, which was released that summer, although another anti-police song, "Smoked Pork," stayed. The album's lyrics, remarked *Rolling Stone's* J. D. Considine, made NWA "seem like the Patrolman's Benevolent Association." Body Count lost several gigs when off-duty policemen refused to provide security, and 400 of them picketed the band at its Chicago gig.

Yet even that furor paled in the fall of 1992, when Warner Bros. lobbied for lyric changes on Ice-T's upcoming *Home Invasion* album. They also objected to its cover of a white teenager imagining violent activity while listening to music.

Tired of such pressures, Ice-T tore up his contract and headed for NWA's old home, Priority Records, which issued *Home Invasion* in spring 1993. Asked why, the hip-hopper said he understood major labels weren't in the anti-censorship business. But, as *Rolling Stone's* Alan Light heard it, Ice-T had learned that "until you make the news, you don't realize that it can lie."

Headlining the violent demise?

As *Home Invasion* made clear, Ice-T

was losing no sleep about being an independent business owner: "I own my own label, put my own [music] out, / So no one tells me what ... to talk about." That held true for "Home Invasion," a reference to white teenagers checking into black culture, or "That's How I'm Living," which *Rolling Stone*'s Anthony DeCurtis called "as introspective and personal a track as rap has ever seen."

DeCurtis praised *Home Invasion* as "a curiously mature work, the sort of album you could make only after establishing a successful, multifaceted career." He gave it a full five-star rating, while expressing concern about some of the more sexually explicit material.

Indeed, Ice-T was maturing into a celebrity as the 1990s progressed. Like rapper **Ice Cube** (see entry), with whom he'd starred in the film, *Trespass,* in 1992, reporters sought his opinions on that year's Los Angeles riots. He took more film roles, playing a drug dealer in *Ricochet* (1991), and a kangaroo in the futuristic epic, *Tank Girl* (1995). With the publication of *The Ice Opinion,* a collection of essays on every imaginable topic, Ice-T entered the ranks of published authors, too.

Return of the Real

Ice-T's next effort, *Return of the Real* (1996), received mixed notices for too much preoccupation with hip-hop credentials in its title track, "I Must Stand," and "Comp Your Style." The following year, Body Count returned on *Violent Demise: The Last Days,* shortly after drummer Beatmaster V died of leukemia.

Once again, a single song drew controversy. "I Used to Love Her" accused ex-football star O. J. Simpson of killing his wife, Nicole Brown Simpson, and a friend, Ron Goldman: "Not guilty? / What ... you talkin' about / You got a bloody glove, bloody car, bloody knife, bloody bitch, bloody carpet, bloody sock, bloody hand!" "White people are saying, 'The black people are gonna get mad,'" Ice-T told the *Los Angeles Times.* "Black people don't [care] about O.J. They don't [care] about O.J. or Rodney King because their brother or father is in jail." *Time*'s Donnally responded to such provocative comments: "Ice-T does not want to be adored. He'd rather be shocking—and well-paid." With that said, Ice-T seems assured of a lengthy run.

Selected Awards

Grammy Award for Best Rap Duo or Group, for *Back on the Block* (by various artists), 1991. (Ice-T was one of four rap artists who won for the album, including Big Daddy Kane, Melle Mel, and Kool Moe Dee; producers Quincy D III and Quincy Jones also won.)

Selected Discography

As Ice-T:

Rhyme Pays (Sire/Warner Brothers), 1987.

Power (Sire), 1988.

Colors (Sire), 1988. Soundtrack; Ice-T contributed the title track.

Freedom of Speech (Just Watch What You Say) (Sire), 1989.

Back on the Block (Warner Brothers), 1990. By Quincy Jones; Ice-T appeared as a contributor.

Original Gangster (Sire), 1991.

New Jack City (Sire), 1991. Soundtrack; Ice-T contributed the title track.

Home Invasion (Priority/Rhyme Syndicate Records), 1993.

Return of the Real (Priority/Rhyme Syndicate Records), 1996.

With Body Count:

Body Count (Sire), 1992.

Violent Demise: The Last Days (Priority/Rhyme Syndicate Records), 1997.

Further Reading

DeCurtis, Anthony, "Ice-T Fires: Black Rage, Dope Beats," *Rolling Stone,* April 1, 1993.

Donnelly, Sally B., "The Fire Around the Ice," *Time,* August 22, 1992.

Ice-T, *The Ice Opinion,* St. Martin's Press, 1993.

Light, Alan, "Words from the Home Front," *Rolling Stone,* May 27, 1993.

Patterson, Sylvia, "For Your Demise Only," *New Musical Express,* March 22, 1997.

Sharpe, Jerry, "Eddie Rabbitt Raps Rap," Scripps Howard News Service, November 25, 1992.

Contact Information

Priority Records
6430 Sunset Blvd., Ste. 900
Hollywood, CA 90028

Web Site

http://www.ice-t.com.au/

KOOL MOE DEE

American rap artist

Born Mohandas Dewese, New York City, New York, in 1963

"I think a lot of rappers just rap to go through (a track), while I'm thinking: what message am I trying to get across? What's the most important part of the sentence? I'm always trying to take myself to another level lyrically." –Kool Moe Dee

Kool Moe Dee may not occupy younger fans' minds today, yet he holds a privileged position with his "old school" peers. As one of hip-hop's founding fathers, Dee's self-conscious word-play, outspoken commentary, and outright dance approach have earned him a permanent place in the genre. Long before **Public Enemy** (see entry) championed black independence, Dee did so in "I Go to Work." His creative appropriations, such as swiping Paul Simon's 1970s pop hit ("Fifty Ways to Leave Your Lover"), opened new doors for sampling. Finally, his participation in *Stop the Violence*'s book and record—organized by **Boogie Down Productions**' (see entry) KRS-One to address the problem of black-on-black violence—shone a light at black-on-black crime before mainstream writers did. Dee's battles—first with Busy Bee and later with **LL Cool J** (see entry)—are the stuff of legends.

To hear Dee recount it, it all stemmed from an interest in wordplay. Born Mohandas Dewese in New York City's Harlem area in 1963, Dee and his friends were "the next step from a nerd," he told *GQ*'s Stephen Fried. "Our competition was over vocabulary.

Throw a word in there, and see if anybody can respond. And if the person doesn't respond correctly, it means he didn't understand the word—or sometimes we'd overlook it, and then run home and look it up."

This word-for-word's-sake approach served Dee well on his Enjoy Records debut, "The New Rap Language," on which he, Special K, and Sunshine—The Treacherous Three—supported "old school" rap artist Spoonie Gee.

Trio's wordplay broke ground

The Treacherous Three's name meant to suggest an image of invincibility, a "must" when MCs and DJs regularly "battled" in small clubs before packed crowds. Dee, Sunshine, and Special K had "showed the lyrical and percussive possibilities of hip-hop right up your auditory canal," said the *Village Voice's* Harry Allen.

In 1981, The Treacherous Three broke out with "Heartbeat," whose rhythms floated on a bed of gunshots and hearts—a full decade before "trip-hop" did those things. The group stayed hot for 1982's "Whip It," a parody of the megahit by mechano-rockers Devo, and "Gotta Rock." For 1983's "Yes We Can-Can," the group added multisyllabic words, using their voices to blend against each other's style.

By this point, Dee and company had signed to Sugar Hill Records, for whom they kept recording into 1984 with "Get Up" and "Xmas Rap (Uncensored)," until their new label ran out of steam. By the

year's end, Dee had already gone solo for "Turn It Up"; then, just as abruptly, he left music for SUNY (State University of New York), Long Island, earning a communications degree there.

Made waves with feuding

But Dee stayed in the business, catching Jive/RCA's attention with "Go to the Doctor" (Rooftop Records, 1985), a comment on promiscuous sex. Dee promptly remade it for his 1986 self-titled debut album, on which Lloyd Richards of *Melody Maker* remarked: "Moe Dee's style is slack-jawed and straight faced, laced with menace."

The follow up, *How Ya Like Me Now?* (1987), broke Dee into million-selling territory, especially for its rants against LL Cool J. Its cover showed a jeep crushing LL's trademark Kangol hat, while Dee graded himself at the top of hip-hop on *How Ya's* inner sleeve (with categories for articulation, word usage, and "sticking to themes").

On "Let's Go," Dee claimed LL's initials stood for "lackluster, lower-level, last, least, limp lover." (Not to be outdone, LL retaliated with his "Jack the Ripper," which blasted Dee as "an old school sucker punk.") The thumping title track, yet another anti-Cool J rant, gave Dee a smash hit—and a reported 900,000 sales.

In *Knowledge Is King* (1989), Dee expressed his hope for black autonomy and power. The shining example came in "I Go to Work," a production of "New Jack Swing" wizard Teddy Riley: "You wanna know my occupation? / I get paid to rock the nation." Calling *Knowledge* "too clean" in sound, the *Village Voice*'s Havelock Nelson concluded: "Everything on the first half ... hits hard, along with one solid uppercut in the second." *GQ*'s Fried hailed it as rap's most important record since Public Enemy's "Fight the Power."

Next efforts sold fewer copies

Despite these praises, *Knowledge Is King* sold 650,000 copies—less than *How Ya Like Me Now?*—but Dee kept busy with appearances on "The Arsenio Hall Show" and British Knights shoe commercials. Two "hits" compilations slipped out, including *The Best* (1987), soon eclipsed by a fifteen-song *Greatest Hits* (Sequel, 1989) that included virtually all Dee's significant tracks to date. (Not to be outdone, Jive came back with *The Greatest Hits*—considered Dee's best compilation effort—in 1993.)

Dee's star shone bright as ever on Quincy Jones's Grammy-winning *Back on the Block* album, released in 1990. He shared the title track's rapping with **Ice-T** (see entry) and Melle Mel, another 1970s founding father of rap. He also contributed to KRS-One's gold "Self-Destruction" single. Writers around America picked up on its most cutting lyric: "I never had to run from the Ku Klux Klan / And I shouldn't have to run from a black man."

Dee also addressed black-on-black crime in the book, *Stop the Violence: Overcoming Self-Destruction,* where he asserted rap artists "are into something besides making money. It's at the point where we're trying to show that we really

care about the fans ... because that's where rap music is generated from, and for." Only by setting a positive example, concluded Dee, "can we utilize this to become young black leaders ... since they don't have any real positive images to identify with." But young people didn't relate to Dee's EP, *God Made Me Funke,* which bombed in 1990.

Returned with funk "Wisdom"

When *God Made Me Funke* flopped, Dee returned with *Funke, Funke Wisdom* in 1991. Armed with familiar samples from soul/funk artists such as James Brown, Sly & the Family Stone, and Parliament/Funkadelic, Dee's latest offering jacked up the beats—without compromising his commentary.

"Rise 'N' Shine" resembled a "hip-hop summit," having been cut with Public Enemy's Chuck D, and Boogie Down Productions' KRS-One, while "Death Blow" once again hit out against LL Cool J. Once again, critics lined up to praise the album; Fried found it "a great followup" to *Knowledge Is King.* "Its slower songs," he added, "capture a sound that is a perfect basis for a rapper who tries to jam as many clever words as possible" into each line.

Rolling Stone's Alan Light felt similarly. "The record's stripped-down beats move the rapper's crisply enunciated delivery to the fore," he said, "and the samples ... are funky and flexible." Reflecting on a new album without Ted Riley's production skill, Dee's biography said he'd survived "because unlike other old school rappers, I pay attention to what people like. I make music for them. You can't get caught up in yourself."

Not so, felt the public; in sales terms, LL Cool J's platinum string had long surpassed Dee's track record, while the new "gangstas" (Ice-T, NWA, **Snoop Doggy Dogg**, **Tupac Shakur** [see entries]) pushed old school performers into nostalgia-driven package tours, articles, and reissues.

Dee's money problems surfaced in 1992 when *Jet* magazine reported the Internal Revenue Service had sold his Mercedes for $20,300, against an estimated $181,660 in back taxes. As a result, Dee's profile slipped; reportedly working as a bicycle messenger, he did appear in the 1993 HBO film *Strapped*. Coming at the time of *The Greatest Hits*, it reminded buyers of an artist only one smash away from returning to their minds—and shelves.

Selected Awards

How Ya Like Me Now? certified platinum, 1987.

Grammy Award, Best Performance by a Rap Duo or Group, for "Back on the Block" from Quincy Jones's album of the same name, along with rappers Ice-T, Melle Mel, and Big Daddy Kane, 1991.

Selected Discography

Kool Moe Dee (Jive/RCA), 1986.
How Ya Like Me Now? (Jive/ RCA), 1987.

The Best (Jive/RCA), 1987.
Greatest Hits (Sequel), 1989.
Knowledge Is King (Jive/RCA), 1989.
God Made Me Funke EP (Jive/RCA), 1990.
Funke, Funke Wisdom (Jive/RCA), 1991.
The Greatest Hits (Jive/RCA), 1993.

As Contributing Artist:

"Self-Destruction" single, Stop the Violence projects (Jive/RCA), 1989.
Back on the Block, Quincy Jones (Qwest/ Warner Brothers), 1990.
Zebrahead Soundtrack (Ruffhouse), 1992.

Further Reading

Fried, Stephen, "Rap A La Moe Dee," *GQ*, June 1991.

George, Nelson, editor, *Stop the Violence: Overcoming Self-Destruction,* Pantheon Books, 1990.

Heibutzki, Ralph, "Time Enough for the Old School: The Hip-hop Revolution, 1970-1990," *Goldmine,* May 1996.

Jet, "Kool Moe Dee Loses His Car to Internal Revenue, February 17, 1992.

Light, Alan, "Kool Moe Dee: Funke, Funke Wisdom," *Rolling Stone,* July 11-25, 1996.

McAdams, Janine, *Billboard,* July 22, 1989; July 27, 1991.

Contact Information

Jive Records
137-139 West 25th Street
New York, NY 10001

RCA Records
1540 Broadway
New York, NY 10036

LL COOL J

American rap artist
(East Coast, hardcore, and lovers-oriented rap styles)

Born James Todd Smith on August 16, 1968
(some sources say January 14, 1968) in Queens, New York City

"I want everyone to be able to get into what I'm doing. But I'm not trying to compromise. I'm not trying to be white, and I'm not trying to be black. I'm just being LL, just being me."

For a hip-hopper nearing thirty, LL Cool J has had numerous "firsts" in his fifteen-year-career—first rap artist to reach number one on *Billboard*'s Black Singles chart; first to go acoustic for an acoustic MTV "Unplugged" album; and first to rack up four straight platinum albums. Yet, despite these and other imposing milestones, LL has often felt a lack of respect from hardcore fans, who question his "street" credentials and shirtless strutting onstage. They may not know LL was pioneering rap label Def Jam's first release, kick-starting a 1980s sound admirers considered brash, even if lacking gangsta rap's graphic urgency.

Such a position suits LL fine, as he informed *Rolling Stone*'s Alan Weisel in 1996: "I have a right to make the kind of music I want to make. At the same time, I have a responsibility to think about kids, too." Having seen younger peers like **The Notorious B.I.G.** (see entry) fall to bullets, drugs, or declining sales, LL's profile remains sturdy, expanding into sitcoms (UPN's "In The House"), movies (*Krush Groove, The Hard Way*), and a projected autobiography.

Yet LL admits to paying a price for avoiding political issues. "I like my music to relieve pressure and get rid of life's tensions," he told *Rolling Stone*. "I don't want to give people problems." When he does, it's from the inner perspective of tracks like "Illegal Search," which has been keeping his career alive in the 1990s.

Artistic drive started early

Born James Todd Smith in New York City's Queens borough, LL claims his artistic drive started at nine, when he heard the first "old school" records. "In this neighborhood, kids grow up on rap," he reminded Stephen Holden in the *New York Times Magazine*. "It's like speaking Spanish if you grow up in an all-Spanish house." Actually, LL grew up in the black middle-class confines of St. Albans, where his grandmother, Ellen Griffiths, raised him. Thanks to LL's late grandfather—who had bought $2,000 in DJ equipment for the thirteen-year-old boy—his ambition got a major boost. When not performing with neighborhood groups at roller rinks and block parties, LL was bombarding record labels with crude demos.

"If you see me smiling, standing straight up, gold around my neck, it's not because I'm conceited. It's because I'm proud of what I achieved. I made this. That's what this is all about."

One of LL's targets—original "old school" label, Sugar Hill Records—got *nine* demo tapes from him, recalled rap promoter Van Silk, without any responding. But two partners in a new hip-hop label, Def Jam, felt differently. Russell Simmons, older brother of **Run-DMC's** (see entry) Joseph "Run" Simmons, and Rick Rubin, picked LL's "I Need a Beat" as their first single release.

The resulting 100,000-plus sales encouraged LL to quit Andrew Jackson High School. The followup, "I Want You," won him national exposure on the New York City Fresh Fest tour. Encouraged by Rubin to simplify his raps—and rework them into a verse-chorus-bridge pop format—LL's *Radio* (1985), became Def Jam's first album release, rocketing him to fame.

Between the B-boy [break-boy, referring to the use of breaks in rap music] swagger of "Rock the Bells," and "I Can't Live Without My Radio"—which declared, "I'm sorry if you can't understand/But I need a radio in my hand"—LL dropped trademark ballads in "I Can Give You More," and "I Want You." Such material, declared *Rolling Stone*, was "heralding the arrival of a superb rapper," while the *Village Voice*'s Robert Christgau called *Radio* "the most engaging and original rap album of the year."

It's all in the beats

Rubin put *Radio*'s appeal down to the beats, which relied on tension and release between LL's raps, and their rhythmic drive. Hence, Rubin told *Musician*, "LL Cool J's album is a rock 'n' roll album even though there are no guitars on it."

Members of LL Cool J, left to right: Bobcat, E. Love, Cut Creator, and LL

LL quickly followed with his first film appearance, in *Krush Groove*, and a summer 1986 slot on Run-DMC's *Raising Hell* tour. However, nothing prepared critics for his next album, *Bigger and Deffer* (1987), which stayed in *Billboard's* Top Ten for two months, boosted by the unlikely hip-hop ballad, "I Need Love." The first such track to reach number one on *Billboard's* Black Singles Chart, "I Need Love" established LL as the ultimate ladies' man who cared about his partner's needs, instead of being a sexist, superficial conquerer. (His rap name, LL Cool J, stands for Ladies Love Cool James.) Two other hits, "I'm Bad" and "Go Cut Creator Go," followed what *Rolling Stone* called

"the hippest bedroom monologue since [soul singer] Barry White's heyday."

Billed as "The Crown Prince of Rap," LL spent the summer of 1987 headlining a seventy-city tour over Doug E. Fresh, Public Enemy, Stetsasonic, and Whodini. "If you see me smiling, standing straight up, gold around my neck," he told Fab Five Freddy, "it's not because I'm conceited. It's because I'm proud of what I achieved. I made this. That's what this is all about."

Champagne, gold chains not well-received

LL's early success opened doors unimaginable to other hip-hoppers. He

Parents Aren't Supposed to Like It

did "Go Cut Creator Go" on NBC's *Saturday Night Live*; Nancy Reagan asked LL to headline her Just Say No Foundation anti-drug concert; *Playgirl* named him one of its "Ten Sexiest Men." Yet LL's celebration of material success—not to mention his penchant for gold chains and champagne—made him a target in hardcore circles, who questioned his lack of social consciousness. Those feelings came to a head in September 1989, when LL endured booing at a voter registration rally in Harlem, while *Rolling Stone* questioned if "being the boaster with the mostest" would suffice. LL took those concerns coolly, telling the magazine: "I think people were searching for weakness [on *Panther*]. It was a timing thing; it was my time to get it in the back."

In 1990, however, LL rebounded with a harder-hitting album, *Mama Said Knock You Out*, whose title cut saluted his parents for giving him the will to succeed. Fans kept *Mama* in the Top Twenty six months after its release, and made it his fourth platinum album. The title track became another crossover smash for LL, making Top Fifteen and Twenty of the R & B and pop charts, respectively. By January 1992, *Mama* had spun off six top-selling singles, including "Six Minutes Of Pleasure," and had been certified double platinum (two million sold).

Commitments kept piling up

LL kept busy with a supporting role in the 1991 film *Toys,* playing opposite actor Robin Williams. His emerging social consciousness didn't stay idle, either.

LL Cool J's Selected Film Appearances

Krush Groove, 1985 (includes LL performing "I Can't Live Without My Radio").

MTV "Rapumentary" (with Afrika Bambaata, Jazzy Jeff; also includes vintage clips of "old school" act The Sugarhill Gang), 1991.

The Hard Way (with Michael J. Fox), 1991.

Toys (with Robin Williams), 1992.

He taped a series of public service announcements ("I'm here to say your dreams can come true if you stay in school!") for Project Literary U.S. (PLUS), and the "Rappers Save Libraries" radio campaigns.

That same year, LL pulled off an artistic coup with acoustic takes of "Mama Said Knock You Out" and "Jingling Baby" for MTV's "Unplugged" series—then a new concept. When asked by *Rolling Stone* why he never repeated it, LL responded: "Sometimes when you have a great moment, you just have to let it be that. I don't know about trying to recapture it."

On *14 Shots to the Dome* (1993), LL seemingly stumbled in some critics' eyes. *Rolling Stone* decided platinum success had "encouraged LL to recycle," drawing unfavorable parallels between "Mama Said Knock You Out" and *Dome*'s "How I'm Comin'," for one example. While *Dome* offered an adequate take on LL's crossover strengths, Toure also felt its star "may continue to live in the shadow of those early [Def Jam] recordings forever." The artist responded by firing his management—including his father—and issuing *Mr. Smith* (1996), which critics ranked as a decided improvement over its predecessor.

Asked, "Who calls you Mr. Smith?" by *Rolling Stone*, LL joked: "Bill collectors." Dismissing *14 Shots* as "a bad day at the office," LL offered a more realistic view of what fans termed yet another comeback: "One thing I've learned about the music industry is it comes in waves—there's ups and downs. Every album isn't going to be killer."

As the 1990s progressed, LL seemed determined to keep his plate varied. He continued to read scripts that interested him ("I'm not running down the street with an Afro and a TV"), and has begun Youth Enterprises, a foundation for troubled teenagers in his neighborhood. There may even be a "Camp Cool J," if he gets his way.

Yet LL has no intention of competing with anybody but himself, as his latest Internet biography made clear: "You know what, I've been doing this for so long I don't really [care] about who's coming out. Doesn't really matter. That's because I gotta stay on my game. There's a lot of good chefs, but I gotta keep my kitchen straight."

Selected Awards

Bigger and Deffer certified double platinum, 1987.

Radio certified platinum, 1988.

Walking with a Panther certified platinum, 1989.

Mama Said Knock You Out certified double platinum, 1992.

Record-setting fifteen New York Music Awards, 1990-1991 (including Artist of the Year, Album of the Year, Song of the Year, for *Mama Said Knock You Out*).

Soul Train Music Awards, Best Rap Album (*Bigger and Deffer*) and Best Rap Single ("I Need Love"), 1988.

Mama Said Knock You Out, *Village Voice* Album of the Year, 1990.

"Mama Said Knock You Out," Grammy Award, Best Rap Solo Performance, 1991.

"Mama Said Knock You Out," MTV Video Music Award, Best Rap Video, 1991.

Billboard Music Award, Top Rap Singles Artist, 1991.

"Hey Lover," Grammy Award, Best Rap Solo Performance, 1997.

Selected Discography

Radio (Def Jam/Columbia), 1985.

Bigger and Deffer (Def Jam/Columbia), 1987

Walking with a Panther (Def Jam/Columbia), 1989. Double album.

Mama Said Knock You Out (Def Jam/Columbia), 1990.

14 Shots to the Dome (Def Jam/Columbia), 1993

Mr. Smith (Def Jam/Columbia),1996.

Further Reading

Freddy, Fab Five (Fred Brathwaite), "LL Cool J," *Interview*, December 1987.

Light, Alan, "Heavyweight: LL Cool J Throws a Perfect Combination of Raw Rap and Pure Pop," *Rolling Stone*, October 3, 1991.

Nelson, Havelock, "Rick Rubin: Def Jam's Man with the Plan," *Musician,* May 1987.

Toure, *14 Shots to the Dome* album review, *Rolling Stone,* May 13, 1993.

Weisel, Alan, "Q & A" interview column in *Rolling Stone,* June 27, 1996.

Contact Information

Def Jam
160 Varick St., 12th Fl.
New York, NY 10013-1220

Web Site

http://www.defjam.com/artists/llcoolj/
llcoolj.html

NAUGHTY BY NATURE

American rap group (East Coast and hardcore rap styles)
Formed in East Orange, New Jersey, in 1987 as The New Style

> "Treach is just a regular brother from around the way, rippin' the mike and doin' it because he loves his craft. [Treach] *is* hip-hop: in dress, in talk, in spirit."
>
> —music critic Kevin Powell, *Vibe*

Naughty by Nature achieved what few other rap groups have managed to do when their first single, "O.P.P.," reached the Top Ten on the pop chart. Although their music has "crossed over" and been accepted by mainstream music fans, Naughty by Nature hasn't varied much from its street-based hardcore style of rap over the course of releasing three albums. As Ed Lover, co-host of *Yo! MTV Raps*, described the group's lead rapper and unofficial head in *Vibe* magazine: "Treach is the first authentic hip-hopper I've seen in a long time.... Yeah, he wants to get his, like everybody else, but there's a sincerity there too. Look at him; you can see that he's had a hard life, and it comes out in his music. His hard-core ain't made-up; it's real."

Talent was evident at the high school talent show

Treach (Anthony Criss) and his Naughty colleagues, DJ Kay Gee (Kier Gist) and rapper Vinnie (Vincent Brown), have maintained their street credentials, in part by continuing to live and es-

Treach

Treach (Anthony Criss) and his Naughty colleagues, DJ Kay Gee (Kier Gist) and rapper Vinnie (Vincent Brown)

tablish their own businesses in the East Orange, New Jersey, neighborhood where they grew up. Treach and Vinnie both grew up in the 1970s in poor, single-parent homes just a few blocks apart. With his mother having to work, Treach later became a strong supporter of birth control and a strong family. He's often expressed his belief that his father's absence contributed to his years on the street.

In high school, Treach and Vinnie first collaborated in order to enliven a junior-year health class: whenever the class became unbearably dull, they would break into an improvised rap, Treach rapping and Vinnie providing the beat.

Friend Kay Gee, who was a year ahead of Treach and Vinnie in school, in the meantime had been polishing his skills as a DJ. When the senior talent show came up, Kay Gee asked his "homeboys" to perform with him. They walked away with the adulation of their audience.

Outside of school, the three friends made money at occasional jobs and from hanging out with their neighborhood gang in East Orange, the 118th Street Posse. That life offered some income, largely from the drug trade or other illegal sources, and plenty of risk: fights, shootings, and jail time. One time when Treach got in trouble, his mother wouldn't let

Members invested their profits

Naughty by Nature's instant stardom did not lead to the "fat" life that many associate with success in the music industry—testimony to the principles of the Naughty trio; all three reinvested their profits from the first album, pursuing a variety of business ventures. Naughty Gear, a line of merchandise renowned for its underwear sporting the band's logo, has taken off under Kay Gee's guidance. They also began their own label, Itown Records, and management company, 118th Management, in order to widen the market for rap. Kay Gee set up his own production company, 118th Productions, and subsequently produced "Hit Em Hard" for rap greats **Run-D.M.C** (see entry). After participating in the production of Naughty by Nature's videos, Treach began directing clips for other artists. And Naughty by Nature have insisted on reserving positions in their businesses for friends from the neighborhood—especially those finishing prison sentences—since they know firsthand the scarcity of legitimate, decent-paying jobs in the ghetto.

him come home, and he found himself out on the streets.

Motivated by their talent show success, the trio dubbed themselves the New Style and began performing locally. Rap music represented a chance to escape the dead end of the ghetto, and in 1988 the group released an independent record on a small label. When it didn't go anywhere, they turned to hustling drugs on the street to raise money for their music career. They were able to put enough money away within one year. As Treach explained to Tom Sinclair of *Spin,* "I did what I had to do on the street so I could get mine and not have to do it no more.... We didn't put our money into jewelry or cars or anything like that. We put it into studio time. And, once we got signed, we cut [drug dealing] out completely."

Queen Latifah helped secure a recording contract

After changing their name, Naughty by Nature sent out its new demo tape to every label that handled hip-hop—but none were interested until the group came to the attention of rapper **Queen Latifah** (see entry) and her management company, Flavor Unit. Mightily impressed, she signed Naughty by Nature to the Flavor Unit and secured them a deal with Warner Bros. for a debut album that was eventually released by rap label Tommy Boy.

Their self-titled debut album hit record stores in 1991; it had been preceded that June by the single "O.P.P." Driven by an irresistible sample of the Jackson Five's "ABC," the song did more than top the charts and sell two million copies; it entered into street slang across the country and inspired a variety of merchandise, including t-shirts and hats, that declared "Down Wit O.P.P." "O.P.P.," which stands for "Other People's Property," is a song about cheating on one's lover despite the best of intentions not to.

"Hip Hop Hooray"

When "Hip Hop Hooray," the lead single from Naughty by Nature's second album, *19 Naughty III*, was released in the spring of 1993, it became a sensation akin to "O.P.P." two years earlier. The song climbed to the Top Ten of the pop charts and was universally recognized as the hip-hop anthem of the summer. Although it did not have quite the video success of "O.P.P.," which had risen to Number One on *Yo! MTV Raps*, the "Hip Hop Hooray" video enjoyed the distinction of having been directed by Spike Lee, the filmmaker responsible for such films as *Do the Right Thing* and *Malcolm X*. *19 Naughty III* was as successful as the group's debut, selling more than two million copies and reaching number one on *Billboard*'s rhythm and blues chart.

Poverty's paradise

Critics for the most part continued their love affair with the group. *Spin*'s Tom Sinclair, for example, fondly noted Naughty by Nature's dedication to their music, explaining, "There's a zealousness in NBN's embrace of hip-hop as a musical form, a stance, a life-style that eclipses all else. They're lifers." He described them as "homies with heart, happy to have left behind the world of drug-dealing to bring their message of hope through hip-hop."

In 1995 Naughty by Nature released their third album, *Poverty's Paradise*. Writing in *Entertainment Weekly*, critic James Bernard gave the album an "A" rating. He found it "dominated by rollicking bass lines, chant-along choruses, and the catchy, tight rhyme schemes that are Naughty's trademark." Treach and Vinnie's reality-based lyrics made it seem "almost like being right on the street with them," according to *People Weekly*'s Jeremy Helligar.

Having used their success to boost local businesses in their hometown of East Orange, Naughty by Nature continued to send a message of hope to their less fortunate brothers and sisters. The group has remained close to its sources of inspiration, and in so doing has provided inspiration to those around them.

Selected Awards

American Music Award, Best New Rap Group, 1991.

Source Award, New Artist of the Year, 1991.

Poverty's Paradise, Grammy Award, Best Rap Album, 1996.

Selected Discography

Naughty by Nature (Tommy Boy), 1991.

19 Naughty III (Tommy Boy), 1993.

Poverty's Paradise (Tommy Boy), 1995.

Further Reading

Cohen, Rich, "The Hood, the Bad, and the Ugly," *Rolling Stone*, August 19, 1993, p. 66.

Coker, Cheo H., "Poverty's Paradise," *Rolling Stone*, June 15, 1995, p. 80.

Criss, Anthony, "Talking with Naughty by Nature's Treach," *People Weekly*, May 29, 1995, p. 22.

Helligar, Jeremy, "Poverty's Paradise," *People Weekly*, May 29, 1995, p. 22.

"Naughty by Nature Uses Success to Help Boost Business in N.J. Hometown," *Jet,* June 5, 1995, p. 38.

Spin, April 1993.

Vibe, fall 1992.

Contact Information

Tommy Boy Music
1747 First Ave.
New York, NY 10128

Web Sites

http://www.naughtybynature.com/

http://flavorunit.com/naughty.htm

THE notorious B.I.G.

American rap artist (East Coast, gangsta, and hardcore rap styles)

Born Christopher Wallace in Brooklyn, New York, May 21, 1972; died March 9, 1997, of gunshot wounds in Los Angeles, California

H e never expected to be a platinum-selling artist. Yet, that's just what happened to Christopher Wallace, "The Notorious B.I.G." Just when pundits were declaring East Coast hip-hop commercially dead, his *Ready to Die* (1994) and *Life after Death* (1997) albums forced listeners to rethink that notion.

In the end, however, not even Wallace's clear, commanding baritone—which freed him from a drug dealer's life in New York City's Bedford-Stuyvesant area—saved him from the bullets that cut his life short at age twenty-four. For himself, Wallace seemed almost to take that ending for granted, telling *Rolling Stone*: "Every true hustler knows that you cannot hustle forever."

The brief nature of Wallace's contributions hardly made them less powerful, as *Entertainment Weekly*'s David Browne commented on B.I.G.'s second, and final album *Life after Death,* with its unforgettable titles "Somebody's Gotta Die" and "You're Nobody (Til Somebody Kills You)." "Business as usual has never been so usual and unusual," Browne remarked, putting his finger right on the 300-pound hip-hopper's appeal.

"I had a master plan/I'm in a caravan/On my way to Maryland/With my man Two Techs/to take over these projects."–from the song "Everyday Struggle," on *Ready to Die* (1994)

Claimed he was "Ready to die"

Born in New York City's borough of Brooklyn, Wallace made a living selling crack cocaine on Fulton Avenue in his Bedford-Stuyvesant neighborhood. To residents, the street is known as "The Ave," and that's where Wallace became a fixture from the age of fifteen. He took his original pseudonym, "Biggie Smalls," from a hustling character in Bill Cosby's 1970s action comedy, *Let's Do it Again*. The film might well have suited Smalls' flashy lifestyle, he told *Rolling Stone*. But hooking up with DJ 50 Grand for some wild hip-hop sessions in Wallace's own basement convinced him a different future lay in store.

One of their tapes went to New York-based hip-hop magazine *The Source*'s "Unsigned Hype" column, which publicized unsigned rap artists, and to a projected compilation of the magazine's brightest prospects. The album never came out, but rap groups Back II Back, Common Sense, Mobb Deep, and Wallace—now calling himself The Notorious B.I.G.—wound up with record deals. Hip-hop promoter Sean "Puffy" Combs saw something in B.I.G.'s tape that merited an Uptown Records deal. While there, B.I.G. enjoyed underground attention with his "Party & [B.S.]" on Uptown's *Who's the Man?* soundtrack.

"Puffy helped a lot with the A & R [Artists & Repertoire]," B.I.G. recalled in his Internet profile. "It was a lot of stuff he made do over. He wasn't trying to rush nothing. He treated my album like an R & B [rhythm & blues] album."

However, when they finished that album, Uptown refused to accept it—so Combs started over with his own Bad Boy Entertainment label. Released in 1994, and produced by Easy Mo Bee, B.I.G.'s debut claimed he was *Ready to Die*.

Became center of East Coast/West Coast feud

All during his debut album's creation, B.I.G. kept on dealing drugs, "just risking my life every day on the street, you know what I'm saying?" he told *Rolling Stone*. That point-blank view of life surfaced on songs such as "Gimme the Loot," an account of his first stickup; "Everyday Struggle," which described a drug-selling expedition he attempted down South; and the closing track, "Suicidal Thoughts," on which the listener could hear gunshots following B.I.G.'s discussion with Combs of his own self-inflicted death.

Critical praise for B.I.G.'s effort was nearly unanimous. Not since rapper **Ice Cube's** (see entry) work "have hip-hop and cinema verite been combined so effectively," raved *Rolling Stone*'s Havelock Nelson, while Toure offered a somewhat more measured view in the *New York Times*. In her view, B.I.G. "is not the best vocalist among the recent crop of rap starts," but he stood out "because his lyrics mix autobiographical details about crime and violence with emotional honesty." The album went platinum instantly, selling one million copies.

Ready to Die also touched another nerve—namely, a feud between the East Coast hip-hop school, as represented by B.I.G. and Combs, and their chief West

Coast rivals, Death Row Records' **Tupac Shakur** (see entry) and chief executive Marion "Suge" Knight. The war of words escalated following a 1994 robbery attempt against Shakur in New York City. Severely wounded, Shakur blamed B.I.G., or Combs, for setting up the affair, which would only end with both men's violent shooting deaths some two years later.

Rivals exchanged "disses"

In 1995, B.I.G. celebrated winning *Billboard*'s Rap Artist of the Year Award for his single, "One More Chance"/"Stay with Me." *Entertainment Weekly*'s David Browne celebrated "One More Chance" for turning a "standard dis—stealing a rival's girl—into an excuse for clever, tongue-rolling rhymes." He had less admiration for its "penthouse-pad soul" and "cooing female backup singers," which were "far less distinctive than Biggie's throat."

West Coast rapper Shakur responded with his most vicious putdowns yet against B.I.G. On his double CD, *All Eyez on Me* (1996), Shakur attracted notoriety for a claim that he'd slept with B.I.G.'s wife, rhythm & blues singer Faith Evans. By that year, B.I.G. himself had built up his own police record. Early in the year, he pled guilty to criminal mischief and fourth-degree harassment, after allegedly chasing away fans with a baseball bat. In summer 1996, he was arrested after police found firearms and marijuana at his Teaneck, New Jersey, home. That fall, Brooklyn police charged B.I.G. with drug possession after they found him smoking marijuana in a parked car.

Notorious B.I.G. tribute single went platinum

Following B.I.G.'s death, Sean "Puffy" Combs and B.I.G.'s widow, R &B singer Faith Evans, released a tribute song, "I'll Be Missing You." The song, based on the melody to the Police's 1983 megahit "Every Beath You Take," sold over one million copies, and some reports called it the fastest-selling single in history. The song debuted on May 14, 1997, following a day-long vigil during which more than 200 radio stations held a moment of silence for the slain rapper. The video also received heavy airplay on MTV.

Police considered slaying "payback"

Fears about the cost of East and West Coast-related violence escalated with Tupac Shakur's September 13, 1996, death in Las Vegas, Nevada, following a "drive-by" shooting there. However, when leading hip-hop figures called "a summit" in Harlem after the slaying, B.I.G. remained notable for his absence.

In January 1997, B.I.G. made his final court appearance, after being ordered to pay $25,000. A man claimed that B.I.G. had beaten him over a canceled Camden, New Jersey, performance, following the artist's acquittal of robbery charges in the same incident. B.I.G.'s life ended on March 9, 1997, following a party held after the Soul Train Music Awards, in Los Angeles, California. According to witnesses, B.I.G. was shot by unknown men while sitting in his parked car; police counted five bullets in the passenger's front door.

"He died as he lived," belief ran

B.I.G.'s instant death made him the second high-profile "gangsta" slain in a six-month period. Once again, fear rose to new levels, as one insider told *Rolling Stone* afterwards: "It's a call for the East Coast rap labels to go to war, and that's really scary for us. And probably to them, too."

B.I.G.'s own feelings were apparent on the sprawling, 110-minute *Life after Death...'Til Death Do Us Part* album, completed just weeks before his murder. Its cover showed him next to a hearse, and the double-CD opened with Combs pleading against a heart monitor: "Damn, we was supposed to rule the world, baby. We was unstoppable. [This] can't be over. You got too much living to do." Tracks like "My Downfall" ("You wanna see me locked up, shot up/Mom's cracked up over my casket screaming") and "You're Nobody ('Til Somebody Kills You)" set the overwhelming tone and caused the greatest comment.

Writers like Browne found B.I.G.'s death doubly tragic, since his tone "is mellower and less in-your-face," he wrote, while *Rolling Stone's* Anthony De-Curtis wondered if such relentless realism meant to ask "when all this will end. Or when the shots will ring out again."

The attendance at B.I.G.'s April 7 funeral, held in New York City, amounted to a virutal short list of the hip-hop nation, including **Dr. Dre** (see entry);

DMC, of **Run-DMC** (see entry); Treach, of **Naughty by Nature** (see entry); Flavor Flav, of **Public Enemy** (see entry); Arista Records President Clive Davis, who'd distributed Bad Boy's product; and former mayor David Dinkins. Combs delivered the eulogy, while B.I.G.'s instrumental, "Miss U," ended the 350-person ceremony. Shaken by rumors of gang involvement with Bad Boy, Combs vigorously denied these charges. While vowing to change, Combs even promised to donate more profits to worthy community causes. "I'm building a legacy here," he said. "I'm not going to go down in history for some stupid gangster B.S. No way, man," he told the *Los Angeles Times*. Meanwhile, his top-selling artist's murder remained unsolved.

Selected Awards

Billboard Music Awards, 1) Rapper of the Year, and 2) Rap Single of the Year for "One More Chance," 1995.

"Hypnotize," Best Rap Video, MTV Video Music Award, 1997.

Selected Discography

Who's the Man? (Uptown), 1993. Soundtrack; B.I.G. contributed "Party & [B.S.]."

Ready to Die (Bad Boy/Arista), 1994.

Life after Death...'Til Death Do Us Part (Bad Boy/Arista), 1997.

Further Reading

Allen, Kyle, "Life after Death," Spin Online, April 1997.

Browne, David, "The Last B.I.G. Thing," *Entertainment Weekly*, April 15, 1997.

Browne, David, "One More Chance," *Entertainment Weekly,* August 18, 1995.

Coker, Cheo H., "Notorious B.I.G.: Ready to Die," *Rolling Stone,* November 3, 1994, p. 96.

DeCurtis, Anthony, "Life after Death," *Rolling Stone* online, April 1997.

Fernando, S. H., Jr., "The B.I.G. Payback: Notorious B.I.G. Is Living Large—The Legal Way," *Rolling Stone,* June 1, 1995, p. 24.

Haring, Bruce, "Bullet-Riddled Rap," *USA Today,* March 10, 1997, p. D1.

Hendrickson, Matt, "Notorious B.I.G., 1973 [sic]-1997," *Rolling Stone,* April 17, 1997, p. 29.

Michel, Sia, "The Notorious B.I.G.: Last Exit from Brooklyn," *Spin,* May 1997, p. 65.

Nelson, Havelock, "B.I.G.: Rap's Next Big Thing," *Interview,* November 1994, p. 82.

"Rappers Pay Last Respects to Notorious B.I.G. at Funeral Service in Manhattan," *Jet,* April 7, 1997.

Toure, "Biggie Smalls, Rap's Man of the Moment," *New York Times,* December 18, 1994, p. 42, section 2.

Web Sites

http://aristarec.com/big/

http://www.wallofsound.com/artists/thenotoriousbig/

PUBLIC ENEMY

American rap group
(East Coast, hardcore,
social/political consciousness styles)

Formed c. 1985 at Adelphi University,
Long Island, New York

"Rap should dare to be different and not [care] about the charts." –Chuck D

As hip-hop's most prominent socially and politically conscious group, Public Enemy have been subject to contradictions throughout the band's career. While striving to unite black youth against social and political wrongs, Public Enemy itself has come under fire for negative statements about Jewish people made in its songs and to the media. And, while often uncompromising in his lyrical urgency—"I'm interested in politics and social commentary, " Chuck D told the *Los Angeles Times*'s Robert Hilburn in 1988 —Public Enemy's militant imagery has often been dismissed as "radical chic," or just reckless, ill-considered rhetoric.

Few hip-hoppers, however, command as much respect as Public Enemy's leader, Chuck D, who makes a virtue of sticking by principle. He can lecture college audiences, or show an unexpectedly personal touch, such as dedicating *Muse Sick-N-Hour Mess Age* (1994) to basketball star Michael Jordan's slain father. "When he was killed," Chuck D told *Vibe*, "I felt [it] personally. You have a situation where the structure is teaching the young to disrespect the old." Chuck D and Public Enemy aim to show an alternative for

From left to right: Terminator X,
Flavor Flav, and Chuck D

black youth, a legacy of his mother, a 1960s activist who took him to study programs taught by former Black Panther members.

In the beginning came Griff

Public Enemy began in Long Island, where James Hank Boxley threw his first block party, in ninth grade. His friend, Richard Griffin, helped DJ, but hardly anyone came. One of the few attendees, Carlton Ridenhour, "told me I didn't understand the science of flyers," Boxley told *Spin*. "I didn't want to hear about it."

As the parties continued, Boxley became Shocklee, joined by Griffin—now Professor Griff, occasional MC and later the group's "Minister of Information"—and Ridenhour. Soon the trio formed a farther-reaching concept, Spectrum City sound system, to entertain students at Adelphi University. That year, Griff quit studying music to create an Islamic group, Unity Force, which became S1W (Security of the First World)—Public Enemy's own plastic Uzi-toting dancers and bodyguards.

In this militaristic spirit, Ridenhour became Chuck D, and designed the Public Enemy logo of a youth inside a sniper scope. (Not all fans know, but Chuck's degree came in graphic design.) "When we threw affairs," Chuck recalled for *Spin*, "Griff would have guys dressed up like Black Panthers or FOI [Fruit of Islam], with the berets. And never once did we have one incident."

The momentum picked up when Adelphi DJ Bill Stephney interviewed Chuck, who soon got his own three-hour show. Chuck puzzled listeners by giving his first ninety minutes to William Drayton, who'd become Public Enemy's second MC and comic foil, Flavor Flav (or "The Cold Lamper," "The Joker," "The Juice," and "Sparkplug").

"Bum Rushing" to success

Such madness had its methods, however. Chuck also used the show to air his home demos—because "there weren't enough rap records," Shocklee told *Rolling Stone*. "What we would do was program a beat and make up records on the radio. We didn't have any instruments, so we would use a turntable and scratch when the chorus came in."

When Flav warned that Chuck was losing his edge, he flung back "Public Enemy Number One," a warning that such gossip was misdirected: "It's you they never hire—you're never on flyers/'Cause you and your crew—is only known as good triers." Rick Rubin—who'd just signed a CBS deal to distribute his new hip-hop label, Def Jam—became interested when the song was Adelphi's most requested record.

But Chuck initially wouldn't return Rubin's calls, fearing himself too old to risk his marriage and promotional career to be an MC. Rubin's persistence eventually won him over, though, and Public Enemy's *Yo! Bum Rush the Show* (1987) moved 400,000 listeners to buy it.

From the start, Public Enemy established itself as different. Its debut struck a militant political tone on "Miuzi

Weighs A Ton," which declared, "It was war they wanted,/And war they got,/But they couldn't take the heat when my Uzi got hot!!" They courted controversy on "Sophisticated Bitch," which featured **Living Colour**'s (see entry) guitarist, Vernon Reid, and playfully jibed critics on "You're Gonna Get Yours."

Most importantly, Public Enemy made noise, and sound effects, a major part of its approach. A faster flow also let Chuck express his complex ideas more easily, since most hip-hop records "were doing 98 to 100 beats a minute," he told *Rolling Stone*. "We did 'Bring The Noise' at 109 beats a minute. At the time it was unheard of."

Anti-Semitic charges nearly derailed group

"Bring the Noise" showcased a harsher sound on *It Takes A Nation of Millions To Hold Us Back* (1988), Public Enemy's breakthrough. "Don't Believe the Hype," though, raised anti-Semitic concerns, as did Chuck's support for The Nation of Islam's black separatist minister, Louis Farrakhan. (Lines from speeches by Malcolm X and Louis Farrakhan can be heard in some of Public Enemy's songs.) Critics like the Jewish Anti-Defamation League felt they'd heard enough in 1989, when Griff (Public Enemy's Minister of Information) told the *Washington Post* that Jews were responsible "for the majority of wickedness that goes on around the world."

The resulting media furor exposed a split in Public Enemy. Despite 800,000 sales for *Nation of Millions,* an ill-advised contract had forced Chuck to support his wife and daughter doing temporary jobs between tours, while Griff became road manager and won a pay raise. When not disagreeing over those issues, the group found itself pounded with anonymous phone calls, boycott threats, and media debates over its intentions.

As a result of these pressures, Public Enemy asked Griff to leave the group, and he played his last gig in March 1990, at London's Brixton Academy, on the eve of the group's European tour. Griff later claimed Chuck had abandoned basic principles for success, something Public Enemy's leader refused to accept. "He went outside the group strategy, outside the pyramid," Chuck told *New Musical Express*'s Ian McCann.

Greatest hits (and misses)

Despite these distractions, Public Enemy kept busy, having contributed the anti-government anthem "Fight The Power" to *Do The Right Thing,* Spike Lee's controversial 1989 film on race relations. The next album, *Fear of a Black Planet* (1990), ignited more controversy with tracks such as "Meet The G That Killed Me," which Chuck claimed meant "girls," not "gays" in the AIDS era. "911 Is a Joke" hit at response to black-on-black crime; "Burn, Hollywood, Burn" and "Who Stole the Soul?" asked whether blacks owned their original culture.

But "Welcome to the Terrordome" attracted the most attention for its lyric about the group's media tiffs: "Apology made to whoever pleases / Still, they got me like Jesus." Jewish groups again complained, while Chuck referred them to the album's title. "Blacks see the problem of racism in America very clearly because they have to live it every day," he told the *Chicago Tribune's* Greg Kot.

Public Enemy kept up its heated pace for 1991, with six new tracks for its *Greatest Misses* compilation, and another platinum-selling album in *Apocalypse 91...The Enemy Strikes Back*. That album's best-known track, "By the Time I Get to Arizona," criticized the state for not accepting Martin Luther King's January 15th birthday as a state holiday. "Anybody who would listen to this kind of trash would not be beneficial to Arizona, or to any state," declared Governor Evan Mecham, who was later impeached. But 60 percent of MTV's viewers polled about the song's video considered it an effective protest.

The group also issued its second video compilation, *Tour of a Black Planet*, and completed an unsuccessful tour with Goth-rockers Sisters of Mercy, among others. On a more upbeat note, the group redid "Bring the Noise" with metallic band Anthrax, recording it in the studio and playing New York City's Madison Square Garden, "proving wrong those who predicted that the Public Enemy rappers would be booed off stage by this supposedly bigoted audience," wrote *New York Newsday's* Frank Owen.

The enemy struck back?

Public Enemy kept a low profile over the next few years, until Flav's November 1, 1993, arrest at his South Bronx apartment for attempted murder and illegal weapons charges. The following July, af-

ter completing a drug rehabiliation program, Flav was again arrested for 43 license suspensions—going back to 1989, police claimed—and fighting with the mother of his first three children.

Such problems, Flav claimed in *Vibe*, had only strengthened his own resolve. Any black man could fall prey to crack cocaine addiction, famous or not, he told Kevin Powell: "I was around the right people, but I hung out with the wrong people. I let them lead me into that." Despite those conflicts, work continued on the next Public Enemy album.

Released amid rumors of another split, Public Enemy's *Muse Sick-N-Hour Mess Age* (1994) drew raspberries from reviewers, who heard weak beats and few insights. To *Rolling Stone's* Toure, Chuck was not breaking new lyrical ground—even on "Hitler Day," which hit the racial hypocrisy of holidays like Thanksgiving, or "Living in the Zoo," which slammed the music industry.

Instead, Toure scolded Chuck for firing too many blanks against the press: "If you find a critic dead/Remember what I said/Who killed a critic/Guess the crew did it." "So, Chuck," she sarcastically responded, "does that mean that because your album is wack, I should fear for my life?" Leaving those questions unanswered, Public Enemy declined to tour behind *Muse Sick* in America, and traveled to Europe, where sales were better.

Breakup rumors persisted

Yet the group seemed unable to shake persistent breakup reports, which gathered steam after Flav broke both arms in Italy, following a motorcycle mishap. On returning home, Chuck blasted journalists for dismissing *Muse Sick*. "If you feel two or three [albums] are fantastic, why waste your time dissin' some [thing] you don't like?" he fumed to *Vibe*'s Kevin Powell. Powell responded that *Muse Sick* "is neither a great album nor as bad as some people make it out to be." The album's sixty-eight minutes needed something special to stand out, yet much of it "barely holds one's attention," he found. Chuck sidestepped such comments by saying, "They can dis PE all they want, 'cause it'll bounce off me."

Promoter and RCA executive Van Silk expressed no doubts about Chuck's ability to bounce back. "I don't think Chuck was angry," he told *Goldmine* in May 1996, "he was just telling it like it is. The kids think, 'Oh, ... Chuck's angry.' Is Martin Luther King angry when he was trying to tell you something?"

Chuck slams back into spotlight

Chuck D returned in fall 1996 with his own label, Slam Jamz. With Sony Music's support, Chuck wished to record artists who might not fit "gangsta" formulas being exploited by "Big Willie," Chuck's metaphor for black executives profiting off the so-called "gangsta" rappers they created. Instead, Slam Jamz would use singles and EPs to showcase genuinely radical hip-hoppers, he told *Rolling Stone*'s Matt Diehl. Rather than spending $800,000 on a video, he promised to "go underneath [that scene]

and have anti-stars." Thus, the hockey mask-wearing Hyenas in the Desert— who mixed hip-hop and industrial beats—became Slam Jamz's debut release.

That same year saw Chuck's solo debut, *The Autobiography of Mistachuck*, which began with dialogue from Spike Lee's *Clockers* ("clockers" referred to street drug dealers), in which street kids wondered if Chuck had anything to say. He responded with "Mistachuck," a "State of the Hip-hop Union address," as *Rolling Stone*'s Anthony DeCurtis described it. Wherever Chuck glared, DeCurtis noted, he found much to fault, whether in the gangstas of "Generation Wrekked," the junkies of "Horizontal Heroin," or blacks ignoring their roots. DeCurtis raised the same criticisms of *Mistachuck* that had dogged *Muse Sick*. For example, he said that even *Mistachuck*'s better tracks, like "Talk Show (Created the Fool)," had been addressed more creatively on Public Enemy's "She Watch Channel Zero." That said, "It's time for this 'incredible rhyme animal' to go on a fresh hunt," DeCurtis suggested.

But Chuck remained undaunted, touring persistently with Public Enemy, who promised a forthcoming 1997 album tentatively titled *Afraid of the Dark*. "The way Chuck views rap music is that it's global," Slam Jamz general manager Phil Nelson said to *Goldmine*. "It's natural that PE got accepted internationally. They toured in thirty-eight countries. He did that for a reason, to establish rap on the international level." As Chuck has previously stated, he wants nothing less than a hip-hop Motown, including a clothing line (Rapp Style), Internet site, and talk show. He's even discussed forming a community foundation that would reach out to the same youth who found inspiration in the track that started it all: "Known as the poetic lyrical son/I'm public enemy number one."

Selected Awards

It Takes a Nation of Millions To Hold Us Back certified platinum, 1988.

Fear of a Black Planet certified platinum, 1990.

Rolling Stone Readers' Picks, Best Rap Group, 1991.

Apocalypse 91...The Enemy Strikes Back certified platinum.

Apocalypse 91...The Enemy Strikes Back, Soul Train Music Award for Best Rap Album, 1992.

Greatest Misses certified gold, 1992.

Yo! Bum Rush the Show certified gold, 1994.

Muse Sick-N-Hour Mess Age certified gold, 1994.

Selected Discography

Yo! Bum Rush the Show (Def Jam/Columbia), 1987.

It Takes a Nation of Millions to Hold Us Back (Def Jam/Columbia), 1988.

Fear of a Black Planet (Def Jam/Columbia), 1990.

Apocalypse 91...The Enemy Strikes Back (Def Jam/Columbia), 1991.

Greatest Misses (Def Jam/Columbia), 1992.

Muse Sick-N-Hour Mess Age (Def Jam/Columbia), 1994.

Selected Home Videos:

Fight The Power (Sony Music Video), 1989.

Tour of a Black Planet (Sony Music Video), 1991.

The Enemy Strikes...Live (Sony Music Video), 1992.

Selected Solo Albums:

As by Professor Griff (and the Last Asiatic Disciples), *Pawns in a Game* (Skyywalker Records), 1990.

As by Professor Griff, *The X Minista* (Def Jam/Columbia), 1993.

As by Flavor Flav, *Flavor Flav* (Def Jam/Columbia), 1993.

As by Terminator X, *In the Valley of the Jeep Beats* (Def Jam/Columbia), 1993.

As by Chuck D, *The Autobiography of Mistachuck* (Mercury Records), 1996.

Further Reading

Cole, Lewis, "Def or Dumb?," *Rolling Stone,* October 19, 1989.

DeCurtis, Anthony, "The Autobiography of Mistachuck," *Rolling Stone,* October 3, 1996.

Diehl, Matt, "Chuck D Is Back with More Agendas Than Ever," *Rolling Stone,* October 17, 1996.

Heibutzki, Ralph, "Time Enough for the Old School: The Hip-hop Revolution, 1970-1990," *Goldmine,* May 1996.

Hewitt, Paolo, "PE's Griff in New Jew Storm," *New Musical Express,* March 31, 1990.

Hilburn, Robert, "Public Enemy's Chuck D: Puttin' On the Rap," *Los Angeles Times,* Feburary 7, 1988.

Kot, Greg, "A+ for Chuck D: Public Enemy Is a Textbook for Race Relations," *Chicago Tribune,* June 9, 1990.

Leland, John, "Do the Right Thing," *Spin,* June 1989.

Toure, "Bust This," *Rolling Stone,* July 14-28, 1994.

Contact Information

Def Jam
160 Varick St., 12th Fl.
New York, NY 10013-1220

Web Site

http://www.defjam.com/artists/

QUEEN LATIFAH

American rap artist
(East Coast and rhythm and blues-flavored rap styles)
Born Dana Owens in Newark, New Jersey, on March 18, 1970

Dana Owens' stage name means "delicate and sensitive" in Arabic, but fans see something else behind it—a shrewd businesswoman and role model with a penchant for African-style clothing and speaking her mind. While hip-hop has often seemed like a "boys' club," Latifah has done things her own way, and sold records, too.

This means leading by example. On her debut, she only allowed two of fifteen tracks to be co-mixed and produced, despite a wealth of collaborators in **Boogie Down Productions'** (see entry) KRS-One and Stetsasonic's Daddy-O. Yet Latifah declines to be called a feminist, fearing it's a limited label. She even supports artists like Two Live Crew, well-documented for poor attitudes on women, on First Amendment free speech grounds.

Most importantly, said *Mother Jones's* Dominique DiPrima, Queen Latifah "teaches female pride without preaching ... she is the Queen, never the victim." Armed with a formidable wit and track record, Latifah encourages black females to think, and

"Me, MC Lyte, Roxanne Shante, we got record deals because we're good, we deserve them, not because we're women." –Queen Latifah

speak, for themselves. Her run as self-styled "hip-hopreneur" of Flavor Unit Records and Management aims to achieve that goal by "controlling the dollars," she told *Essence*.

Early start proved invaluable

Born in Newark, New Jersey, on March 18, 1970, everything in Dana's past signaled a head start—even her stage name, given by father Lance Owens at age eight. Latifah did not add the "Queen" until later in her teens; it was meant, she said, to salute long-forgotten African-American royalty.

A policeman's daughter, she showed an early performing flair, appearing in her second grade production of *The Wizard of Oz*. At sixteen, she split time between working at the local Burger King and performing as the "human beatbox" for Ladies Fresh, an all-female trio who took after The Fat Boys.

But Latifah expressed more serious ambitions, feeling that hip-hop was often closed to women. To fix such problems, she reasoned, a major record deal would be necessary. Latifah made that vow good when she signed with Tommy Boy Records, aged just seventeen, after giving *Yo! MTV Raps* host Fab Five Freddy (Fred Brathwaite) a tape.

This meant postponing journalism studies at Manhattan Community College—and issuing her explosive debut, *All Hail the Queen*. Backed by a variety of house, jazz, reggae, and vocal choruses, Latifah proved herself an able and compelling performer, winning attention for

her "Ladies First" duet with British colleague MC Lyte. It reached number six on *Billboard*'s R & B (rhythm and blues) charts, while *All Hail the Queen* sold 400,000 copies.

Style matured on second album

Sprinkled with tongue-in-cheek "royalty" raps like the title track, or "Dance with Me," *All Hail the Queen* (1989) also pushed Latifah into a swelling female pack. While few old school hip-hoppers beyond The Funky Four Plus One's Sha-Roc—and all-female Sugar Hill trio Sequence—had grabbed the 1970s spotlight, the 1980s climate had changed.

Latifah now found herself joined by MC Lyte, Monie Love, **Salt-N-Pepa** (see entry), and **Ice Cube's** (see entry) partner, Yo-Yo—among the better-known competition. Thus, Latifah felt a special obligation to issue strong messages against casual sex, drugs, racism, and violence, as she recalled her mother's struggle to escape a Newark housing project. Following a one-off remix of "Fame" with rocker **David Bowie** (see entry), Latifah put her concerns at the forefront of 1991's *Nature of a Sista*.

The album showed Latifah developing her celebrated vocal skills—which had once included opera—into "How Do I Love Thee," "'Nuff of the Ruff Stuff," and "Fly Girl," among other tracks. She also employed live musicians, as opposed to hip-hop's normal dependence on sampling. On the whole, *Nature of a Sista* hoped "to weave subtle messages into every song instead of confining social comments to a few tracks," *Rolling Stone*'s Alan Light wrote.

> **"I have been extremely lucky in my life to have strong models, like my mother, helping me developing a strong sense of self-worth."**

Not everyone bought into the album. Where Light had found *Nature of a Sista*'s title track "more commercial and more accessible," *Rolling Stone*'s Diane Cardwell felt Latifah's lyrical axe could use some sorely-needed sharpening: "'Love Again' doesn't say much more than racism is a bad thing, and 'Give Me Your Love' is just another love song."

Broadened into acting

Such comments suggested a broader approach was necessary, one now coexisting with an acting career. The latter work began with a small role as a racist waitress in Spike Lee's *Jungle Fever* (1991). Other parts followed in *House Party 2* (1992), *Juice* (1992), the hip-hop comedy *Who's the Man?*, and *My Life*, with Michael Keaton.

These roles came as a welcome relief after *Nature of a Sista*'s failure to make a commercial dent in hip-hop—whose audiences reacted to its R & B "cross-over" production. Latifah's biggest breakthrough came in 1992, when she landed the role of magazine editor Khadijah Jones in Fox TV's smash series, *Living Single*. The sitcom centered on the struggles of Latifah and three friends to make it in New York City.

Described as a "black forerunner of *Friends*," Latifah had "made the leap from the counterculture fringe into the mainstream of television stardom," in the *New York Times*'s opinion. "In the past," agreed Steve Pond of *TV Guide*, "Latifah played angry young women, but now she is trying to balance that anger with hopefulness."

By showing young blacks as lawyers and business people, Latifah hoped to change audiences who had no trouble packing her gigs. "This is a business where you sell off your talent," she told *Mother Jones*'s Lisa Kennedy, "and to me the proof is usually at the show. There is no double standard with your fans."

Tragedy struck in 1992 when Latifah's older brother, Lance, Jr.—a policeman like his father —died in a motorcycle accident. She poured her grief into *Black Reign* (1993), which would become her biggest-ever album with sales topping one million copies. She featured more singing than before, paying tribute to her brother in "Winki's Theme." Better yet, the single "Unity" won Latifah her first Grammy Award for Best Rap Solo Performance.

Worked on becoming CEO, author

That same year, in 1993, Latifah added "CEO" (Chief Executive Officer) and manager to her ever-growing job description. With her mother installed as vice-president, Flavor Unit Records/Management unveiled a compilation, *Roll Wit This Flava*, to start off. **Naughty by Nature**'s (see entry) Treach was its biggest name among Flavor Unit's seventeen signings.

In 1995, tragedy struck again when a July night in Harlem degenerated into a carjacking nightmare. Two men stopped Latifah's BMW and shot friend Shawn Moon in the chest. Moon eventually recovered, and Latifah picked out the two assailants from a police lineup, sending them to prison. Suitably scared, Latifah found herself packing a handgun—which earned her a bust in Los Angeles, following a stop for speeding. She paid a small fine.

Latifah continued acting, playing a lesbian bank robber in 1996's *Set It Off*, and continuing her long-running success on *Living Single*. In the summer of 1997, William Morrow announced its intention to publish her book, *From the Heart of a Queen,* which would zero in on self-esteem issues, Latifah said: "I have been extremely lucky in my life to have strong models, like my mother, helping me developing a strong sense of self-worth."

Selected Awards

"Latifah's Had It Up to Here," Grammy Awards Nomination, Best Rap Solo Performance, 1993.

"Unity," Grammy Award, Best Rap Solo Performance, 1995.

Selected Discography

All Hail the Queen (Tommy Boy Records), 1989.

Nature of a Sista (Tommy Boy Records), 1991.

Black Reign (Motown Records), 1993.

Other Recordings

"Fame" single remix, with David Bowie (EMI Records), 1990.

Further Reading

Cardwell, Diane, *Nature of a Sista, Rolling Stone,* October 31, 1991, p. 92.

"Get Out or You're Dead," *People Weekly,* July 31, 1995, p. 50.

Gregory, Deborah, "The Queen Rules," *Essence,* October 1993, p. 56.

Gregory, Deborah, "Girlz 'N' The Hood: Watch Out! Four Sisters are 'Setting It Off' on the Big Screen," *Essence,* October 1996, p. 56.

Gliatto, Tom, "Loss of a Brother," *People Weekly,* November 29, 1993, p. 73.

Light, Alan, "Queen Latifah, *(All Hail the Queen),*" *Rolling Stone,* February 22, 1990.

Light, Alan, "Queen Latifah's New Gambit," *Rolling Stone,* October 17, 1991.

Meisler, Andy, "The Ever-Expanding Role of Queen Latifah," *New York Times,* January 9, 1994, p. 29 (Section 2).

Pond, Steve, "Hail to the Queen," *TV Guide,* October 16-22, 1993, p. 23.

Webb, Veronica, "The Lady Won't Be Restricted," *Interview,* November 1996.

Contact Information

Flavor Unit
155 Morgan Street
Jersey City, NJ 07302-2932

Web Sites

http://www.lifetimetv.com/tv/Intimate/queen.html

http://www.motown.com/motown/artists/Queen_Latifah/QL_M.html

RUN-DMC

American rap group
(East Coast, hardcore, rap/soul styles)

Formed 1982 in Queens, New York

Fifteen years after exploding from their original Queens stomping grounds, Run-DMC remain a vital reminder of hip-hop's roots. They're also one of the genre's most entertaining paradoxes. At various times, Run-DMC have been rap orators confessing to addictions; upbeat lyricists whose songs frequently carry brash, violent overtones; and uncompromising artists who've captured black and white audiences' affections. At times, these contradictions have cost Run-DMC their credibility. When their *Raising Hell* album hit number three on the 1986 pop charts and sold three million copies, violence marred several tour dates. The resulting fallout ignited one of the earliest backlashes against hip-hop.

When Run-DMC tried to broaden its appeal through its own film, *Tougher Than Leather* (1988), critics dismissed the results as bad, 1970s "blaxploitation" fare. And later, when the group's sales began to fall, critics began writing Run-DMC's obituary—until their return on *Down with the King* (1993), which made references to their new-found Christianity. Despite those setbacks—which

> "We're not scary. Kids look up to us and we give them something good to look up to. I'm a great guy. I went to school. I don't do drugs. So it's no problem for me to be a role model." –Run (Joseph Simmons), *New York Talk*, 1986

included admissions to dabbling with alcohol and marijuana during their "down time"—Run-DMC's peers were forgiving, since nobody could overlook their influence. "They've learned a lot," rap group A Tribe Called Quest's Q-Tip told *Rolling Stone*. "They made mistakes—just like we all do. I'm proud of them, because once again the black man is triumphant."

"We were dealing with Christian principles before, we just didn't have the whole thing," said Run. Run and DMC can often be found on Sundays at Zoe Baptist Ministry, a nondenominational church where they may even perform "Down with the King" as part of the service.

It all seems a lifetime away from the mid-1980s, when Run-DMC traded B-boy (Break-boy, referring to the use of breaks in rap music) boasts with Aerosmith's leering, skinny vocalist Steven Tyler for a brassy, sassy remake of the latter's "Walk This Way." Yet, when the group performs for today's crew, "It's like they never went away," said *Rolling Stone*'s Matt Diehl of a February 24, 1997, Madison Square Garden gig. "Don't call it a comeback," he concluded, "until you see it for yourself."

Group had middle-class origins

Despite Run-DMC's hardened "street" image of black, "gangster"-style hats, dungarees, and sneakers, Joseph "Run" Simmons, Darryl "DMC" McDaniel, and Jason "Jam Master Jay" Mizell, grew up in Hollis, a middle-class section of Queens, New York. Simmons made the earliest entry into the music business through his older brother, Russell, a promoter of early pioneers like Kurtis Blow and Grandmaster Flash and The Furious Five.

Run found himself particularly taken with Blow, whom his older brother also managed through his company, Rush Productions. As Blow told *Goldmine* in 1996, Russell "taught him [Run] how to rap, and he became my DJ, and we called him 'Son of Kurtis Blow.'" But a broken arm halted Run, then all of sixteen, from accompanying Blow, who was then supporting R & B/soul group The Commodores on tour.

Despite this glamorous introduction to the music business, Run's father, Daniel—a New York Board of Education employee—insisted his son finish high school, and get a "real" job. (In fact, some sources attribute this lifestyle to Joey's nickname—because he had to "run" home early from any party.)

Run-DMC formed in college

With those expectations, Run enrolled at LaGuardia Community College for mortuary science, where a new rap occurred to him while studying a cadaver in class: "One thing I know is that life is short, / so listen up, home boy, and give this a thought / The next time someone's teaching, why don't you get taught / It's like that, / and that's the way it is."

Simmons showed these lines to childhood friend Darryl McDaniel (DMC), himself a St. John's University student, and their first extended rap, "It's

Early fans identified with Run-DMC's "new school" look, in their sneakers and t-shirts

Like That," sold 250,000 copies for a new independent label, Profile, in 1983. Their next, "Hard Times," was equally successful, convincing the pair—now accompanied by Mizell (Jam Master Jay) as onstage DJ—to adopt their "street-tough" image. The group's name, Run-DMC, came from combining Joey's and McDaniel's nicknames.

Run-DMC were well-timed for success, as RCA executive and promoter Van Silk said in *Goldmine*: "The door was already open for the crossover market, but the Sugarhill artists were more into their outfits. Run came out with sneakers and dungarees: 'I'm like you, I'm from a neighborhood like yours.'"

Hip-hop publicist Bill Adler took that logic one step further, noting Run-DMC essentially ended Sugar Hill Records's dominance of hip-hop: "They were self-consciously 'new school,' which was how the old school felt: 'Who are these interlopers from Queens?' [Who needs them?] It came in their attitude."

"That's a lot of the appeal," Russell Simmons told *New York*'s Peter Blauner in 1986. "It's not for the Bill Cosbys. People talk about how there aren't black role models around, but what they mean is there aren't enough white black people on television. Rap groups like Run-DMC aren't like that."

Group rocked into big leagues

In Profile Records, Run-DMC had a white rock and roll label whose owners had jumped into hip-hop as something new and fresh. Goosed along by the rapid-fire guitar stutter of ace sessioneer Eddie Martinez, *Run-DMC* (1984) showcased their crunchy, early singles ("Hard Times," "Rock Box") and became the first gold record by a hip-hop group.

Run-DMC's early hints of rock-oriented influence exploded on their second album, *King of Rock* (1985), which took more chances. The group collaborated with Jamaican reggae artist Yellowman on "Roots, Rap, Reggae," and explored the boundaries of white noise in "Rock the House"'s mixture of beats. Martinez's guitar powered the thundering title track, which bragged, "I'm the king of rock, there is none higher / To break my kingdom you must use fire / I won't stop rockin' till I retire!"

The group also won praise for its takes on daily life, like "It's Not Funny"'s catalogue of letdowns, and "You Talk Too Much"—whose subject "told the cavity creeps / To watch out for Crest." *King of Rock* achieved another first, when it became hip-hop's first platinum album in 1987.

With *Raising Hell* (1986), however, Run-DMC entered a new, multiplatinum level. They became the first hip-hop group with an album that sold three million copies. Its chances were undeniably aided by remaking "Walk This Way" with Aerosmith's vocalist Steven Tyler and guitarist Joe Perry, in a salute to Run-DMC's roots. The album was also the first rap album to top *Billboard*'s R & B (rhythm & blues) chart, and the first rap album to make the U.S. Top Ten.

After all, Run had once rapped over the original's guitar breaks as a twelve-year-old, back in 1976—and was hardly the only one, as he reminded *Rolling Stone*: "There were lots of hip-hoppers rapping over rock when I was a kid." While some hip-hop purists felt Run-DMC went "soft" to get airplay, insiders like Silk felt differently: "If that record was a drug, they could not say 'no.' That was a hell of a collaboration."

Album raises trouble

Raising Hell's other tracks weren't slight, either. "It's Tricky" talked about the perils of fame, where people "even bother my poor father, / 'cause we're on TV." "My Adidas" hailed the group's deal with the sneaker maker, while "You Be Illin'" mocked drug abuse. As far as the critics were concerned, Run-DMC had arrived, proving hip-hop's longevity as an art form.

"There were lots of hip-hoppers rapping over rock when I was a kid."

The resulting 1986 tour, however, proved more problematic, as violence broke out at several stops, including Long Beach Arena, California, where rival gangs—hiding their "colors" under tracksuits like Run-DMC wore—slugged it out, injuring forty-two people. Run-DMC never made it onstage, and they drew fire from music conservatives like

Tipper Gore, who claimed the group's music "says it's okay to beat people up."

As *New York Talk* described it, Run-DMC's *Raising Hell* tour had become "the all-hell-breaks-loose" tour—and forced the group into calling a press conference to defend themselves. Run—a family man, like his colleagues—took pains to criticize the violence.

"The broke crackheads can make money if they come out and beat up on my little fan who's got $30 in his pocket because he wants a Run-D.M.C. T-shirt or a booklet," he told *Newsweek,* "which leaves me hurt. They come to make money. They come to fight. They're scum." He also found the press scrutiny unfair, especially when reporters overlooked similar disturbances at heavy metal gigs.

The group rebounded with an album and a film, both titled *Tougher Than Leather* (1988). However, the film—hyped as a cross between *48 Hours* and *Rambo* and involving a plot of violent revenge—did not find box office favor. The accompanying album was more accepted. It included a reworking of the Temptations' "Papa Was a Rolling Stone" in "Papa Crazy," and continued *Raising Hell's* rock-influenced leanings overall. Comic actor Dana Carvey made an offbeat cameo appearance in the group's video, "Mary Mary," which aired on MTV.

Group experienced leaner years

Run-DMC found itself experiencing some leaner years in the late 1980s—because a leaner, meaner, and faster sound had emerged, with a harder, more up-front social consciousness. Groups like **Public Enemy** (see entry)—whose frontman, Chuck D, often described himself as a Run-DMC admirer—and KRS-One's **Boogie Down Productions** (see entry) led the charge. In their fans' eyes, Run-DMC had become "old school" overnight, and therefore, old hat.

The group also encountered business problems when it attempted to break its Profile contract. Their efforts failed, dooming the next album, *Back from Hell* (1990), which still remains a cult favorite among Run-DMC fans. In tracks like "What It's All About," "Kick the Frama Lama Lama," and "Word Is Born," Run-DMC found themselves meeting old and new styles halfway—without sacrificing their trademark down-to-earth fan appeal.

Run made that goal plain to the *Village Noize* fanzine, accusing MC **Hammer** (see entry) of making it on their backs: "In his first ['Let's Get It Started'] video he stepped on D's [DMC] hat and pushed around guys with gold chains. To get into the business he dissed us. He knows it. He can't say nothing."

Hoping *Back from Hell* would hit the Number One slot for black and pop music charts, Run thought the group could still reach across all levels, for one simple reason: "You don't know [anything] about Hammer. With a $90,000 outfit, he ain't like your main man."

Back with a new look

With the exception of *Together Forever: Greatest Hits* (1991)—which gathered all of Run-DMC's biggest-known gems—fans heard little from the group, though Mizell had expanded into production for new rap groups The Afros and Onyx. In 1993, however, Run-DMC broke its silence on *Down with the King,* an album intended to showcase their newfound Christian beliefs—and a new image, too.

Gone were the black hats, gold chains, and dungarees of old; in came shaved heads, black jail suits, and Timberland boots. DMC had even surrendered his trademark "owl" glasses, because they'd gotten "too big for my face," as he told *Rolling Stone's* Toure. Run and DMC confessed to substance abuse and bouts with depression, which they put down to their recent failures. (Mizell, on the other hand, expressed no overt Christian beliefs, but claimed he'd "always been into God.")

When "Down with the King" became Run-DMC's biggest single in years—debuting at Numbers One and Seven, respectively, on *Billboard's* R & B and pop charts—Run-DMC wasted no time attributing its success to their new-found faith. "We believe and know that's why we're back," Run told Toure. "He [God] guided us to be large this time around."

A measure of Run-DMC's long-standing respect came from all the producers recruited to help *Down with the King,* including rap group EPMD; KayGee, of **Naughty by Nature** (see entry); A Tribe Called Quest's Q-Tip; Pete Rock; and, of course, Public Enemy's Chuck D, who supervised "3 in the Head," and "Ooh, Whatcha Gonna Do."

"I didn't do any actual producing. If anything," Chuck claimed, "I was a cheerleader, a fan. They were the group that made me feel like rap was worth building a career on as an artist." These sentiments have been seconded by many—such as they were in an April 22, 1997, advance concert write-up in the University of Iowa's paper, the *Iowan.* Comparing Run-DMC to the Beatles in terms of impact, Brian Sutherland had no trouble explaining why: "My friends and I knew every line of the *Raisin' [sic] Hell* album. So it is with nostalgia, as well as the anticipation of seeing walking rap history, that I await the coming show."

Rolling Stone's Matt Diehl, catching Run-DMC at New York City's Madison Square Garden in 1997, more than agreed: "Run-DMC rely solely on beats, lyric skills and showmanship, something sorely lacking in today's hip-hop." In his eyes, when the group "exhorted the crowd to 'put your hands up in the air [if] you love old school,' Run-DMC reveled in the past only to sound curiously present."

While the group has recorded only sporadically in recent years, Jay has little trouble defining their goals, fifteen years after their humble start in Hollis. "We gotta do this for another ten or twenty years," he told *Rolling Stone.* "We gotta be Michael Jackson, Stevie Wonder. What I got to prove is longevity. Rap is here to stay."

Selected Awards

Run-DMC, certified gold, 1984.

Raising Hell, certified gold and platinum, 1986; certified triple platinum, 1987.

King of Rock, certified platinum, 1987.

Parents Aren't Supposed to Like It

Soul Train Music Awards: 1) Best Rap Single and 2) Best Rap Album, 1987.

Tougher Than Leather, certified platinum, 1988.

Down with the King, certified gold, 1993.

Selected Discography

Run-DMC (Profile), 1984.

King of Rock (Profile), 1985.

Raising Hell (Profile), 1986.

Tougher Than Leather (Profile), 1988.

Back from Hell (Profile), 1990.

Together Forever: Greatest Hits 1983-1991 (Profile), 1991.

Down with the King (Profile), 1993.

Further Reading

Blauner, Peter, "Run-DMC," *New York,* November 17, 1986.

Diehl, Matt, "Run-DMC Concert Review," *Rolling Stone,* April 17, 1997.

Heibutzki, Ralph, "Time Enough for the Old School: The Hip-hop Revolution, 1970-1990," *Goldmine,* May 1996.

Newsweek, September 1, 1986.

Sutherland, Brian, "Run-DMC Is a Reminder of Rap's Great Beginning," *The Iowan,* University of Iowa, April 22, 1997.

Toure, "Run-DMC: Back on the Throne," *Rolling Stone,* July 8-22, 1993.

Wielander, Eric, "Raisin' Hell, Back from Hell, What the Hell?" *Village Noize* fanzine, issue #11, circa 1990.

Contact Information

Profile Entertainment, Inc.
740 Broadway, 7th Fl.
New York, NY 10003

Web Site

www.users.interport.net/~tjbeat/code/rd main.html.

Salt -N- Pepa

American female rap group
(East Coast, pop, and rhythm and
blues-flavored rap styles)

Formed 1985 in Queens,
New York City

"We don't do hard-
core rap music,
because not
everyone understands that.
We're not just out to please
our own crowd. Rap is for
everyone." –Salt-N-Pepa

Salt (Cheryl James, born March 28, 1968), Pepa (Sandy Denton, born November 9, 1969), and DJ Spinderella (Deidra "Dee Dee" Roper, born August 3, 1971) are members of the first female rap group to cross over to the *Billboard* Pop Chart with the gold single "Push It" from their first album, *Hot, Cool & Vicious* (1986), which went platinum for selling over one million copies two years later. Regarded as something of a phenomenon in the record industry, Salt-N-Pepa put women in the forefront of male-dominated rap music with the critically and financially successful, "Push It."

Salt-N-Pepa call their particular brand of street poetry, "pop-rap." Combining elements of pop, rhythm & blues (R&B), disco, rap, and other musical styles in their (for the most part) sexy songs, the group went on to become one of the most popular female rap groups of the 1990s. Their 1993 album, *Very Necessary*, yielded two Top Ten hits in "Shoop" and "Whatta Man" (recorded with **En Vogue** [see entry]) and the Grammy-winning "None of Your Business." The album went on to sell more than five million copies.

Rap queens came from Queens

James and Denton grew up in the middle-class, urban environment of Queens, New York, one of the five boroughs of New York City. In 1985, the duo attended Queens Borough Community College, where one was in nursing, the other in liberal arts. Not long afterwards, they both took jobs as telephone customer-service representatives for Sears Roebuck, where they met fellow employee Hurby "Luvbug" Azor, a student at New York City's Center for the Media Arts. When he needed to make a record to fulfill a class assignment, he asked James and Denton to record a number to "answer" a big hit rap single at the time, "The Show" by rappers Doug E. Fresh and Slick Rick. Azor called the girls' group Supernature and their recording "The Showstopper." When the single was pressed and released by Pop Art Records in October 1985, it quickly sold over 250,000 copies. When record label Next Plateau Records, Inc., took notice of Azor and the group, James and Denton decided to quit their telephone sales jobs at Sears. They launched a new career under the name of Salt-N-Pepa, a phrase taken from a line in "The Showstopper."

Hot, cool, and vicious

The group's first album, *Hot, Cool & Vicious,* was released in 1986. In addition to "The Showstopper," the album contains "I'll Take Your Man," the single "My Mike Sounds Nice," a cover of the Otis Redding/Carla Thomas hit "Tramp," and the group's first Top Forty hit, "Push It." "Push It" was orignally the B-side to "Tramp," but when DJs started featuring it in their shows, it became a crossover hit for the group (with help from a sexy performance video) and made them the leading female rap group of the time.

Hot, Cool & Vicious was recorded with the "first" Spinderella, Latoya Hanson, who was replaced by Dee Dee Roper in 1987. Hanson lost the use of the name "Spinderella" and later worked as a solo artist under the name, "The Original." Roper was still in high school when she auditioned and won a spot with Salt-N-Pepa for their 1987 tour. At this time, Salt-N-Pepa's live performances found them wearing black spandex body suits under oversize leather jackets, and choreographed dance routines accompanied each song.

Salt with a deadly Pepa

With Hurby "Luvbug" Azor writing and producing most of their material at this point, Salt-N-Pepa went back to the studios to record their second album, *A Salt with a Deadly Pepa,* in 1988. Although the album was a rushed affair, it sold over 500,000 copies to earn gold certification. *Rolling Stone* wrote, "There's nothing as galvanizing as 'Push It' on S & P's new album, but Cheryl James, Sandy Denton, and Dee Dee Roper remain fixed on kicking rap in the pants.... In the best rap tradition, Salt-N-Pepa balance humor, arrogance and practicality." Songs on the album included a new version of the Isley Brothers R&B classic "Twist and Shout," "Shake Your Thang" (a rewrite of another Isley Brothers R&B classic "It's Your Thing"), and "Everybody Get Up."

Salt-N-Pepa helped put women in the forefront of male-dominated rap music

Add a dash of magic

With their producer busy with other projects, Salt-N-Pepa began taking more control of their music. For their third album, 1990's *Blacks' Magic,* Salt produced three songs and co-produced a fourth, Spinderella co-produced one, and all three worked on the songwriting.

Several songs on the album were devoted to the themes of self-reliance, independence, and female pride. Singles from the album included Salt's productions of "Expression" and the follow-up "Independent." Those two songs opened and closed the album, projecting images of black pride and the strong female.

But it was "Do You Want Me" that gave the group its next Top Forty hit. Telling listeners to slow down and get to know somebody before committing to sex, the song reached number twenty-one on the pop chart in the spring of 1991. Salt-N-Pepa followed that up with "Let's Talk about Sex," a song with a positive message about not being afraid to discuss sex. With a new, upbeat mix, the single climbed to number thirteen on the charts in 1991, making it Salt-N-Pepa's biggest hit to date.

AIDS awareness took off in 1992

When basketball star Earvin "Magic" Johnson announced he had contracted

Parents Aren't Supposed to Like It

the HIV virus that leads to AIDS, it served as a wake-up call to the nation. Then, news anchor Peter Jennings of ABC-TV heard and liked the message of "Let's Talk about Sex," and he convinced Salt-N-Pepa to record a similar AIDS public service announcement (PSA) called "Let's Talk about AIDS." With new words by Salt, the single was released in the spring of 1992 to raise money for AIDS charities.

Salt-N-Pepa were very necessary

After working on their next album for more than a year, Salt-N-Pepa released their fourth album of new material in the fall of 1993, *Very Necessary*. Again, Salt, Pepa, and Spinderella took more active roles in writing and producing the album. The album went on to become the group's biggest seller, moving more than five million copies by 1995.

"Shoop," the first single from the album, became the group's first Top Ten hit when it peaked at number four. Produced by Salt with help from Pepa on the writing, "Shoop" was another "turn-the-tables" song, which found the girls checking out the guys and voicing their approval or disapproval.

The next single, "Whatta Man," was recorded with R&B group En Vogue and originally appeared on an En Vogue EP, *Runaway Love*, before being on *Very Necessary*. The words of the song praised a man who never disrespected women, while the girls wished they could marry such a man. It became the group's biggest hit, peaking at number three in 1994.

Three mothers

1994 was a big year for Salt-N-Pepa. The group topped off a year that included two Top Ten hits and a Grammy-winning single by performing at Woodstock '94 in front of 300,000 people. By this time all three members of the group were single mothers. Salt had a daughter Corin, Pepa had a son Tyran, and Spinderella a daughter Christenese. They told Life that being single parents had helped all three of them deepen their "sisterhood" relationship, although it has also complicated their working lives.

The third and final single from the album was a double-sided hit, "Heaven 'N' Hell"/"None of Your Business." Although it didn't reach the Top Ten, "None of Your Business" earned Salt-N-Pepa its first Grammy in 1995.

Something new

The band's pace of recording slowed down in 1995 and 1996, with all of their work appearing on movie soundtracks, compilations, and records by other artists. In 1995 they recorded the title track for the female rap compilation album, *Ain't Nuthin' but a She Thing*, which raised money for charities. During the year they signed a new contract with MCA Records which allowed them to start their own label, Jireh, for the development of other artists. Pepa opened a clothing store called HollyHood in Atlanta, Georgia. On November 19, 1995, the group sang "Whatta Man" at Frank Sinatra's eightieth birthday celebration.

For most of 1996 and part of 1997, Salt-N-Pepa fans heard rumors of a new album to be called *Flavor in Your Ear*. Meanwhile, they had to be content with only two songs released on movie soundtracks, "Champagne" from the movie *Bulletproof* and "Upside Down" from the Michael Jordan/Bugs Bunny film *Space Jam*. The new Salt-N-Pepa album was to be released in August 1997 under the title, *Brand New*.

Selected Awards

Hot, Cool & Vicious certified platinum, 1988.

Blacks' Magic certified platinum, 1992.

"Whatta Man," MTV Video Music Awards for 1) Best Dance Video, 2) Best R&B Video, and 3) Best Choreography, 1994.

Rolling Stone Critics' Pick, Best Rap Group, 1995.

"None of Your Business," Grammy Award for Best Rap Performance by a Duo or Group, 1995.

Entertainer of the Year, Soul Train Lady of Soul Awards, 1995.

Very Necessary certified multi-platinum for sales of five million copies, 1995.

Selected Discography

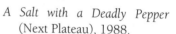

Hot, Cool & Vicious (Next Plateau), 1986.

A Salt with a Deadly Pepper (Next Plateau), 1988.

Blacks' Magic (Next Plateau), 1990.

A Blitz of Salt-N-Pepa Hits (Next Plateau), 1990.

Very Necessary (Next Plateau), 1993.

Brand New (Next Plateau), 1997. Originally announced as *Flavor in Your Ear*.

Further Reading

Adato, Allison, "Hip-hop's Reigning Queens Celebrate Mummy's Day," *Life,* May 1997, p. 74.

Cain, Joy Duckett, "The Growing Pains of Salt-N-Pepa," *Essence,* October 1994, p. 86.

Dunn, Jancee, "The Spice of Life," *Rolling Stone,* June 30, 1994, p.21.

"Salt-N-Pepa," *Jet,* April 3, 1995, p. 54.

Wilson, Mary, "Salt-N-Pepa's Unshakable Conviction," *Interview,* October 1995, p. 136.

Contact Information

Next Plateau Records
1650 Broadway, Suite 1201
New York, NY 10019

Web Site

http://execp.com/~mwildt/snp.html

Parents Aren't Supposed to Like It

Sir Mix-A-Lot

American rap artist

Born Anthony Ray; birthdate unknown

nthony Ray grew up in one of Seattle's poorer neighborhoods. Even so, Ray was taught responsibility. "In my day, when I was growing up, everybody was your mom and dad. If I broke a window down the street, someone else's momma would beat my behind and bring me home.

"I think that's the problem in America today, we all duck responsibility. I shoot you right now, and they want to analyze me. I committed a crime, put me in jail! I don't walk around the street like I'm some sort of tough guy, because there's always one tougher. I think acting responsibly is very important."

Sir Mix-A-Lot

And Sir Mix has always tried to act responsibly throughout his career. Taking on the name Sir Mix-A-Lot, Ray began by DJing at the Rotary Club, then graduated to the exhibition hall. "That's back in 1981, when hip-hop was something new, and everybody thought it was just a fad. Music was my first love, and rap was

"Hip-hop was fun, entertaining, a release, something different from R & B, something the kids could relate to, and I try to keep that in all my songs."

secondary, initially. I knew I couldn't sing, so I started out more really as a DJ."

In 1985, Sir Mix signed to the newly formed Seattle indie label, Nasty Ness, and released his first single, "Square Dance Rap." Along with a remix, the record sold 100,000 copies, an amazing amount for a new artist on a small label.

Stardom

Sales of "Square Dance Rap" financed Sir Mix's debut album, *Swass*. When it came out in 1988, the young rapper became a star. His album went platinum, and he was a rap sensation. What made Sir Mix so popular was that he filled a gap in the pop rap world. His music was perfect for people who didn't like gangsta rap, but who found artists like Vanilla Ice too wimpy. "Hip-hop was fun, entertaining, a release, something different from r'n'b, something the kids could relate to, and I try to keep that in all my songs," Sir Mix explains.

His next album, *Seminar*, sold almost as well as *Swass*, and earned a gold record. The single from the album, "My Posse's on Broadway," also went gold.

Def American

Sir Mix and his label should have been on the top of the world. Instead, the label owners were in court fighting each other. To make things even worse, Nasty Ness began arguing with the rapper over his image and music. "The label was seeing everything as pop and glitzy, and that's not how rap sells. It sells by looking like the bad animal. That's why kids buy it, they like the rebellious aspect of rap. We started disagreeing about what I should come out with, the image, everything, and in the midst, my record contract lapsed."

So, in 1991, he moved from a tiny indie label onto a large major label, Def American. "I was terrified, I'd never been on a major. And I'd always been given so much creative control over my projects. Rick Rubin [head of American] would call and say, 'maybe this,' and everything he told me to do, made the song better."

Baby Got Back

The result was 1992's *Mack Daddy*, the album that spawned his greatest hit to date, "Baby Got Back." That single sold a whopping three million copies, earned three platinum records and a Grammy, and made Sir Mix a household name.

That was why the rapper was asked to star in the short-lived UPN series, *The Watcher*. It wasn't a happy experience. "Egos, oh my God, everyone has an ego. We were the number-two rated show on the network, and they cut it." But that may have been a mercy killing, for Sir Mix describes the show as, "Twilight Zone-ish, with three stories going at the same time, but the stories were stupid."

The Watcher

He was in the midst of filming when *Chief Boot Knocka* was released, which was partly why the album sold so poorly. Sir Mix also blames himself. "I thought I could slap a record together, throw it down there, and sell a million. But it doesn't work like that. Now, I realize that."

Parents Aren't Supposed to Like It

So, he took a lot more care when recording *Return of the Bumpasaurus*. That record was a return to the Sir Mix of old. It was funny, scathing, and very pop, with lots of phat bass (the big, booming bass that blares out of boomboxes and rattles windows). "I'm serious, but I still want to entertain. I still have fun with my songs, but I maintain a certain amount of credibility. I don't try to get respect at the expense of creativity."

Respect

However, some people think Sir Mix has respect for himself, but not women. For as the Tacoma, Washington, *News Tribune* noted, "Mix likes to sing about women's physical attributes. He knows it's not politically correct, but he believes it's not disrespectful." Most of the songs on *Bumpasaurus* are either funny attacks on his detractors or about women's bodies. He may belittle the first group, but he never belittles women or calls them names. That's because Sir Mix loves women and everything about them. For him that's the basis of respect.

Selected Awards

American Music Awards, Favorite Artist Rap/Hip Hop.

Grammy Award for Best Rap Solo Performance for "Baby Got Back," 1993.

Selected Discography

Swass (American), 1988.

Seminar (American), 1989.

Mack Daddy (American), 1992.

Chief Boot Knocka (American), 1994.

Return of the Bumpasaurus (American), 1996.

Further Reading

Coleman, Mark, "Sir Mix-A-Lot: Mack Daddy," *Rolling Stone,* April 16, 1992, p. 86.

Dunn, Jancee, "Sir Mix-A-Lot," (interview), *Rolling Stone,* October 20, 1994, p. 44.

Hunt, Dennis, "Sir Mix-A-Lot Says His Critics Have Got His Message Backward," *Los Angeles Times,* July 19, 1992.

Jamison, Laura, "Chief Boot Knocka Sir Mix-A-Lot Rides Again," *Vibe,* August 1994.

Reader, Stephanie, "Rap's New Mix," *(Tacoma, WA) News Tribune,* July 19, 1994.

Contact Information

American Recordings
3500 W. Olive, Suite 1550
Burbank, CA 91505-4628

Web Site

http://american.recordings.com/American_Artists/Sir_Mix-A—Lot/mix_home.html

SNOOP DOGGY DOGG

American rap artist
(West Coast, gangsta, and hardcore rap styles)

Born Calvin Broadus (some accounts say Cordavar Varnado),
in Long Beach, California, May 9, 1971

"If I'm gonna come back, I wanna come back right. I was chosen, and I know that. A lot of people follow me and respect me. Now I'm gonna step up and handle my position, as far as trying to be the role model I tried to deny (being) at the beginning of my career." –Snoop Doggy Dogg, after his acquittal on murder charges

In hip-hop, few rules are as ironclad as "keep it real," even if that means staying in a neighborhood that had claimed friends and relatives. Given a choice, Snoop Doggy Dogg claimed he would have gotten a decent job, possibly by going to junior college. But such aspirations were snuffed in Snoop's 21st Street neighborhood near Compton, California, one of America's most violent inner-city areas. "I was always good at rap," Snoop told *Vibe*'s Kevin Powell, "but I really had no study habits, because I didn't think nobody would put no money into me or my talent —my true talent."

Born Calvin Broadus in East Long Beach, California, on May 9, 1971, Snoop was the second of three half brothers. Like many black families, Snoop's parents had left the Deep South for better opportunities elsewhere. They never got them in Long Beach. According to the "Wall of Sound" Internet page, Snoop's father nicknamed him after the *Peanuts* cartoon character Snoopy. "That's the key to my life," Snoop told Powell, while refusing to reveal his real name. "I snoop. I don't like nobody snoopin' on me."

Such sense of personal mystique came in handy when Snoop was "selling every kind of narcotic you could think of" in North Long Beach, where he'd moved by age fifteen. Weighing his parents' lack of success, Snoop decided the flow of instant drug profits outweighed any prison time he might serve.

Drug conviction marked turning point

For Snoop, his graphic lyrics reflected what he'd lived. "The other day I was looking at an old picture from back when I used to play," *Melody Maker* quoted him saying, "and like of twenty-eight homies on the team, twelve are dead, seven are in the penitentiary, three of them are smoked out."

Snoop's turn came in 1990, when police caught him selling drugs, just one month after graduating from Long Beach Polytechnic High School. Over the next three years, he became a county jail fixture, which forced him to mature quickly. Snoop told *Melody Maker*: "You can't show no weakness, 'cause then you'll be stuck [stabbed]."

Despite such setbacks, Snoop claimed in *Vibe* true friendship could, and did, exist on the streets: "[Street friends] will do anything for you, do time for you, take a bullet for you, kill for you." After he got out of jail, Snoop formed his first rap group, 213, named after a Los Angeles area code. With Warren G (**Dr. Dre's** [see entry] younger brother) and Nate Dogg, 213 gained some local notoriety but little else, despite support—and free equipment us-

age—from VIP Records owner Kelvin Anderson, who distributed 213 demo tapes to no avail. Few knew it, but Snoop had been rapping since high school, keenly following hardcore artists like Eric B & Rakim, NWA, and his alltime favorite, Slick Rick. Claiming fellow inmates had urged him to change direction, Snoop began handing out demo tapes to whoever might listen.

His big break didn't come until 1990, when Warren G gave a tape to his brother, NWA's **Dr. Dre** (see entry). That led to Dre's invitation for Snoop to watch the sessions for NWA's second, and final album, *Efil4zaggin'*. It was a period during which he survived off his friends' money and good graces: "That's what you call paying dues, you know? But that's [what] I had to go through after I gave up selling dope."

Snoop stayed single-minded

Snoop had experienced some early brushes with fame before meeting Dre. While living with an aunt in Long Beach, he'd turned down a ninety-day deal, because "I didn't want to be wearing no flat-tops and all that other R & B [stuff]," he remembered. "That ain't me. I want my [music] to be 100 percent gangsta [style]."

Snoop's persistence paid off handsomely on the *Deep Cover* (Solar Records, 1992) soundtrack album. "Deep Cover," which attacked crooked police, became an underground hit, largely due to its chorus of "1-8-7 on an undercover cop." The number comes from California's pe-

Snoop Doggy Dogg in court in Los Angeles, June 1995

of women and his casual attitude toward graphic lyric content. To *Vibe* he chalked up any profanity as the cost of building up an image.

Nor did he lose sleep over content. A gangsta, Snoop claimed, "don't listen to nobody but himself, and he programs himself around being intelligent and staying above the rest of the competition out there." Alternative rocker Kelly Deal of The Breeders agreed; she cited *The Chronic*'s "Ain't Nuthin' But A 'G' [Gangsta] Thang" among 1993's top tracks in *Rolling Stone.*

Murder was the case, police claimed

By summer 1993, Snoop had established himself as one of hip-hop's biggest and brightest new hopes. The "West Coast" sound of 1970s funk samples and ace studio musicianship had established its supremacy over hip-hop's original East Coast brethren with little difficulty. Snoop almost lost that promise on August 25, 1993, when police claimed he had helped bodyguard McKinley Malik Lee escape arrest after fatally shooting a man. Police alleged Lee had fired two bullets into 20-year-old Philip Woldermariam, a member of the By Yerself Hustlers street gang, and fled the scene. To make matters worse, Snoop was out on bail on a concealed weapons charge at the time.

If convicted, Snoop and Lee faced twenty-five-years-to-life in prison. Ironically, such problems boosted sales of Snoop's solo debut, *Doggystyle,* which *Melody Maker* termed "the unacceptable face of contemporary rap." It became the

nal codes for murder. Solar later sued Snoop's ultimate home, Death Row Records, for $125 million in 1997, alleging they'd been cheated out of a potential partnership.

Snoop's next assignment, rapping on four tracks of Dr. Dre's triple-platinum solo debut, *The Chronic* (1993), cemented his status as "gun-toting renegade" in the tradition of Jimi Hendrix and Bob Marley, *Vibe* observed. To *Rolling Stone*'s Jonathan Gold, *The Chronic* portrayed a world in which "women are attractive nuisances, and guns are waved at enemies from a safe distance." Snoop, in fact, took a bit of heat for his portrayals

Parents Aren't Supposed to Like It

first debut album to enter the charts at number one, selling 800,000 copies during its first week. By spring 1994, *Doggystyle* would sell four million copies and eventually gross $40 million for Death Row.

The singles performed well, too. "What's My Name?" and "Gin & Juice" both made number eight in America, becoming gold roughly a week after their releases. While preachers and politicians thought Snoop a hip-hop symbol run amok, critics like *Time*'s C.J. Farley said "the album's music is irresistible, though the lyrics are often unnecessarily graphic and downright obscene." *Rolling Stone*'s Toure found *Doggystyle* had a unity lacking in most rap; its fifty-five minutes, she believed, showed "the pain and lurking paranoia that have resulted from his success."

Apart from those troubles, Snoop had a banner year. In September, he won Best Rap Video at MTV's eleventh annual Video Music Awards (where detectives had waited outside), and Top Male Artist at *Billboard*'s fifth annual Music Awards. That same fall, *Murder Was The Case*—a soundtrack album built on an eighteen-minute video clip —entered the charts at number one.

1995 was a quiet year

As pretrial motions dragged on, Snoop spent much of 1995 preparing for trial and recording with his rap group, Tha Dogg Pound. Police charged him in January 1995 for possessing drug paraphernalia (following a late 1994 arrest in Louisiana). But he won more trophies,

too; *Rolling Stone* readers named him Best Rapper in the magazine's annual poll, and Snoop also claimed another for Favorite Artist, Rap/Hip-hop at the twenty-second Annual American Music Awards.

On February 20, 1996, a Los Angeles jury acquitted Snoop and Lee of first- and second-degree murder charges. The judge called a mistrial when they deadlocked on a separate charge of voluntary manslaughter. "People think this ... is cool," he told *Rolling Stone,* "that I like being notorious. It ain't none of that. This is nothing cool, nothing fun, nothing to laugh about. This is stressful."

Observers believed the contradictions among twenty-four prosecution witnesses had freed Snoop. Two had claimed Woldermariam was unarmed, only to admit retrieving a weapon from the victim. The victim's family felt Death Row had "bought" an acquittal with its four lawyers, a claim label head Marion "Suge" Knight dismissed. Plenty of innocent people had been convicted in local courts, he argued to *Rolling Stone*: "Just check the letters from the penitentiary."

Snoop considered the verdict a "wakeup" call and released a long-awaited second album, *Tha Doggfather,* later that year. Despite a consensus that it broke little new ground, *Doggfather* sold strongly—though Death Row's mushrooming legal problems had pushed Dre out, leaving Snoop to handle its music himself. Fans hoped for a stronger effort next time, as Augustus wrote on the "Wall of Sound" home page: "Snoop needs some fresh hits ... maybe some good will come out of this past year."

Acquittal changed lifestyle

After his acquittal, Snoop kept a lower profile. In November 1996, and then in March 1997, the simmering East-West Coast hip-hop feud claimed the lives of **Tupac Shakur** (see entry), and **Notorious B.I.G.** (see entry), respectively. They also ended a projected Death Row Family Tour, to feature Snoop, Tupac, and Tha Dogg Pound.

Nor did Snoop's plans for a thirty-eight-city Doggfather Fresh Fest go ahead in spring 1997. Citing security reasons, Snoop scuttled his own tour, claiming he'd promote a peace and unity message on the next outing—complete with film tributes to Tupac and B.I.G. In April 1997, Reuters reported that artists from both coasts, including Snoop, had buried their differences at Chicago's Nation of Islam headquarters.

That summer, Snoop married longtime girlfriend Shantay Taylor, and agreed to appear in the alternative rock festival Lollapalooza. The tour was set to begin June 25, 1997, in West Palm Beach, Florida, with Snoop inheriting the rap slot graced in the past by **Ice Cube** (see entry) and **Ice-T** (see entry). As for Death Row, it hadn't folded, despite grand jury investigations and Knight's March 1997 nine-year prison sentence for probation violations. Instead, Knight's family was running Death Row, with Suge himself reportedly signing checks in prison.

The new Death Row regime promised another Snoop album, possibly with Dr. Dre's production, in summer of 1997.

They didn't explain how it would happen, following a June 2, 1997, suit against Snoop by Knight's estranged wife, Sharitha. That claim alleged the artist owed millions of dollars in back commissions to her, and 20 percent of all his income.

Anyone needing proof of Snoop's arrival only had to scan *Variety's* announcement, that same month, of his upcoming film role with **LL Cool J** (see entry), in *The Real*. Neither artist was expected to rap, but "hopefully, they'll do a soundtrack," explained producer Scott Heller. Such projects, as Snoop had reminded *Vibe* so long ago, served an important purpose: "I'm still breathing. Stop trying to make me dead before it's my time."

Selected Awards

Doggystyle certified platinum, 1994.

"What's My Name?" and "Gin & Juice" certified gold, 1994.

Best Rap Video, MTV Video Music Awards, 1994.

Top Male Artist, *Billboard* Music Awards, 1994.

"Gin & Juice," Grammy Awards Nomination, Best Rap Solo Performance, 1995.

Best Male Rapper, *Rolling Stone* Readers' Picks, 1995.

American Music Award, Favorite Male Artist/Rap or Hip-hop, 1995.

Selected Discography

Doggystyle (Death Row/Interscope), 1993.

Tha Doggfather (Death Row/Interscope), 1996.

Doggumentary EP (Death Row), 1997.

Guest Appearances/Soundtracks

Deep Cover Soundtrack (Solar Records), 1992 (Snoop contributes "Deep Cover").

The Chronic, Dr. Dre (Death Row Records), 1993.

Murder Was the Case Soundtrack (Death Row), 1994.

Above the Rim Soundtrack, 1994.

A Thin Line Between Love & Hate (Warner Brothers), 1996.

Further Reading

Berman, Eric, "What's New at the Dogg House?" *Interview*, December 7, 1996, p. 106.

Farley, Christopher J., "Snoop Doggy Dogg: Doggystyle," *Time*, November 29, 1993, p. 73.

Fields-Myer, Thomas, "Facing the Rap: Snoop Doggy Dogg Comes to Trial for a 1993 L.A. Murder," *People Weekly*, November 20, 1995, p. 193.

Gold, Jonathan, "Day of the Dre," *Rolling Stone*, September 30, 1993, p. 38.

Leland, John, "Criminal Records," *Newsweek*, November 29, 1993, p. 60.

"Popjournal," edited by Eric Boehlert, *Rolling Stone*, p. 42.

Powell, Kevin, "Hot Dogg," *Vibe*, September 1993.

Samuels, Allison, "Man of Peace," *Newsweek*, October 28, 1996, p. 128.

Smith, Mat, "Ruff Justice," *Melody Maker*, February 5, 1994.

Toure, "Snoop & Cube," *Rolling Stone*, January 27, 1994, p. 51.

Wielenga, Dave, "Tha Dogg Walks," *Rolling Stone*, April 4, 1996, p. 23.

Contact Information

Death Row Records
10900 Wilshire Blvd., Suite 1240
Los Angeles, CA 90024-6532

Web Site

http://www.wallofsound.com/artists/
snoopdoggydog/index.html

TUPAC SHAKUR

American rap artist
(West Coast, gangsta, and hardcore rap styles)

Born June 16, 1971; died September 7, 1996

♪ "Don't shed a tear
for me ... /I ain't
happy here / I hope
they bury me and send me
to my rest / Headlines
readin' murdered to
death." –from "If I Die Tonight" on
Me against the World, 1995

With his tattoo-splattered physique, piercing deep-set eyes, and shaved head, Tupac Amaru Shakur came across as middle America's worst nightmare, the darkest strain of hip-hop. To fans, Shakur was only "thuggin' against society, thuggin' against the system that made me," as he once rapped. Like some other rappers, Shakur was criticized for his sexist lyrics He celebrated his mother, Afeni, but was equally capable of debasing women in his music. The contradictions hardly ended there. In his last video, "I Ain't Mad at Cha," Shakur—newly arrived in Heaven—saluted an old friend for quitting the "thug life." In "Only God Can Judge Me," Shakur foresaw death bearing down on him, yet seemed unable to tolerate his rival, **The Notorious B.I.G.** (see entry) and B.I.G.'s mentor, Sean "Puffy" Combs. Shakur's "Hit 'Em Up," the last single issued during his twenty-five-year lifetime, set new highs of profane rage against B.I.G., who was later gunned down after Shakur's own untimely death.

Yet millions of fans found something meaningful in Shakur's troubled life and lyrics, like a thirty-two-year-old Detroit accountant buying her first Shakur album. "I've never supported that kind of music," she told the *Detroit News,* "but there was something so tragic about the way he died ... It's almost like I'm looking for answers." Politician Jesse Jackson also tried to explain Shakur's downfall and apparent appeal, telling the *Los Angeles Times*: "Sometimes the lure of violent culture is so magnetic that even when one overcomes it with material success, it continues to call."

Acting bug bit early

From his June 16, 1971, birth in New York City, Shakur's life read much like an epic melodrama. His mother, Afeni, and father, Billy Garland, belonged to the Black Panthers, a militant group dedicated to achieving racial equality. Just two years earlier, in 1969, Afeni and then-husband Lumumba Adbul Shakur were among twenty New York Panthers arrested for multiple felonies. While out on bail, she dated Garland—a Panther from Jersey City, New Jersey—and a low-level gangster known only as "Legs."

Although Afeni lost bail in 1971, she and thirteen codefendants beat the charges in May; in June, Tupac was born. His first and middle name (Tupac Amaru) come from an Inca prince, while his surname (Shakur) means "thankful to God" in Arabic. By then, Garland was no longer seeing Afeni, and he didn't see Tupac until his son filmed *Juice* in 1992.

Tupac always cited his family background as a source of underlying conflict —along with the gap between his mother's revolutionary ideals and living with relatives or in homeless shelters. "Here we was," he told *Rolling Stone,* "kickin' all this [talk] about the revolution—and we starvin'. That didn't make no sense to me." He held greater admiration for Legs, an associate of reputed Harlem druglord Nicky Barnes, until Tupac discovered that it was Legs who had introduced Afeni to crack cocaine. (Legs later died of a crack-induced heart attack.)

But Tupac showed a flair for performing; at fifteen, he won enrollment to the Baltimore School for the Arts, taking roles in several productions there. "I was writing poetry," he told *Rolling Stone,* "and I became known as MC New York, because I was rapping, and then I was doing the acting thing.... It was the freest I ever felt in my life." That ended at seventeen, when his family moved to Marin City, California—a ghetto called "The Jungle"—and Tupac's relationship with Afeni broke down completely. He survived by hustling on the streets and selling drugs.

"Everybody's gonna know me"

In 1989, life began looking up when Shakur met Shock G, leader of West Coast hip-hop group Digital Underground, whose "Humpty Dance" and "Sex Packets" singles were about to hit. Hired as a dancer/roadie, Shakur appeared on their *This Is an EP* and *Sons of the P* (Tommy Boy, 1991) releases. As a result, Shakur established his own distinct voice long before his peers did. "Everybody knew me even though my album wasn't out yet," he told *Vibe.* "I never went to bed. I was working it [recording] like a job. Everybody's gonna know me."

This early start ignited controversy when a Texas inmate claimed "Soulja's Story," off Shakur's *2Pacalypse Now* solo debut (Interscope Records, 1991) incited a state trooper's murder. The lyrics depict a fugitive who decides to shoot a police officer.

While federal courts dismissed the inmate's lawsuit, a number of politicians, including Vice President Dan Quayle, wanted the track removed from the CD. Back in his adopted hometown of Oakland, California, Shakur sued local police, alleging brutality over a jaywalking arrest. His "posse" also made unwelcome news in Marin City, when a six-year-old boy died there after a gunfight. His label, Interscope, allegedly paid $300-500,000 to settle out of court.

These distractions didn't stop Shakur from pursuing his acting career, though. He won raves in Ernest Dickerson's *Juice* (1992), playing the role of Bishop, a youth addicted to the "highs" of violence. He also reaped praise in John Singleton's *Poetic Justice* (1993) as pop singer Janet Jackson's boyfriend, Lucky. Reviewers felt the film weak, but hailed its supporting star's work.

Rap acts became rap sheets

As 1993 rolled on, Shakur's life and art were growing dangerously blurry. He beat allegations of punching out a limo driver and shooting at two off-duty policemen in Atlanta, but he served a ten-day jail sentence for allegedly hitting a competing hip-hopper with a baseball bat. Shakur's troubles continued into 1994, when he served another fifteen-day sentence for hitting filmmaker Allen Hughes. But the most serious charge came from a Brooklyn woman claiming that Shakur and three friends sexually abused her.

Still, Shakur found time to turn in another acclaimed role in *Above the Rim*. *Entertainment Weekly* led the praise by saluting Shakur as "the most dynamic young actor since Sean Penn." The soundtrack, featuring Shakur's new band, Thug Life, sold two million copies.

Thus encouraged, Shakur formed a spinoff label (Out Da Gutta) for *Thug Life, Vol. One*, a "ten-song meditation about life under the gun," as *Entertainment Weekly* described it. The phrase suited Shakur's next misfortune, when unknown rivals shot him with .22-caliber bullets as he got ready to rap on another album. Shakur survived multiple injuries from the shooting, but he was robbed of $40,000 in cash and jewelry. From then on, he claimed B.I.G. and Combs were responsible, or at least had set him up. It was a charge Shakur would air on his 1996 CD, *All Eyez on Me*. For his sentencing on the sexual abuse charges, Shakur appeared in a wheelchair, but he still drew eighteen months to four-and-a-half years in prison.

On ice, but defiant

To some, Shakur's eight-month stay in jail had made a lasting impression. "It really shook him up," one associate recalled to *Newsweek*. "He seemed to un-

Parents Aren't Supposed to Like It

derstand how sacred life was." But others disagreed, especially looking back after the artist's death: "He said he wanted to get away from the violence and live a calmer life. But those were only words."

Bankrupted by legal fees, Shakur emerged from prison with his newest patron, Death Row Records boss Marion "Suge" Knight, who wooed him to the label. Knight reportedly paid Shakur's $1 million bail, something disputed in future accounts, and helped his newest artist buy his mother, Afeni, a house.

Making up for lost time with a vengeance, Shakur wrapped up another role in the film *Bullet,* with Mickey Rourke, and released his third solo CD, *Me against the World,* which took his popularity to another level. It sold 500,000 copies on release and yielded "Dear Mama," a heartfelt tribute to Afeni, now off crack and working for her son's production company. The single went Top Ten.

Afeni also appeared in the video, watching her son's work on TV. *Rolling Stone* found the album a compelling display of pain, whether in "If I Die Tonight" ("Addicted to drama so even mama couldn't raise me") or "Lord Knows" ("...and if I wasn't high, I'd probably blow my brains out"). Like him or not, Shakur "remains one of the most compelling characters in black popular culture," the magazine concluded. Others counted the approaching storm clouds. On September 24, 1995, Knight's friend Jake Robles died after being shot in an Atlanta, Georgia, nightclub. Next, record promoter Mark Bell claimed to have been beaten with champagne bottles, while Knight demanded to know where Combs, and Combs's mother, lived.

End of a thug life

Further ugliness erupted at the 1996 Soul Train Music Awards, when a gun appeared after a confrontation between Combs's (Bad Boy Records) and Knight's (Death Row Records) employees. By then, Shakur's "Hit 'Em Up" had already appeared. It taunted B.I.G. and Combs with the lyric, "Who shot me? / But ya punks didn't finish / Now you're about to feel the wrath of a menace."

The 1996 double-CD *All Eyez on Me,* on which "Hit 'Em Up" appeared, showed no letup of Shakur's trademark anger. *Rolling Stone's* Mikal Gilmore called it "one of the most melodically and texturally inventive albums that rap has ever produced—and one of the most furious." In tracks like "2 Of Amerikaz Most Wanted," Shakur seemed to predict his own doom. "He was his own most attentive audience," observed *Newsweek.*

Death arrived as Shakur sat beside Knight, stuck in Las Vegas, Nevada, traffic after the Mike Tyson-Bruce Seldon bout. Two men walked up to Knight's vehicle and blasted away with semiautomatic pistols, hitting Shakur four times while only grazing Knight's scalp. In his fight to escape, Shakur lost two fingers and a testicle. Doctors cut out one lung, but this failed to stop Shakur from sinking into a coma. He died six days later, on Friday, September 13, 1996.

Did Tupac lead nine lives?

Incredible as it seems, not all Shakur fans believe their hero died in Nevada. As faithful disciples, they await his return, pointing to several different "clues" and coincidences:

• Shakur's last album adopted the name Makaveli, after a sixteenth-century Italian political philosopher (spelled: Machiavelli) who suggested faking one's death to deter enemies.

• Authorities released no pictures from the hospital, and Shakur's family had him cremated without an autopsy. Big funeral ceremonies were planned, then canceled.

• Shakur was shot on the 6th, he died seven days later on September 13th. His age, 25 (2 + 5), and time of death (4:03, or 4 + 3), added up to seven. He also died seven months after his All Eyez on Me double CD came out. Its producer is listed as Simon (Peter), an apostle in The Bible and a witness to Jesus's resurrection.

Shakur's own "disciples" think he may return seven years after his death, and sightings have peppered the media. Listeners told a San Francisco radio station that 500 people had reputedly seen Shakur in Cuba after the shooting.

Others claim to have seen him in Arizona, Montana, the Caribbean, Europe, and South America. Shakur sighting remained a hot Worldwide Web topic. "I think people still want him to be around," said Kansas City high schooler Todd Leblanc, who keeps his own Shakur site, "and it's [the death] gotten to them so much that they believe the impossible."

Questions remain unanswered

Shakur's slaying remained officially unsolved, though police and record industry sources checked several angles—including the East Cost/West Coast feud. Informants told police in Compton and Los Angeles, California, that a gang rivalry seemed more likely. They claimed Death Row had ties to Los Angeles's Bloods, while Combs's Bad Boy Entertainment had employed rival gang Crips for concert security.

Knight's refusal to talk about the slaying, or post a reward, also attracted attention. By October 1996, Knight was back in prison, after police saw a videotape of him kicking a man in a casino shortly before Shakur's murder. This, in turn, earned him a nine-year prison sentence for parole violations. (For more on Knight, see **Notious B.I.G.** entry and box on Death Row Records, pp. 334-335.)

When not accusing police of lacking any desire to arrest her son's murderers, Afeni Shakur was suing Death Row Records, claiming Shakur's estate had been swindled out of millions in royalties. By then, producer **Dr. Dre** (see entry) had left the fold, telling *Newsweek*: "The negative element there was just too strong."

When B.I.G. himself died in a March 9, 1997, shooting incident, which some regarded as "payback" for Shakur, a shaken Combs vowed to change. Fans struggle to make sense of what read like the script of hip-hop's own demise. In the end, *Esquire*'s Ivan Solotaroff found no "gangsta" glamor on visiting Knight's Club 662 shortly after Shakur's murder, "just a sad, ugly feeling, very creepy, very hollow," he said. "No art, no life, just ashes."

Larger-than-life

Vibe chief executive Kevin Clinkscales, however, advised fans against anymore "rumor-mongering," which he found disrespectful to Shakur's family. "These are not comic-book heroes," he told *USA Today*. "These are real people."

That said, however, most agree that Tupac Shakur has won the larger-than-life immortality he craved so much. The sightings and resurrection theories place him in a select club that includes the late Kurt Cobain, Doors singer-poet Jim Morrison, and Elvis Presley.

On that score, fans need not fear, as poet Nikki Giovanni acknowledged in her own tribute, "All Eyez on You": "don't tell me he got what he deserved he deserved a chariot and / the accolades of a grateful people / he deserved his life." Nor did Giovanni stop there, getting her own "Thug Life" tattoo to honor Shakur's memory, telling the *Chicago Tribune*: "Young black men are in a holocaustic situation." So long as that persists, fans insist, Tupac Shakur's musical legacy will be hard to deny.

Selected Awards

2Pacalypse Now certified gold, 1993.

Strictly for My N.-G.G.-Z. certified platinum, 1993.

Me against the World, Grammy Award Nomination, Best Rap Album, 1996.

"Dear Mama," Grammy Award Nomination, Best Rap Solo Performance, 1996.

Selected Discography

With Digital Underground:

This Is an EP Release (Tommy Boy), 1991.

Sons of the P (Tommy Boy), 1991.

With Thug Life:

Above the Rim (Death Row/Interscope Records), 1994 Soundtrack; Thug Life contributed "Pour out a Little Liquor").

Thug Life, Vol. I (Out Da Gutta/Interscope), 1994.

As a solo performer (2Pac):

2Pacalypse Now (Interscope), 1991.

Strictly For My N.-G.G.-Z. (Interscope), 1993.

Me against the World (Interscope), 1995.

All Eyez on Me (Death Row), 1996.

Makaveli...Don Killuminati: The 7 Day Theory (Death Row), 1996.

Further Reading

Bailey, David, "Tupac Lives," *Detroit News,* October 26, 1996.

Biema, David Van, "What Goes 'Round...," *Time,* September 23, 1996.

Coker, Cheo H., "Me against the World," *Rolling Stone,* May 4, 1995.

Hendrickson, Matt, "Notorious B.I.G. 1973-1997," *Rolling Stone,* April 17, 1997.

Leland, John, and Alison Samuels, "Trouble Man (Death of Tupac Shakur)," *Newsweek*, September 23, 1996.

McDonnell, Evelyn, "Beyond the Tracks," *Interview*, July 1995.

Oldenburg, Ann, and Kevin V. Johnson, "Pac Man: Is Tupac Shakur Alive, or Is This Just a Game Some Fans Are Playing?" *Detroit News*, April 5, 1997.

Powell, Kevin, "Bury Me Like A G: The Short Life and Violent Death of Tupac Shakur," *Rolling Stone*, October 31, 1996.

Solotaroff, Ivan, and Veronica Chambers, "Gangsta Life, Gangster Death," *Esquire*, December 1996.

Wiltz, Teresa, "Chapter and Verse: Ex-'60s Firebrand Reflects on Life, Tupac And Pig's Feet," *Chicago Tribune*, May 29, 1997.

Web Site

There are numerous memorial web sites dedicated to Tupac Amaru Shakur and his memory.

Index

Italic type indicates volume numbers;
boldface type indicates featured entries and their page numbers;
(ill.) indicates photographs.

Parents Aren't Supposed to Like It

231 (ill.), **232-236**, 239,
271, 400; 3: 614, 655
Bowie, David, with Nine Inch
Nails 1: 91; 2: (ill.) 231
Bowman, Steve 3: 557
Boxley, James Hank 2: 393
A Boy Named Goo 1: 58
The Boys 3: 507
Boyz in the Hood (film and
song) 2: 332, 339, 361, 362
Boyz II Men 3: 503, **511
(ill.) 512-514**
Bradley, Owen 3: 636
Break A Dawn 3: 526
Breakdancing 2: 277
Bridge School benefit concerts
1: 207
Brill, Dmitry 2: 283-285
Brion, Jon 3: 613
Bristol (England) Sound 2:
299-301
Brit Pop 2: **219-222**, 238,
255
British press 1: 39
British new wave music 1:
154; 2: 253
British Invasion 3: 543
Broadus, Calvin (see Snoop
Doggy Dogg)
Brodsky Quartet 2: 245
The Brown Album 1: 133
Brown, Andre 2: 331
Brown, Bobby 3: 503, **516
(ill.) 517-519**
Brown, James 2: 276, 304; 3:
502, 503
Brown, Mark (see Brown Mark)
Brown Mark 3: 529
Brown, Rex "Rocker" 3: 491
Brown, Vincent 2: 382, 383
"Bruise Violet" 1: 18
Brutal Truth 3: 468
Bryan, Mark 3: 572
Bryson, David 3: 556
Buchignani, Paul 1: 9
Buck, Peter 1: 154
Buckley, Jeff 3: 441 (ill.),
442, **443 (ill.), 444-445**
Buckley, Tim 3: 442
Budd, Harold 2: 297
Buddhism 2: 231
Buffalo Springfield 1: 204
Bullet 2: 427
"Bullet in the Head" 1: 135
Bulletproof 2: 414
Bumstead records 3: 635
Burrell, Stanley Kirk (see Ham-
mer)

Burton, Cliff 3: 486, 487
Burton, James 2: 244
Busby, Jheryl 3: 513
Bush 2: 222, **237 (ill.)**, **238
(ill.)**, **239-240**
Bush, Dave 2: 256
Bush, George 2: 340
Bustin' Records (label) 2: 350,
352, 353
Busy Bee 2: 372
Butcher Brothers 1: 188
Butler, Bernard 2: 270, 272
The **Butthole Surfers** 1: 3, **33
(ill.), 34 (ill.), 35-36**
The Buzzcocks 1: 139; 2:
253
The Byrds 2: 221; 3: 543

C

Caine, Michael 2: 272
Cajun music 2: 243
Cale, John 3: 654, 656
Calhoun, William 3: 480
Calire, Mario 1: 200
Cameron, Matt 1: 118, 172,
173
Campbell, Sterling 1: 170
Campbell, Tevin 3: 503, **520
(ill.) 521-523**
Cantrell, Jerry 1: 11 (ill.), 12,
14
Capitol Records 3: 484
Captain Beefheart 2: 222
Carey, Mariah 2: 277; 3: 513
Caroline Records 1: 163
The Cars 2: 277
Cash, Johnny 1: 194
The Castilles 3: 597
Cauty, Jimmy 2: 295, 296
Cave, Nick 2: 222
CBGB's 1: 139
CBS/Columbia Records 3: 598
Cease, Jeff 3: 546
Censorship and freedom of
speech issues 1: 62, 76, 79; 2:
310, 361, 368, 369, 394-
395, 399; 3: 655-656
Chamberlin, Jimmy 1: 164
(ill.), 165, 167
Chapel Hill, North Carolina 1:
4
Chapman, Tracy 3: 439 (ill.),
441, 442, **446 (ill.), 447-450**
Charles, Ray 3: 501 (ill.), 502
Cheap Trick 2: 277
Cheeba, Eddie 2: 304

Chemical Brothers 2: 278,
280-282
Cherone, Gary 3: 468
Cherry, Nenah 2: 300
Chic 2: 276, 308
Chicago, Illinois 1: 165, 188
Childress, Ross 3: 553
Chilli 3: 536
Chipperfield, Sheila 2: 256
Christianity 2: 291
Christianne F 2: 233
Christian Right 2: 292, 293
The Chronic 2: 336
Chrysler Corporation 3: 600
Chuck D 1: 27; 2: 305, 362,
374, 392 (ill.), 394-396, 408
"Cinnamon Girl" 1: 204
Civil rights movement 3: 439
Clarke, Gilby 3: 477
The Clash 1: 1, 60, 139, 154;
2: 219, 225, 308
Clash of the Titans tour 1: 13
Classical music 2: 245
Claypool, Les 1: 130 (ill.),
131-133
Clayton, Adam 1: 190, 191,
192 (ill.)
Clearmountain, Bob 3: 476
Clemmons, Clarence 3: 598
Clifford Ball 3: 589
Cline, Patsy 3: 635
Clink, Mike 3: 474, 476
Clinton, Bill 1: 193; 2: 315
Clinton, George 1: 149; 2: 276,
285; 3: 503, 541
Clockers (film) 2: 396
Clouser, Charlie 3: 499
Cobain, Kurt 1: 49, 50, 65-
67, 94, 96 (ill.), 97, 98, 175,
206, 208; 2: 238; 3: 573
Cobra Verde 3: 570
Codling, Neil 2: 272
Coed rock 1: 196
Coffey, King 1: 36
Collective Soul 3: 543, **552
(ill.), 553-555**
Colley, Dana 1: 81, 82
Colling, Bootsy 3: 507
Collins, Judy 3: 440
Colt, Johnny 3: 546
Columbia Records 3: 444
Colvin, Douglas 1: 138
Combs, Sean "Puffy" 2: 310,
388-390, 424, 426, 428
"Come Out and Play" 1: 108
Comedy, musical 1: 20
Comess, Aaron 3: 595
The Commodores 2: 404

Parents Aren't Supposed to Like It

I

Iacocca, Lee *3:* 600
Ibold, Mark *1:* 111
Ice Cube *2:* 310, 332, 336, 339, **360 (ill.), 361, 362 (ill.), 363-365,** 400, 422
The Ice Opinion (essays) *2:* 370
Ice-T *1:* 3; *2:* 307, 310, **366 (ill.), 367, 368 (ill.), 369-371,** 422
"If I Had $1,000,000" *1:* 21
Iggy Pop *1:* **69 (ill.), 70 (ill.), 71-74;** *2:* 232; *3:* 616
Igloo Record Company *3:* 619
Iha, James *1:* 164 (ill.), 165
Illtown Records *2:* 384
Incesticide *1:* 98
Independence Day (film) *2:* 328
Indies (independent record companies) *1:* 3
Indigo Girls *3:* 441, 442, 451-453
Industrial music *1:* 78, 87, 90; *2:* 278, 287, 297
I Need More (autobiography) *1:* 70, 73
INET festival *1:* 125
Inez, Mike *1:* (ill.) 11, 14
Inspiral Carpets *2:* 266
International Harvesters *1:* 207
Internet *1:* 22
"Interstate Love Song" *1:* 180
Interview with the Vampire (film) *3:* 477
In Utero *1:* 98
Iovine, Jimmy *2:* 330, 334
Ireland *1:* 37, 190-193
Irons, Jack *1:* 116, 148
Isbelle, Jeffrey (see Izzy Stradlin)
Ivey, Antis, Jr. (see Coolio)
"I Wanna Be Sedated" *1:* 141
Ixnay on the Hombre *1:* 108

J

Jackson, Michael *2:* 292; *3:* 627
Jackson, O'Shea (see Ice-T)
Jaffee, Rami *1:* 200
Jagger, Mick *2:* 233; *3:* 480
Jam *1:* 1; *2:* 225
Jam 80 *3:* 622
Jam, Jimmy *2:* 277; *3:* 512
Jamaican music *1:* 184
James, Alex *2:* 228

James, Cheryl *2:* 410
James Dean Isn't Dead *2:* 260
James, Elmore *2:* 306
Jane's Addiction *1:* **75 (ill.), 76-77,** 123, 166
Jar of Flies *1:* 14
Jean, Wyclef "Clef" *2:* 344
Jello Biafra *1:* 34; *2:* 368
Jennings, Peter *2:* 413
Jerky Boys *3:* 554
Jerry Maguire (film) *3:* 601
Jesus Lizard *2:* 240
Joannou, Chris *1:* 160
John, Elton *3:* 613
Johns, Daniel *1:* 161
Johnson, Max *3:* 608
Johnson, Scott *3:* 563
Johnston, Freedy *3:* 613
Jones, David (see David Bowie)
Jones, George *2:* 243
Jones, Maxine *3:* 524-526
Jones, Quincy *2:* 307, 374; *3:* 521
Jones, Steve *3:* 478
The Joshua Tree *1:* 192
Joy Division *2:* 221
J.R.S. Records *3:* 573
Judas Priest *3:* 466
Juice *2:* 425, 426
Jump blues *3:* 501
Jungle *2:* 235, 278
Just a Gigolo *2:* 233
"Just a Girl" *1:* 101
Justified Ancients of Mu Mu (JAMS) *2:* 295

K

Kain, Gylan *2:* 305
Kannberg, Scott "Spiral Stairs" *1:* 110
Kato, Nash *1:* 187, 188
Katruud, Nathan *1:* 188
Katzenberg, Jeggrey *1:* 81
Kay Gee *2:* 382, 383, 408
Kelly, R. *2:* 277, 324
Kennedy, John F. *2:* 275
Kerplunk *1:* 61
Kerrville Folk Festival *3:* 441, 462
Kershenbaum, David *3:* 448
Kettle Whistle *1:* 77
Kid Creole (Nathaniel Glover) *2:* 308
Kiedis, Anthony *1:* 148 (ill.)
Kimble, Paul *3:* 565, 566
Kinchla, Chan *3:* 549
King Bees *2:* 231

King, Dee Dee *1:* 142
King, John *1:* 26
King, Kerry *3:* 493-495
King's Blank *2:* 238
Kinks *1:* 60; *2:* 221, 227; *3:* 465
Kinney, Sean *1:* 11 (ill.), 12
Kirby, Kier (see The Lady Miss Kier)
Kiss *2:* 232; *3:* 466
KLF *2:* 296
Kling Klang *2:* 288
Knight, Gladys *2:* 306
Knight, Marion "Suge" *2:* 333, 334, 335, 353, 389, 421, 422, 427, 428
Kool Moe Dee *2:* 307, **372 (ill.), 373-375**
Koppelman, Brian *3:* 447
Koppelman, Charles *3:* 447, 448
Korn *3:* 469
Kowalczyk, Ed *3:* 576 (ill.), 577-578
Kraftwerk *2:* 277-279, **287 (ill.), 288-289**
Krasnow, Robert *3:* 448
Kravitz, Lenny *3:* 541, 542, 613 (ill.), 614, **630 (ill.) 631-633**
Kreisel, Greg *1:* 105
Krez, Eric *1:* 179
Krizan, Anthony *3:* 596
Kross, Kris *1:* 188
KRS-One *2:* 304, 309, 317 (ill.), 374, 399, 407
Kukl *3:* 622

L

L7 *1:* 5
La Bamba *3:* 581
Lack, Steve *1:* 197
Ladies Fresh *2:* 400
The Lady Miss Kier *2:* 277, 283 (ill.), 284 (ill.), 285-286
LaFace Records *3:* 508, 536, 538
Landau, Jon *3:* 598, 599
lang, k. d. *3:* 615, **634 (ill.), 635, 636 (ill.), 637, 638**
Lang, Kathryn Dawn (see k. d. lang)
Langer, Clive *2:* 239
LaRock, Scott *2:* 304, 317
The Last Poets *2:* 305
Leary, Paul *1:* 33
Led Zeppelin *3:* 465, 542